LEADING AND IMPLEMENTING BUSINESS CHANGE MANAGEMENT

Being change capable is the *new normal* for today's growth-minded organizations. The "do more with less" strategies of the past are no longer effective in preparing organizations to meet the increasing challenges for growth, competitiveness, and innovation required of them in this new era. Business change challenges including customer and market shifts, legal and regulatory requirements, strategic redirection, acquisitions, strategic partnerships, and cultural transformation are demanding that organizations effectively and efficiently manage change across multiple dimensions. To reach this level of change capability, organizations must adopt an integrated, balanced, and customized approach to change management.

Change management is addressed from the unique perspective of both its foundational concepts as well as practical application. Using an integrated, scalable, and flexible framework, this book provides tools which can be readily customized and applied to initiatives across or within stages of the Business Change Management life cycle, from assessing the need for change, through planning the change initiative, designing a balanced change solution which integrates the people, process, and project management elements, through deploying and institutionalizing the change. Common risks associated with failed or stalled change initiatives are presented with best practices, and key topics associated with change management are explored and illustrated through real-life case studies.

Aimed at professionals within organizations and post-graduate students and researchers of business strategy, organizational behavior and change management disciplines, this book will provide a conceptual understanding of change management and a road map with a supporting toolbox for leading and implementing change that sticks.

David J. Jones is a Managing Partner with TKG Healthcare Consulting. Mr. Jones designs and facilitates change management approaches for organizations in the health care industry. His 25 years of business change experience as a business architect, methodologist, and project leader include designing and leading initiatives in change management, business process reengineering, knowledge management, and business change methodology development, for corporate and government organizations. He can be reached at www.tkghealthcare.com or dave@ tkghealthcare.com.

Ronald J. Recardo is the Managing Partner of The Catalyst Consulting Group, LLC, a professional services company that provides strategic planning, M&A advisory, operations improvement, and organization effectiveness consulting services. He has over 30 years of experience as both a corporate executive and management consultant. Mr. Recardo has worked in a variety of industries with over 100 different global clients including General Electric, Sandoz, Shire Pharmaceuticals, Nielsen, The Stanley Works, Schick Wilkinson Sword, Bi-Lo, and Philip Morris International. He can be reached at www. catalystconsultinggroup. org or rrecardo@catalystconsultinggroup.org.

'Recardo and Jones offer up a true masters class in change management. This text goes beyond standard remedies to help change leaders, practitioners and students grasp the root challenges and foundational aspects of business change, and apply integrated change management best practices through an engaging "you are there" approach. A real no nonsense guide for getting business change done effectively and efficiently and making it stick.'

Tim Toterhi, *Senior Director, Global Talent, Development & Engagement, Quintiles, USA*

'Ronald Recardo and David Jones have done a great job identifying critical issues associated with organizational changes, but then go much further by providing valuable tools to help address these issues. This is the most comprehensive book I have seen to date addressing change. Everyone talks about change, but few really know what it means and how to harness its transformational capabilities. This book is a game changer in that it presents simple tools to help any manager understand and harness the value of possible change and fight the battles raised by those opposing change.'

Gil Fried, *University of New Haven, USA*

'Ronald Recardo and David Jones have created a unique roadmap jam-packed with actionable and practical tools. *Leading and Implementing Business Change Management* is my go-to guide for relevant resources to help implement a variety of change challenges. It can be used as a comprehensive playbook for navigating any major change, or for cherry-picking specific activities, tools or templates for a variety of business needs.'

Janet Macaluso, M.Ed., MSOD, *Head of Global Learning and Development, Shire Pharmaceuticals, USA*

'This book is a valuable tool, especially for those who are new to Change Management. The authors link theory to practice with their extensive consulting work in the field, and clearly demonstrate the essential differences between project management and change management.'

Anthony Macari, *MBA Director and Clinical Assistant Professor, Sacred Heart University, USA*

'The biggest challenge with Change Management is the struggle many have to link it to concrete numbers and business performance. *Leading and Implementing Business Change Management* moves the needle forward on this. It not only offers a pragmatic step-by-step method on how to break up the work into manageable pieces, it remains focused on one core purpose: how to identify and roll out the necessary changes you need to grow your business.'

Kleigh Heather, *Director Organization Development, Philip Morris International, USA*

'Jones and Recardo bring the occurrence of change to light with believability. The timing and content of this book are especially relevant due to significant changes that will take place in all business environments with the speed of globalization. The book has uniqueness in approach, and provides motivation with precise direction. You will be empowered *to be the change!*'

Robert P. Hanlon, *President, RPH Financial Services, Inc., USA*

LEADING AND IMPLEMENTING BUSINESS CHANGE MANAGEMENT

Making change stick in the contemporary organization

David J. Jones and Ronald J. Recardo

Routledge
Taylor & Francis Group

LONDON AND NEW YORK

First published 2013
by Routledge
2 Park Square, Milton Park, Abingdon, Oxon OX14 4RN

Simultaneously published in the USA and Canada
by Routledge
711 Third Avenue, New York, NY 10017

Routledge is an imprint of the Taylor & Francis Group, an informa business

© 2013 David J. Jones and Ronald J. Recardo

British Library Cataloguing in Publication Data
A catalogue record for this book is available from the British Library

Library of Congress Cataloging in Publication Data
Jones, David J.
Leading and implementing business change management : making change stick in the contemporary organization / David J. Jones and Ronald J. Recardo.
p. cm.
Includes bibliographical references and index.
1. Organizational change--Management. I. Recardo, Ronald J. II. Title.
HD58.8.J657 2013
658.4'06--dc23
2012033107

ISBN: 978-0-415-66060-0 (hbk)
ISBN: 978-0-415-66061-7 (pbk)
ISBN: 978-0-203-07395-7 (ebk)

Typeset in Bembo
by Saxon Graphics Ltd, Derby

CONTENTS

FIGURES

TABLES

PREFACE

"To change and to improve are two different things."

German proverb

Business change has become the *new normal* for creating organizational growth, competitiveness, and innovation. Increasing economic volatility and intensifying global competition have placed new demands for managing change on organizations of all types: businesses, not-for-profits, institutions, and governments alike. In order to achieve sustainable change effectively and efficiently, organizational change capability has been elevated from a "nice-to-have" low, tactical priority, to a "must-have" high, strategic priority. Leading and implementing business change initiatives has become less of a sub-function of HR and IT departments and more of a cross-organizational discipline deserving of its own seat at the senior management table.

Despite the heightened recognition of business change as a critical competency, the challenge for many organizations is that they do not have a good track record in managing change and "making it stick." Major studies have cited the high failure rate of change initiatives. We took on the challenge in developing "Business Change Management" for leading and implementing change initiatives in an integrated, balanced, and applied manner to deliver sustainable business impact.

"Change management" means different things to different people, despite its general association with an approach to organizational business change. This lack of common agreement and understanding around such a seminal concept in business change affects the probability of successful sustainable outcomes, since perceptions of change management invariably shape how change initiatives are planned and carried out. By adopting the concept of Business Change Management, leaders can design and implement change initiatives that are clear, consistent, unified, and effective.

Our research and experience of over 50 years of combined consulting with more than 200 clients reveal that there are multiple themes and dimensions related to change management, including loose collections of change practices, which are widely distributed across the "white space" of change literature. Among the variety, books often focus on a specific type of approach to business change (e.g. organizational change, business process reengineering, process improvement, business transformation) and aim at either a general, theoretical level or a granular, technique level. The structural dimension of change is often emphasized at the expense of the people dimension, or vice versa. And depending on the approach, either the early or later stages in the change life cycle tend to receive more attention.

We draw upon the rich heritage of change management and our experience to unify these change themes and practices into a conceptually grounded, balanced, and easy-to-apply methodology with supporting tools. In developing an integrated approach for leading and implementing Business Change Management, we also share our passion for helping leaders effectively change their organizations. Our philosophy on approaching business change is admittedly more progressive than improving the status quo of a current organization. Embedded in Business Change Management are these core principles:

- **Change should be strategic and sustainable.** Change initiatives should tightly align with goals for advancing the business of the organization in the long term and the change should be made to stick.
- **Change should serve a meaningful purpose.** Change should go beyond just improving financial results to creating a bigger-picture impact that enriches the organization, its customers, and stakeholders.
- **Change management should be transformational.** Both hearts and minds need to be engaged so that the organization can embrace a new way of thinking and acting, not just conforming.
- **Change approaches should be balanced.** Change initiatives should address, integrate and reinforce both the structural and people dimensions of change to make the change stick.
- **Change must be integrated into an overall, aligned solution.** Change management cannot operate as a silo and create independent deliverables.
- **Change management is not "one-size-fits-all."** A change management approach should be adapted and scaled to the specific context of the organization, including its culture and its business needs.
- **Change should be viewed as a continuous learning cycle.** Change should not be treated as a "once-and-done" project but as an ongoing process.
- **Change is ultimately about people**. Change should serve the interests and improve the lives of customers and employees in addition to meeting the needs of financial stakeholders.

These principles are incorporated throughout the chapters of this book and the appendices.

Chapter 1 addresses change management from a foundational perspective, which we believe is a precursor to effective practice. The well-reported difficulties in creating and sustaining business change in organizations often start from misunderstandings and biases concerning what change management is and how it should be undertaken. In this chapter, we first examine the multiple and often differing perspectives on the concept of change management. We explore the fundamental challenges individuals and organizations have with change that makes change management continue to be such a difficult and often volatile endeavor in organizations. We then survey the prominent and often competing themes associated with approaches to business organizational change over the last century. Within an evolutionary framework, we depict the origins and influences of change practices that ultimately began to loosely coalesce into change management. We conclude the chapter by presenting an updated model, Business Change Management, which integrates, focuses and balances the key elements of change management's diverse heritage in a holistic, applied and adaptable framework.

In Chapter two we describe the primary, commonly experienced change risks that are inherent in change initiatives, which can lead to significant problems. Change risks are insufficiently managed in failed or stalled change efforts. We present Business Change Management best practices, culled from experience, as an effective strategy for anticipating, preventing, mitigating, and controlling change risk during the planning and execution of change initiatives. A case study shows how a global corporation applied Business Change Management best practices to manage change risk and successfully deliver a change initiative.

Chapter three explains the role of leadership and management in change initiatives, including the important distinctions between the two. We explore important areas of focus for change leaders, including engagement and stakeholder management. Specific competencies and responsibilities of the change leadership team needed to drive the change are described. We conclude the chapter with "hot spots" for applying change leadership on an initiative. Key actions for change leaders are identified within six areas called "change levers" and across the phases of the Business Change Management life cycle.

In Chapter four we address a significant challenge for change initiatives, *resistance*. The root causes of organizational change resistance are explored and its various types are distinguished. Models are presented for identifying resistance and addressing it through specific change interventions and enablers. A case study discusses how a well-known non-profit organization overcame considerable resistance that was standing in the way of its regional goals for advancing the organization.

In Chapter five we explore the critical role culture plays in organizational transformation effort and in making change stick. The core elements which make up culture are examined. We discuss the relationship between an organization's change capability and culture change, as well as other key success factors for creating and sustaining culture change. Models for understanding culture patterns and measuring the progress of culture change are presented. The chapter concludes with a case study that illustrates how a privately-held company transformed its culture from one entrenched in its past success as a leader of pharmaceutical marketing solutions to a forward-thinking culture focused and operating around the needs of today's rapidly-evolving healthcare marketplace.

In Appendices A and B we provide the ready-to-use methodology and supporting toolset.

Appendix A provides an overview of the Business Change Management methodology life cycle, followed by an explanation of each task within each life cycle phase. Tasks are described in terms of responsible role, task steps, the venue in which the task is performed, supporting tools, and deliverables, where applicable. The format of the phases and tasks are presented so that the reader or practitioner can readily apply and customize them to fit their needs for a change initiative.

Appendix B provides thirty-three ready-to-use tools which support the Business Change Management methodology for use on a change initiative. Tool types include change topic primers, techniques and deliverable templates. Most tools include a brief description, when the tool is most likely used in the change methodology, the steps for effectively using the tool, and a completed example that can be customised to support a "real world" organizational change initiative.

Appendix C presents a more detailed comparison of the evolutionary stages of Business Change Management approaches that are summarized in Chapter 1. Expressed in a table format, attributes for comparison include: key theorists and thought leaders who founded or contributed to the stage; causes and trends that led to the stage; change approach themes representative of the stage; and key attributes, strengths and issues or weaknesses associated with the stage.

This book was written for managers, change leaders, change practitioners, consultants, teachers, and students of change management and business change. We are hopeful that this book serves as a "go to" reference for your change initiatives now and in the future.

David J. Jones, Ronald J. Recardo
March 2013

ACKNOWLEDGEMENTS

Business Change Management is about the journey of people whose hearts and minds are engaged in bringing about a positive new direction in an organization. From conception to publication, this book has been a journey that reflects the passion of people who care about meaningful change and helping others create it.

I would like to thank the many individuals and teams with whom I have worked over the last two-and-a-half decades who contributed to the insights and learning about managing business change. The fuel for this book arose from their tireless efforts conceiving and designing change in their organizations, surmounting change challenges and sharing stories and learning of what worked, and what could work better. In particular, Ron and I are indebted to those leaders who contributed their organizations' experiences with a strategic business change initiative: Renée Selman, Julie Manganella, Tim Toterhi, and Allen Gouse. Their change leadership is represented in the book's case studies.

I would like to acknowledge those whose inspiration and belief in our project supplied energy during the writing journey. In particular, Dr. Paul Nutkowitz was a source of enlightenment during our discussions on advancing human progress through knowledge and learning. I am also grateful to my grandparents and parents for stimulating in me a desire to ask questions, think independently, and exercise my curiosity regarding the human condition and the importance of change.

Most of all, I would like to thank my loving wife and business partner, Maria Kirzecky, whose lasting encouragement for me to write was fulfilled through this book. Her patience, support and insights gave me sustenance during my many hours spent on this project. Maria's love of family, her belief in empowering people to create meaningful impact, and her commitment to ensuring that patient interests are always represented at the table in healthcare have created a compelling context for positive change in our consulting work as well as our personal lives.

Last but not least, Ron and I thank the faithful, highly professional efforts of our colleagues at Routledge publishing, especially David Varley and Rosemary Baron. Their belief in the need to address Business Change Management from a perspective that integrated practice and theory was invaluable in sharpening our focus for the book's audience. Our work with the members of the Routledge team was a pleasure.

David J. Jones

I would like to acknowledge two sets of individuals who were invaluable in the writing of this book. The first group of individuals are the over 130 different global companies that I have successfully completed projects for. These sponsoring executives have provided me with a venue to sharpen my skills, challenge my thinking, and ultimately become an effective "thought leader." These clients had the confidence in my abilities to work on strategic, complex business issues and provided a "real world" environment to refine the methodology and tools in this book to achieve "fast cycle" results in a playing field that has been historically characterized as "touchy-feely" and "conceptual."

The other set of individuals I would like to acknowledge are my family. My parents provided me with a loving environment to grow up in and instilled in me a very strong work ethic, a dedication to excellence, and a belief that you control your own destiny. Their sacrifice will never be forgotten. I would be remiss if I didn't take this time to acknowledge my best friend and wife Diane Pricone-Recardo. Although she has never written a book, I honestly believe she is a much better writer than I and has been a great person to bounce ideas off. Even after the many years we have been together I am still often pleasantly surprised by her dedication to her family, the success she has enjoyed in her own right as an animal rights activist for stray animals, and her support to many philanthropic causes. When I first met her I was attracted to her beauty but as the years have passed I am even more impressed by her intelligence. She is a much better person than I will ever be and I am very lucky to have her in my life. I also wish to acknowledge my incredibly inquisitive son Dylan. Many times while I was working on the computer he would sit by my side and ask many questions about consulting and business that demonstrated intelligence far beyond the average nine-year old. They both provide me with love and companionship and keep me grounded.

Ronald J. Recardo

1

THE EVOLUTION OF ORGANIZATIONAL CHANGE PRACTICES TO BUSINESS CHANGE MANAGEMENT

"Change is inevitable. Change is constant."[1]

Benjamin Disraeli

The challenge of understanding and embracing change management

Change management is a term that most business leaders and organizational professionals recognize, but its acceptance and application are far from consistent across organizations, resulting in uneven business outcomes. Despite roots that extend well back into the early twentieth century and a mature set of practices, change management as a discipline often invokes fear, confusion, and distrust among both the management and the ranks of organizations. Two fundamental concepts lie behind this uneasiness with change management, inhibiting its common acceptance and consistent use: *understanding* and *embracing*.

Understanding of change management is still an issue despite its important role in today's business nomenclature. A recent informal poll by Prosci, an independent research company that focuses on change management, revealed, "more than 80 percent of respondents experienced at least some confusion with the concepts of change and change management. In fact, 57 percent of those polled said they often experienced this confusion."[2] As change management began emerging as a discipline in the 1990s, a research study by Dean and Linda Anderson found that "most leaders believed that change management was defined as the implementation of a desired outcome that needed to overcome employee resistance (due largely to workforce opposition or emotional upheaval)."[3] Such a limited perception of change management persists today.

The lack of a common and sufficient understanding of change management is due in large part to the fact that the concept is not universally defined. It is often referred to by different names, such as strategic business configuration, business transformation, or organizational development. Many highly respected practitioner-theorists and academics have provided cogent definitions but these vary depending on point-of-view or experiential emphasis that stress the dimensions of change practice which have evolved into the concept of change management. Such variance in definition leaves a lot of room for leaders and professionals in organizations to read into change management only the elements that they are comfortable with or to focus on what they would *prefer* it to be, based on interpretations of their experience with change initiatives, for better or worse.

Leaders and seminal thinkers in change management theory demonstrate the range of emphasis and concentration on different aspects of change practice dimensions. John Kotter described change management as "the utilization of basic structures and tools to control any organizational change effort."[4] Linda Ackerman Anderson divided organizational change into three types: developmental change, transitional change, and transformational change.[5] Sounding very much like more contemporary, broader descriptions of change management, organizational change pioneer Richard Beckhard defined organizational development as "an effort planned, organization-wide, managed from the top that increases organization effectiveness and health through planned interventions in the organization's 'processes' using behavioral-science knowledge."[6] While these descriptions share some elements, their different perspectives reveal the wide range of interpretation surrounding change management.

Why does such a problem of differing perspectives exist for change management? Change management became a discipline through the merging and codification of a collection of practices that had been in use to address various aspects of business change. However, the discontinuity between its two overarching types of approaches to change – structural and people – was not reconciled. As a result, change management is often categorized as "hard" or "soft." Accordingly, change management efforts are often relegated to Human Resources (a function specializing in "people") or Information Technology (a function specializing in "structure-oriented" solutions) departments. Change management is often exalted or disparaged, depending on the predisposition, understanding, and experience of the person viewing it.

More recent evolutions of change management theory attempt to unite the people and structural elements into a holistic approach to business change, as will be discussed later in this chapter. A more complete and unified understanding of change management and its origins should encourage practitioners to use it more objectively, thoughtfully and consistently in their organizations.

A clear and full understanding of the concept of change management alone, however, is not sufficient for achieving more consistent and effective use in organizational change. Change management requires "embracing" change. The word "change" is highly charged, and is a primal element in human nature which often evokes negative feelings, including loss and how to deal with uncertainty and the unpredictable. Such adverse feelings of change typically include:

- fear of the unknown
- fear of the known
- loss of stability and security
- loss of identity
- loss of relationships.

These natural human emotions are magnified in organizations where groups of people are struggling to deal with change on a larger scale and at higher levels of complexity over which they have minimal control. Even more practical and pragmatic concerns about organizational change have deep emotional roots which are not easily appeased. Examples include:

- "How will the change affect me personally?" (e.g. "Will I have a job? Will I still be able to achieve my career objectives?" etc.)
- "What will *I* need to do to make the change work and successfully perform in the changed environment?"
- "How much of my time will the change work take?"
- "Where will I get more resources to implement the changes and operate my group with minimal disruption?"

If these types of concerns are not sufficiently addressed they will lead to a high degree of organizational resistance to change.

William Bridges has prominently focused on the emotional and psychological transitions inherent in organizational change, and the needs for individuals to apply time and interventions to work through the change "wilderness." Embracing change requires helping people let go of what will not be carried forward from the "old" environment, and renewing themselves by helping shape their new environment.[7] A key responsibility for change leaders is to create the conditions and provide support for people to embrace change and shape the new environment, as will be discussed in Chapter 3.

However organizational readiness or resistance is assessed, a change management initiative must account for the natural follow-through of human transition. This cycle, which has been adapted from the "five stages of grief" theory from Elizabeth Kubler-Ross[8] and incorporated into approaches for changing organizational environments, focuses on the need to embrace change:

1. denial
2. anger
3. bargaining
4. depression
5. acceptance.

Because change is personal for affected members of the organization, stakeholders, and the change team, they will be challenged in their efforts to make change happen. The human inclination is to resist change when people perceive that it will negatively impact them. Since resistance is such a significant barrier to realizing transformational change, change management must objectively anticipate, prevent, overcome, and manage change resistance. This will be discussed in Chapters 2, 4 and 5.

Developing a balanced, realistic understanding of change management will lead to more consistent business change outcomes. Over time this knowledge will evolve individuals' perceptions of change management beyond a concept which is "touchy-feely," highly conceptual, or over-engineered. Once change management is understood in a richer context, it can be deployed as a balanced process.

A codification of business practices aimed at an elusive organizational goal

The emergence and growth of change management was in direct response to the increasing complexity of business change. Change in organizations has evolved from simpler to more complex.

- **Simple change:** The targets are well defined, the outcomes are predictable, the approach is usually linear and quickly applied, and the change effort is often of a shorter, fixed duration with few affected stakeholders. The management and integration of diverse change target solution elements and work streams (i.e. "white space") is minimal (e.g. improving labor output on an assembly line process).
- **Complex change:** The targets are more strategic and transformational, the outcomes are more uncertain and unpredictable, the approach is comprehensive and more complex, the change effort is usually larger in scale, and a considerable amount of white space needs to be managed (e.g. changing a business model and transforming the organization).

When the change management discipline began to emerge in the early 1990s, it formalized approaches to business change, which began to incorporate both structure- and people-centric change elements (e.g. tools, interventions, and loosely-defined approaches). These approaches had reached levels of commonly accepted use in organizations. For example, force-field analysis, facilitation of work group dynamics, chartering (from the people-centric approaches), and process and workflow design techniques (from structure-centric approaches). The more complex and comprehensive approaches were needed to counter some of the failings of simplistic and limited approaches used in addressing larger-scale change. According to Dean and Linda Anderson, the demand for change management was heavily influenced by business leaders' demands for more from their significant investments in change consultants. During the late 1980s and early 1990s:

... many leaders began to feel the pinch of not being successful in actually creating the visions and organizational solutions they needed to meet their increasing marketplace demands. Many of those who used big consulting firms to help them design new strategies, structures, technology, services, or products became frustrated at failing to implement the solutions they had purchased. Their frustration centered on difficulties with approaches that were not easy to apply in the real world.[9]

Morale, resistance, speed of change, and resource availability were among the problems that were not adequately addressed.

In response to these challenges, most respected change management approaches have evolved to embody the following characteristics to some degree:

- a formalized effort to move an organization from a current state to a desired future state
- a significant focus on addressing the people and human transition aspects of change (e.g. communications, readiness, resistance, learning)
- incorporation of change management perspective that is top-down (e.g. formalized plans, structured and cascading) or bottom-up (e.g. empowerment)
- structured plans and tools for creating organizational change.

Despite these advances change management still struggles to meet its promise for addressing the increasingly elusive and complex demands of business change. In response we have developed a new model for the next evolution of change management, called Business Change Management (BCM). Before discussing Business Change Management and its aspects that will be expressed throughout this book, we will survey the major trends and transitions in the development of change management from its origins to the present.

The emergence of change management in response to the evolving needs of business change

Change management is a product of multiple disciplines and practices that have emerged in response to business change needs over the course of the modern business era. The approaches to business change that gave rise to change management follow a trajectory similar to that of other sciences.

These approximate stages of change management's evolution can be compared to Kuhn's paradigm shifts and cycle of scientific revolution, with the newly emerging approach to business change countering the excesses of the established, predominant change thinking.[10] These shifts within the change management continuum align with Kuhn's theory in "The Structure of Scientific Revolutions," as eloquently summarized by a former U.S. Health official: "For many reasons, and in many sciences, old frameworks for seeing and solving problems give way to new ones."[11] One point of difference, however, with Kuhn's theory is that while the new thinking on change highlighted weaknesses in their predecessors', the "old schools" of change thinking and practice never went away, but continue to be used and emphasized by specialists and practitioners with a vested interest in applying and evolving them.

Figure 1.1 illustrates a continuum showing the major disciplines or practices of approaches to business change and the emergence of change management. It also shows how the change approaches countered each other in terms of their biases towards either structure- or people-focused change.

Scientific Management, Industrial Engineering, and Process Improvement

The earliest formalized practices for changing or improving business are rooted in Scientific Management, which began at the turn of the twentieth century. Founder Frederick Taylor applied time-and-motion studies and workflow analysis to address the needs for expanding labor productivity in US manufacturing. Also called Industrial Engineering, Scientific Management focused on the structural side of change; it was highly mechanistic, quantitative, and output-based. It was influential, giving ultimate rise to the process improvement and operational engineering approaches that became popular years later through Edward Deming and the Total Quality Management movement.[12] However, Scientific Management's focus was tactical, focused on optimizing the current state of operations, and it did not address the people side of change.

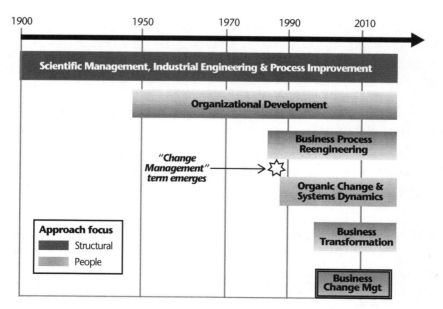

FIGURE 1.1 The evolution of approaches to business change and the emergence of change management

Organizational Development

Organizational Development originated in the 1950s as a response to the post-war service economy boom and the need to address the people aspects of change which were neglected by Scientific Management and Industrial Engineering. Academic disciplines such as behavioral science, industrial and organizational psychology, and sociology were applied to organizational change. Tools, interventions, and concepts were developed to empower individuals in the organizational change and to address the culture change. Kurt Lewin, Edgar Schein, Chris Argyris, Richard Beckhard, and other thought leaders developed methods and techniques. These were focused on understanding change and building awareness, diagnosing resistance, building and chartering teams, and effectively using education and communication as enablers of change. Humanistic and ethical, this work influenced change themes that followed later (e.g. in Organic Change and Human Systems Dynamics), including learning organizations and emotional intelligence. The work of Organizational Development formed much of the foundation of change management, though its lack of a measurable tie to business performance relegated it in many organizations to a Human Resources specialty or a nice-to-have practice. Organizational Development also focused heavily on facilitation and process at the expense of content and outcomes.

Business Process Reengineering

Business Process Reengineering (BPR) emerged to meet the demands for higher-impact "radical" business change that began in the mid-1980s with large global organizations attempting to improve their value to customers by redesigning their business processes and improving efficiencies. BPR was top-down and future-oriented, and it significantly leveraged the explosion in information technology in its process redesign. Michael Hammer, James Champy, Thomas Davenport, Gary Rummler, and Alan Brache were thought leaders.

This approach focused primarily on applying enabling information technology and designing new processes not encumbered by the past way of doing things to obtain order of magnitude improvements in cost, customer service, responsiveness to market changes, and reductions in operating costs. These types of improvements could not be generated from process improvement (a left-to-right process) or initiatives that focused on simplifying what companies did instead of challenging the underlying paradigms and starting with a "white piece of paper." BPR relied heavily on a concept called "reengineering labs" that accelerated solution design and development. This was accomplished by using cross-functional teams that designed the integrated technology, organization, and process solution in real-time and in parallel. When executed properly there were success stories of companies achieving radical performance improvements.

Like most "approaches du jour," the major shortcoming of BPR was that it did not adequately address the myriad of people issues in a proactive and holistic manner.

Despite its successes, including change tools and techniques which were added to the arsenal of change management practice, BPR earned a reputation for large body counts, considerable issues around stakeholder engagement, and often a lack of alignment with the business and corporate culture. BPR's lack of focus on the people aspect of change was highlighted in a widely quoted Wall Street Journal article:

> Gurus of the $4.7 billion reengineering industry like [Michael] Hammer forgot about people. 'I wasn't smart enough about that,' Hammer commented. 'I was reflecting on my engineering background and was insufficiently appreciative of the human dimension. I've learned that's critical.'[13]

Organic Change and Human Systems Dynamics

Organic Change and Human System Dynamics evolved from the collective experiences of BPR and focused heavily on the organization and people aspects of change. Organic Change and Human System Dynamics embodied more of a bottom-up focus to shape organizational change through leveraging the initiative and knowledge of people, as Organizational Development had done previously. This new stage in change management practice incorporated new thinking around patterns of human behavior and paradigm shifts in thinking about models borrowed from the natural sciences, such as complexity theory and chaos theory. This approach was cyclical and continuous, in contrast to linear change approaches such as BPR.

A strong emphasis was placed on fostering healthy teams as the unit for creatively driving change, optimizing relational dynamics, seeding the conditions for change, and, as Argyris had previously emphasized, letting the knowledge workers do the heavy lifting. Peter Senge built on the ideas of his former teacher at MIT, Jay Forrester; Margaret Wheatley popularized complexity and chaos in modeling change; and Daniel Goleman's application of emotional intelligence in business increased the use and development of techniques to break down barriers to empowerment and initiative.

The plethora of new people-focused models and tools-influenced thinking about modeling change and creating environments for high-performing teams resulted in a brief flurry of knowledge management initiatives, but did not become a core part of change management. There were several shortcomings in this body of work. The approaches were typically developed by individuals with minimal experience as change practitioners or in change implementation. The approaches were codified at a model level but often were not documented down to a methodology level. Individuals read the books and their interest was piqued but when they got back to their offices they lacked a cogent, actionable approach for implementing the concepts in a business setting. Additionally, many of these approaches were met by executives down the line with the "eye roll" reaction. They perceived the approaches to be another well-intentioned but "touchy-feely" Human Resources approach that would have very little impact on moving the dials.

Business Transformation

Business Transformation is a synonym for change management as it is used in this book. Business Transformation emerged in the early 1990s in response to greater complexity of large-scale change, as well as an attempt to remedy the excesses from the structure-focused BPR and restore the people-focus from Organizational Development. The intention was to transform the hearts and minds of the organization as well as the organization's structural assets. In addition to rebalancing the structure-people fulcrum, Business Transformation sought to elevate the focus of change management to strategically moving the organization forward to a new place, rather than engaging in incremental change or tactical roles such as supporting systems implementation initiatives.

Business Transformation inadvertently made the change process much more complex by relying on life cycle methodologies and a top down implementation process. Importantly, Business Transformation addressed critical gaps in achieving organizational commitment and a sense of urgency around the organizational change, which included building a strong case for change and "the burning platform," popularized by Daryl Conner.[14] John Kotter and Dean and Linda Anderson are key thought leaders in the area of Business Transformation. William Bridges also became an influential figure for the people focus of Business Transformation, through his attention on creating understanding of how people experience change psychologically and emotionally, and how best to assist them through the process.

Business Change Management

We have conceived Business Change Management (BCM) as the next stage in the evolution of change management. Business Change Management builds on the strengths of Business Transformation while addressing its shortcomings. We define BCM in both a strategic and tactical context as a scalable and adaptable end-to-end process from assessing the need for change (through appropriate data collection), designing a target solution for change that balances technology, organization, and process needs in alignment with overall strategic business direction, through implementing and institutionalizing the integrated change solution by embedding appropriate change best practices into the environment solution and execution.

For a complete reference to each of the primary evolutionary themes see Table C.1 in Appendix C, entitled "Characteristics of business change approach evolutionary stages."

An integrated model for effective change: Business Change Management

Although people use the term "change management" generically, it needs to be distinguished and differentiated as "Business Change Management," not only for the purposes of this book, but also so that it can be built out as a legitimate discipline that has a definite purpose for "sitting at the table" with Operations, Marketing, Sales, R&D, Finance and the other functions. BCM is not an offshoot of HR or IT, but rather has its own purpose and space that embraces those two disciplines. BCM also takes as its point of focus change that transforms an organization from its current state to one that thinks and behaves differently in a new strategic context (i.e. "complex change" described earlier in this chapter). This type of change stands in contrast to making improvements which enhance the status quo, or seek "buy-in" or compliance from members of the organization in response to predetermined business decisions (i.e. "simple change"). These situations demand little in the way of "heart and mind" and collaboration from the organization and can be handled more expeditiously through tactical change improvement approaches and techniques.

Business Change Management:

- **Cascades the change from and is tightly aligned with strategic business direction.** Change is not treated as just implementing after-the-fact goals, plans, or designs which have been independently or previously defined.
- **Addresses business change in a holistic, integrated manner.** Defines, assesses and addresses the impacts to each dimension of architecture: technology, organization, and process. The final solution seamlessly integrates and balances all elements of architecture, which will shorten the implementation timeline, reduce resistance, and enable greater benefits realization.
- **Manages the "white space" between the activities of the change effort as well as the change solution target.** This ensures a unified end result that delivers the intended business impact (i.e. not a silo approach).
- **Utilizes program and project governance to ensure there is an overall change road map, a critical path has been identified, interdependencies between work streams are managed properly**, and strong project process and tools are utilized to keep track of the myriad of details and risks.

The Business Change Management TOPs Model in Figure 1.2 conveys what the change solution can address for a change initiative from a multi-dimensional standpoint. These dimensions include technology, organization, and process (TOP).

Business Change Management uses this TOPs model to determine *what* will be the change impacts to each element of the architecture. The methodology phases and tools in the Appendices describe *how* these changes are designed, implemented, and institutionalized.

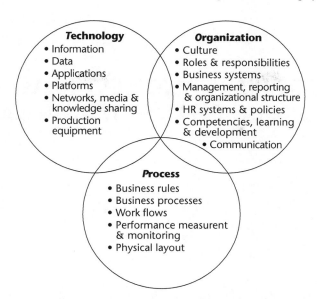

FIGURE 1.2 The Business Change Management TOPs model

Notes

1 http://thinkexist.com/quotation/change_is_inevitable-change_is_constant/145561.html
2 Gans, K. "Should You Change Your Thinking about Change Management?" *Strategic Finance* [serial online]. October 2011; 93(4): 48–50. Business Source Premier, Ipswich, MA.
3 Anderson, D. & Anderson L. (2001). *Beyond change management: Advanced strategies for transformational leaders*. San Francisco. Jossey-Bass/Pfeiffer. 168.
4 Kotter, J. (2011). "Change Management vs. Change Leadership—What's the Difference?" *Forbes* online. http://www.forbes.com/sites/johnkotter/2011/07/12/change-management-vs-change-leadership-whats-the-difference
5 Anderson, D. & Anderson L. (2001). *Beyond change management: Advanced strategies for transformational leaders*. 34–39.
6 Beckhard, R. (1969). *Organization development: Strategies and models*. Reading, MA: Addison-Wesley. 9.
7 Bridges, W. (2009). *Managing Transition: Making the most of change*. 3rd ed. Reading, MA. Addison-Wesley.
8 Kübler-Ross, E. (1969). *On death and dying*. New York. Touchstone.
9 Anderson, D. & Anderson L. (2001). *Beyond change management: Advanced Strategies for Transformational Leaders*. 184.
10 Kuhn, T.S. (1970). *The Structure of scientific revolutions*. 2nd ed. Chicago. University of Chicago Press.
11 Eisenberg, J.M. "Evidence-Based Medicine: A Paradigm Shift is Underway in Health Care." January 2001. Expert Voices.
12 http://en.wikipedia.org/wiki/W._Edwards_Deming
13 Anderson, D. & Anderson L. (2001). *Beyond change management: Advanced strategies for transformational leaders*. 26.
14 http://www.mentoric.com/resource_wall_of_fire.html

2

CHANGE RISKS AND BEST PRACTICES IN BUSINESS CHANGE MANAGEMENT

"A great wind is blowing, and that gives you either imagination or a headache."[1]

Catherine II ("Catherine the Great")

SITUATIONAL CONTEXT FOR CHANGE RISKS AND BEST PRACTICES

You are working with the senior management team to formulate an approach for transforming the organization in alignment with a change in business direction. The goals necessary to achieve the future-state target are conceptually defined, but not much else has been worked out yet. There is a sense of excitement around the table about moving things forward. A few of your management colleagues are pushing the team towards detailed planning for the initiative. One offers a template of a work plan that was used on a systems development project.

You temper your colleagues' enthusiasm by diplomatically asking them to take a step back. Creating a change initiative approach should be customized to the organization's experience with change, and it should not be assumed that one-size-fits-all. You ask the team to reflect on the organization's recurring issues, gaps, and problems with change that are evident from its history. These are key change risks. Overcoming them will be critical for the change initiative's success. You and the team focus the discussion around these change risks and identify the necessary best practices the change initiative approach will need to incorporate. These change practices will form the contextual target around which the change initiative will be conceptualized, staffed, planned, and executed.

Unmanaged change risk leads to problems for change management initiatives

Recognition of change management's importance has grown. However, the ability of organizations to effectively master the discipline has not commensurately advanced, evidenced by the high failure rates of transformational business change initiatives, as reported in landmark studies by both McKinsey and IBM. Confirming research statistics reported by change management thought leader John Kotter a decade earlier, a 2008 McKinsey survey of 3,199 executives around the world found that only one transformation in three succeeds.[2] In another study of more than 1,500 change management executives from 15 countries, IBM reported that nearly 60 percent of projects aimed at achieving business change do not fully meet their objectives.[3] Change management remains a high risk, low benefit realization endeavor.

Our consulting experience suggests that the high risk associated with change management initiatives largely results from not [sufficiently] anticipating and addressing key elements required for the change. Underlying this high risk is the need for the desired change mindset and behaviors to take root in the change leaders, the participating teams, and those in the organization affected by the change. This is the hard nut of organizational transformation. However, this nut can be cracked through early and careful application of Business Change Management best practices, enabling the structural and technical aspects of the change to follow in a concentrated, efficient manner. This chapter describes common problems arising from unmanaged risks on change initiatives and best practices for preventing, mitigating, and resolving them. Successful business change initiatives are distinguished from those which are unsuccessful by their lack of or insufficient use of these best practices.

Framework overview

If you have been involved in a business change or transformational initiative, you have probably seen or experienced several, if not many, of the problems or issues listed in Table 2.1. These problems and issues share key characteristics:

- They arise from risks common to change management initiatives that are uncomfortable to deal with, often avoided or left to resolve themselves, resulting in significant impacts to the change initiative.
- They are clear and self-evident, easily validated through observation and measurement.
- Interventions or practices to address change risks, if applied at all, are employed late, reactively in "crisis mode," or superficially.

Why do these problems persist? Our experience suggests these problems and issues are often ignored despite common knowledge of their risk and impact.

These types of change problems are not confined to simpler, linear solutions associated with structural or technical problems that many leaders and organizational professionals are more comfortable dealing with. Change problems and issues involve "messy" subjects such as uncertainty, ambiguity, risk taking, surfacing, and resolving conflict, not just numbers, objects, or documents.

There is also a requirement for big picture (i.e. strategic) and careful thinking that is heavily qualitative, not solely quantitative or reducible to binary, cut-and-dry measures. Leaders of change initiatives must seek out and interpret input from impacted stakeholders, often reading between the lines, and incorporating their learnings to refine their change plans in real-time.

Additionally, as in life, one ounce of prevention in a business change initiative is worth a pound of cure. If you rush the change initiative towards the more tangible implementation-oriented stages of its life cycle, the moment to capitalize on preventative practices will be lost. These practices then become reactive interventions, seen by the organization as toothless symbols or tokens of an expensive change effort on its way to a crash landing. However, if they had been applied early enough, these practices would have created a softer landing pad.

Our experience suggests that BCM best practices can prevent or mitigate the most common change risks and issues listed in Table 2.1. These BCM best practices evolve the more standard use of similar practices on change management initiatives from primarily process-oriented interventions to *contextual business drivers*. While leveraging the need for process (e.g. keeping participants engaged and motivated during the change process), BCM drivers collectively emphasize the importance of addressing *content* quality of the change target solution and business impact. For example, making sure the big picture and targets for change are clear, understood, reinforced, rewarded, and measured. Similarly, leaders and sponsors must model the behavior of the changes they wish to see in the target transformational change, while making the troops accountable for their initiative and advancement of the change to the new state.

Process-oriented practices are important components as well, for example, to ensure that plan milestones and goals are on track, or to demonstrate consistency of direction and message through communication and reinforcement. BCM's contextual business drivers approach to best practices optimizes their effectiveness in response to specific change management problems by not reducing change practices to transactional processes.

Before exploring the change management problems and the BCM best practices, keep these important points in mind:

- **Apply BCM best practices holistically, not independently.** It is likely that a problem or issue has multiple root causes that need to be addressed. For example, a problem with employee engagement or apathy may not only be related to a lack of a compelling vision and target, but it may also be influenced by the need for leadership behavior modeling as well as individual performance accountability. If you apply only one or a few of the BCM best practices you may send some problems into partial remission, but you will not resolve them.

- **Timing is important.** By the time you've encountered these problems and issues during a business change initiative, a likely cause is that best practices were not put into place at the beginning of the change initiative. Think preventative. Apply the BCM best practices at the outset and throughout the change initiative. If you implement these best practices at the beginning of a project you are more likely to realize much more of the targeted benefits. Apply these BCM practices early and often.

- **Embed these best practices in your business change initiative processes.** Position them as ongoing, not once-and-done, to ensure follow through. Make individuals on the change initiative accountable for applying them to themselves as well as their teams.

- **Do not expect "hard" answers.** Although BCM best practices strive towards concreteness and incorporate quantitative measurements, change-related risks and issues contain an inherent measure of uncertainty which is unavoidable. As in quantum physics, there are no absolute answers, though probabilities exist. Beyond using them to address problems and issues, view BCM best practices as means of gaining valuable information, learning, and course-correcting to help navigate your change management initiative through challenging waters to a new destination: the transformed organization.

- **Be preemptive and customize to the organization.** Another important aspect of best practices is that each initiative is different, and therefore requires thoughtful consideration of unique best practices which address the most important change risks and problems which pre-exist in the organizational environment. In our experience, when assessing a new change engagement, in the pre-planning or definition stages of the initiative we look at what best practices need to be embedded in the initiative from the start, and what could go wrong. In this way, best practices can be viewed as *critical success factors* for the change initiative. It is wise to have early conversations with change leaders and other members of the organization about change risks, problems, and best practices in their areas.

The most common change management risks and issues are organized by categories:

Engagement, resistance, and cohesion (how people respond or do not respond to the change):
1. Little or no engagement and commitment to the change
2. No sense of urgency or momentum
3. Infighting and/or increasing conflict
4. Sabotage or derailment attempts.

Leadership and organization (aspects of the organization which impede the change effort):

5. Lack of unity and cross-functional cooperation (silo effect)
6. Seemingly insurmountable roadblocks and political entrenchment
7. Lack of sponsorship and leadership.

Management and change capabilities (failure to effectively manage the change initiative)

8. Missed goals and milestones
9. Lack of demonstrated evidence for change progress
10. Poor understanding of the change road map, roles, and dependencies.

In Table 2.1, a "√" symbol indicates which of the common change management risks and issues are best addressed through BCM best practices. In this chapter the change risks and issues will be explored first, followed by the BCM best practices for overcoming them, which are:

- make the vision for change clear, compelling, and credible
- identify the problems and probe the causes
- make the tough calls
- model the change
- make the change personal and accountable
- clarify boundaries between the old and new states
- consistently communicate to reinforce the change
- assess readiness and surface inhibitors early and often
- recognize and reward change progress regularly and consistently
- support the transition through the change wilderness
- develop a balanced scorecard and cascade it
- create a change road map and master plan
- manage the white space.

TABLE 2.1 Business Change Management best practices applied to common change risks and issues

Common Change Management Risks and Issues	Best Practices												
	Make the vision for change clear, compelling, and credible	Identify the problems and probe the causes	Make the tough calls	Model the change	Make the change personal and accountable	Clarify boundaries between the old and new states	Consistently communicate to reinforce the change	Assess readiness and surface inhibitors early and often	Recognize and reward change progress regularly and consistently	Support the transition through the change wilderness	Develop a balanced scorecard and cascade it	Create a change roadmap and master plan	Manage the white space
Engagement, resistance and cohesion													
Little or no engagement and commitment to the change	✓		✓	✓	✓	✓	✓	✓		✓			
No sense of urgency or momentum	✓		✓	✓	✓		✓	✓	✓	✓		✓	
Infighting and/or increasing conflict (active or passive)		✓	✓	✓	✓	✓	✓	✓		✓			
Sabotage or derailment attempts		✓	✓		✓	✓	✓	✓					
Leadership and organization													
Lack of unity and cross-functional cooperation (silo effect)	✓	✓	✓	✓		✓		✓	✓		✓	✓	✓
Seemingly insurmountable roadblocks and political entrenchment	✓	✓	✓	✓		✓		✓			✓		✓
Lack of sponsorship and leadership		✓	✓	✓			✓	✓			✓	✓	✓
Management and change capabilities													
Missed goals and milestones		✓		✓			✓		✓		✓	✓	✓
Lack of demonstrated evidence for change progress							✓		✓		✓	✓	✓
Poor understanding of the change roadmap, roles, and dependencies	✓						✓				✓	✓	✓

Ten common change risks (and issues)

Engagement, resistance and cohesion

1. Little or no engagement and commitment to the change

Take a walk down a few hallways, look around the workspaces, and chat for a few minutes with members of your change initiative. Even without a survey it will become apparent what the level of commitment is to the change. Of course there will be outliers, those individuals who can mask their real level of commitment, but your collective impression will register to what degree (if at all) people feel connected to the change and committed to making the effort a success.

Indicators that people are engaged and taking initiative often include:

- **Passion.** Members are excited when they hear about and talk about the change and the possibilities resulting from the change.
- **Interaction/collaboration.** Members are reaching out to others in efforts to discuss and mobilize around the change.
- **Self-initiative.** Members are exploring and contributing ideas for moving the change forward, and taking greater responsibility.

Engagement is the fuel for self-organizing people and teams, which are vital to any change initiative. While individuals' attitudes towards change normally follow natural cycles of rising and falling throughout the course of a change initiative, those cycles can be reduced, smoothed, and to some extent avoided if managed effectively. However, if the engagement is extremely low at the outset and apathy pervades the troops serious problems await. This is foundational. In order for progress to take root people must have their hearts and minds engaged in the change effort.

Lack of engagement differs from other problems related to attitude and behavior in that it is not primarily based on people's fear of change – which causes problems such as infighting, conflict, or sabotage – but a missing sense of "what is in it for me?" (WIIFM), what the big picture looks like and what the consequences will be if immediate action is not taken. These other more energized reactions to change, discussed later, signify that people *care* about something regarding the change, albeit their goals are in conflict, they feel threatened, or they feel compelled to defend something that may be going away.

In contrast, the lack of engagement described here is related to *a lack of care*, apathy, or disconnection about what is going to happen or what individuals need to do to make it happen. And potentially, unlike these other problems, lack of engagement is heavily related to external factors outside of the individual, for example, prior experience with change initiatives, corporate culture, and leadership. In summary, for those who exhibit these signs of a lack of engagement, prior and current stimuli for change do not exert a strong pull. Life is comfortable in the current state, and there is no feeling about the need to change it.

Possible pre-existing contributors to weak engagement include:

- A lack of compelling communication around a "burning platform" or a recognized threat to organizational survival or stability that people can rally around. Stakeholders must understand and have passion for the concept that something is broken and needs to be fixed.
- Weak stakeholder analysis in which most critical stakeholders have not been identified, along with their current level of support, their issues and concerns, and a plan for developing a cascading level of commitment throughout the organization.
- Top-down led efforts that required little of the individuals other than to agree and be polite to one another (someone else is doing it).
- Poor trust between employees and leadership. At times this is an outgrowth of a history of either poor labor/management relations or past resentments from failed change projects.
- An organizational culture that hasn't required much ownership or initiative from employees in the past (no consequences for non-participation).

Address the engagement problem by applying these BCM best practices:

- make the vision for change clear, compelling, and credible
- identify the problems and probe the causes
- develop and execute a commitment plan that uses multiple channels for optimizing support
- model the appropriate behaviors
- make the change personal and accountable
- clarify boundaries between the old and new states
- consistently communicate to reinforce the change
- assess readiness and surface inhibitors early and often
- recognize and reward change progress regularly and consistently
- support the transition through the change wilderness.

Engagement can be achieved through both persuasion and influencing skills and through the use of rewards and consequences to promote desired behaviors and outcomes, including sanctions for non-compliance. Credible and personal persuasion is at the heart of engagement. People are engaged around things that affect them personally, and will be asking themselves, "What's in it for me?" People are also deeply engaged when they find meaning in their work.[4] Possibility, authenticity, and rewards properly applied will engage and inspire, igniting the creativity and self-organizing spirit that is so important to the change initiative.

If you do not perceive a lack of engagement, be sure to examine and regularly clean your filter. We all want to envision that others are as connected to the change as we are, but lack of engagement exists, even if in small pockets, in important "untouchable" places. Comfort and complacency are enemies of change, and they often dwell behind a lack of engagement.

2. No sense of urgency or momentum

Observing and interacting at random with members of the change team will quickly reveal whether or not a general sense of urgency exists around the change, reflective of the overall initiative. Momentum is infectious and members across the organization, in various capacities with the change initiative, either have the spirit or they do not. In contrast to a lack of engagement, change team members may not be apathetic or disconnected from the change, but they may not see the reason for making the change an immediate priority. Such inertia quickly builds to critical mass which becomes the norm on the change initiative, and it is difficult to reconstruct a more compelling case for change once the initiative is already underway.

Creating and sustaining a sense of urgency and momentum is more about the leaders of the change initiative generating the motivation for the change through the vision, decisions, and their behavior than it is about members of the team motivating themselves, although individuals must be held accountable. Competing priorities, often in the form of "day jobs," must be subordinated to the priority for change created at the highest levels of the organization and initiative. A strong burning platform, a clear change road map and "tough calls" around realigning organizational priorities are critical to building and sustaining a sense of urgency on the change initiative.

Possible pre-existing contributors to no sense of urgency or momentum include:

- organization has poor track record with sustaining and completing change initiatives and projects
- the culture has reached a state of complacency
- changes sponsorship is absent or weak.

Address no sense of urgency or momentum through these BCM best practices:

- make the vision for change clear, compelling, and credible
- create a change road map and master plan
- model the change
- support the transition through the change wilderness
- develop a balanced scorecard and cascade it
- create a change road map and master plan.

3. Infighting and increasing conflict (active or passive)

It is not hard to identify conflict across the change initiative and between members of the change team. Infighting and conflict are often symptomatic of frustration and discomfort when people are taken out of their comfort zone, which is rooted in fear of change itself and inability to accept and work through it. Conflict or "noise" may also be a sign that the change initiative is not paying careful enough attention to the human factors involved, which can easily fray under the stress of change. The game of business survival is heightened for some to Darwinian proportions when they are thrust into the unfamiliar, ambiguous, and charged environment of change. This is a mindset issue which requires awareness, accountability and support.

It takes a little more effort to identify the passive behaviors related to fighting change, but they can be uncovered with probing beneath the surface of how people are really feeling. Silence and politeness often mask the fact that people are not dealing with the change-specific issues in effective ways. Since change carries with it the strong scent of human fear, sooner or later it will erupt in some form, potentially disabling the change initiative at a critical juncture. Therefore, it is healthier to encourage people to express their concerns about change from the outset and help them work through them, rather than ignore the subject. Issue identification, inhibitor surfacing, and conflict management are important tools for addressing these reactions towards change. Members of the change initiative and stakeholders must also be made accountable for overcoming their concerns with change and channel their energy to constructive ends for the initiative. If this is not done, primal behavior will often emerge in the form of creating adversaries and taking sides against those imagined to be in opposition to personal interests.

Possible pre-existing contributors to infighting and increasing conflict include:

- an entrenched culture with an inability to work through difficult issues
- a history of tolerating or rewarding manipulation and "leaving dead bodies behind" (i.e. eliminating or punishing people, thus making them afraid)
- lack of awareness and emotional intelligence.

Address infighting and increasing conflict through these BCM best practices:

- identify the problems and probe the causes
- model the change
- make the change personal and accountable
- consistently communicate to reinforce the change
- assess readiness and surface inhibitors early and often
- support the transition through the change wilderness.

4. Sabotage or derailment attempts

Public and covert attempts to undermine change initiatives are not unusual, given the investment people have in their old systems, organizational norms, and ways of doing things. Such attempts may manifest themselves in different ways, but are not hard to pick up with a little vigilance. They include discrediting the change, spreading gossip to immobilize other team members through fear, blocking access to key resources, manipulating through political power, ignoring responsibilities, and backstabbing.

"Toxicity" is a term often associated with the kind of behavior that intentionally seeks to subvert the change effort. Criticizing the change initiative instead of finding ways to help move it forward is a favorite tool of those wishing to derail a change effort. Critical thinking in the form of challenging *why something won't work* is often a function of what Edward de Bono called wearing the "black hat," as opposed to wearing the "green hat," which constructively seeks solutions and growth.[5] While there is a time and place for critical thinking, such as to "kick the tires" of a new idea in order to test and improve it, an overabundance of critical thinking along with reinforcing behaviors will overwhelm the creative, constructive drive needed to propel the change effort forward.

Naysayers and troublemakers can be removed, but it often happens too late, and their anti-change contagion is difficult to remove from the change initiative once it has infected the collective mindset. Positioning themselves as martyrs or heroes in support of a dying culture, saboteurs may have powerful roots and connections deep into the organization which cannot be easily cut. Reason is not an option in this situation, but personal accountability for the change is.

The destructive efforts of an organizational insider (or two or more) will test the change leaders' decisiveness and courage. For example, an influential long-time manager heavily invested in the old system may spread a rumor to members of the change team that the change initiative is masking a job-cutting agenda, which will ignite fear and invite resistance from members of the change initiative and throughout the organization. If the rumor is not true, the sponsor and change leaders must act swiftly and decisively to identify the issue, confront the manager and publicly dismantle the rumor, and outline the consequences of such misleading, fear-provoking behavior including taking action if warranted. It is important that perpetrators of fear who have attempted to attack the change effort not be attacked or silenced, but be immobilized through cooperation with organizational leaders and negated through a positive case for the change.

Possible pre-existing contributors to sabotage or derailment attempts include:

- entrenched culture persists, ruled by controlling individuals
- support for guardians of anti-change is strong, and their connections are far-reaching
- tough calls have not been made in the past to remove these individuals from areas of influence.

Address sabotage or derailment attempts through these BCM best practices:

- identify the problems and probe the causes
- make the tough calls
- make the change personal and accountable
- clarify boundaries between the old and new states
- consistently communicate to reinforce the change
- assess readiness and surface inhibitors early and often.

Leadership and organization

5. Lack of unity and cross-functional cooperation (silo effect)

Assess your change initiative stakeholders and you will likely find that some organizations or functional groups are contributing more to the change initiative than others, when adjusted for expectations. Ask your leaders on the change initiative from different work streams how they perceive the change direction, the dependencies between stakeholders, and their role to collaboratively advance the change. Different answers and different levels of expected contribution may reveal the power of inherent limitations in the organizational structure and culture. Members from different organizations may be strategically aligned on the change initiative direction, but they may not be aligned on how to get there.

Participants in the change effort, especially at the organizational level, need to be marching to (and in alignment with) the same drum on the change initiative. Organizational silos are common barriers to change initiatives. Change initiative members have commitments to their day jobs in their respective organizational "homes." But achieving the full impact of transformational change depends on an integrated, cross-functional effort in which the change is a top priority. An organization with an important stake in the change which becomes absent or silent at a critical stage of the change initiative could block and dissolve the results of the entire effort. In contrast to other problems, lack of unity and cross-functional cooperation may be less of a directional need and more of an alignment need for the change initiative. Decisive leaders who make tough calls, create a clear picture of how organizations must work across the less-specifically defined areas of "white space" to advance the change, and measures for enforcing organization support in a cascading balanced scorecard, are important antidotes for overcoming the lack of unity.

Possible pre-existing contributors to lack of unity and cross-functional cooperation include:

*   Change projects were traditionally driven operationally by a particular stakeholder (e.g. IT, HR), rather than strategically from the top or across business units.
*   Functional organizations operated with a high degree of control, and minimal interdependence.
*   On previous projects, stakeholder organizations performed in a passive or advisory role, rather than as co-drivers of the change, with a seat at the change planning table.
*   Accountability for participating in change initiatives was non-existent or not enforced.

Address lack of unity and cross-functional cooperation by applying these BCM best practices:

- identify the problems and probe the causes
- make the tough calls
- model the change
- clarify boundaries between the old and new states
- assess readiness and surface inhibitors early and often
- recognize and reward change progress regularly and consistently
- develop a balanced scorecard and cascade it
- create a change road map and master plan
- manage the white space.

6. Seemingly insurmountable roadblocks and political entrenchment

Sacred cows can bring change momentum to a near standstill, a situation not uncommon in change initiatives. These roadblocks often involve protection of turf and/or the old ways of doing things in cultures that have been resistant to transformational change. Most roadblocks are known in advance of the change initiative. However, they are underestimated in terms of the change planning and work needed to counter them, or perhaps avoided altogether in hopes that things will sort themselves out once the change initiative is underway. In reality, they never do.

Sacred cows often evoke deep-seeded emotions, since they are longstanding and often rooted in the organization's history and former success. Members of a particular organization may question the value of the change. "What's wrong with what we are doing now?" they may ask. What helped an organization formerly, however, may be holding it back from transformative change. For example, processes to make decisions may have been highly formalized and required gaining consensus from many before proceeding. The future state may require decision-making that is faster, with shorter cycle times and less consensus in order to create a more nimble, customer-responsive culture. In order to overcome such obstacles, a strong burning platform, decisive leadership to make the tough calls, and clear accountability through a cascading balanced scorecard are essential.

Possible pre-existing contributors to seemingly insurmountable roadblocks and political entrenchment include:

- organization has strong silos and a history of turf battles
- culture is not adaptive, the organization has shown little evolution over time
- one organization dominates, or its leaders make most of the decisions for the overall organization
- stakeholders are not vested in strategic change.

Address insurmountable roadblocks and political entrenchment through these BCM best practices:

- make the vision for change clear, compelling, and credible
- identify the problems and probe the causes

- make the tough calls
- clarify boundaries between the old and new states
- assess readiness and surface inhibitors early and often
- develop a balanced scorecard and cascade it
- manage the white space.

7. Lack of sponsorship and leadership

It is not difficult to determine the lack of sponsorship and leadership at various levels of a business change initiative. The momentum of the initiative, and the participation and attitudes towards the change reflected in the change teams, are significantly determined by the quality of sponsorship and the change leadership, or the lack thereof. A sense of clarity, unity, ownership, and confidence pervades the teams of a change initiative with strong leadership. However, given the demand for experience and skill in situations dealing with uncertainty, stakeholder management and tough calls in real-time, it is not uncommon for change initiatives to experience absent or weak change sponsorship and leadership.

Inexperienced change leaders can underestimate the demands of a change initiative, viewing their role as an extension of their management responsibilities in their current or previous positions. Change team members and others affected by the change expect their leaders to guide them through uncertainty and the difficult cycle of change since they are out of the comfort zone of their functional jobs. Consequently, the sponsor and leaders of the change initiative need to be highly visible and influential. The sponsor must be carefully selected for the role on the change initiative, and once there, operating as a hands-on field general. Commitment, authenticity, and passion for the change must be clearly evident in the sponsor and leaders, as these attitudes and behaviors will be picked up by members of the change team. Good communication skills and an ability to articulate the vision and manage the white space are hallmarks of effective change leadership. Importantly, if the sponsor and change leaders are not clarifying change direction, making the tough calls, and removing organizational roadblocks, the trust and confidence of the change teams will quickly erode.

Possible pre-existing contributors to ineffective or insufficient sponsorship and support include:

- assigned sponsor and change leaders lack change management experience
- temperament of the sponsor and change leaders is a poor fit with the change model (e.g. command-and-control or crisis management styles are not typically good fits for transformational change)
- sponsor and change leaders have higher priorities than the change initiative
- sponsor and change leaders focus on narrow aspects of the change initiative that they are familiar with, rather than the big picture.

Address ineffective or insufficient sponsorship and support through these BCM best practices:

- identify the problems and probe the causes
- make the tough calls
- model the change
- make the change personal and accountable
- consistently communicate to reinforce the change
- assess readiness and surface inhibitors early and often
- develop a balanced scorecard and cascade it
- create a change road map and master plan
- manage the white space.

Management and change capabilities

8. Missed goals and milestones

Once the change leadership team lays out the master plan for the business change initiative, you may try to envision where and when the universal problems of delays in the plan schedule and delivery of results will occur. Most projects experience similar issues, which are well documented. However, these problems are even more acute with change initiatives, which are highly and necessarily complex in both their goals and their approaches to achieving them (e.g. interdependent work streams or projects, intangible outcomes like culture). Best practices which derive from the field of change management can be used to mitigate these risks.

Missed goals and milestones in change management are not simply the result of poor planning and execution. The fundamentals of sound program and project management are a given for a change initiative, but the nature of change management is that scope is broad as well as deep. Results are qualitative as well as quantitative, and interdependencies across organizational stakeholders are numerous. The ultimate goal is conceptual, strategic, and longer-term with far-reaching impacts, rather than predictable, tightly bound, and shorter-term, as is the case with many programs and projects which are not change-oriented.

The responsibility for ensuring that goals and milestones are achieved rests firmly on the shoulders of those responsible for leading and managing the initiative. Specific targets and responsibilities must be reflected in the change master plan, and individuals must be made accountable for delivering them. It is important that the change roadmap show how the work streams and the tasks within them integrate to form the change solutions, which drive the milestones and the goals, lest they fall into the white space. Expectations for the change team to achieve these milestones and goals must be communicated consistently and unambiguously, and rewards and consequences should support them.

Possible pre-existing contributors to missed goals and milestones include:

- lack of program and project management skills in the organization
- dismal track record of delivering previous programs and projects
- discipline and accountability for meeting plan targets are missing

- lack of experience in the organization with complex change projects
- no personal accountabilities in performance appraisals for moving things forward.

Address missed goals and milestones by applying these BCM best practices:

- identify the problems and probe the causes
- consistently communicate to reinforce the change
- recognize and reward change progress regularly and consistently
- create a change road map and master plan
- manage the white space.

9. Lack of demonstrated evidence for change progress

Business change initiatives use an infrastructure of program and project management common to most formalized projects. However, traditional program and project management tools often fall short when it comes to measuring progress on a change initiative because of their emphasis on progress in the structural dimension. Change initiatives can be difficult to pin down in terms of progress because they are directed at the human dimension, rather than solely the structural dimension. Artifacts and documentation may be lacking, which makes it difficult to address the integrated or white space connections with other areas of the initiative.

If change initiative progress is hard to define, it is often the result of weak or poorly applied business change methodology. Change methodology should contain a rich, integrated set of tools and activities for addressing the multiple dimensions of a change initiative: people, organization, process, technology, and subsets within them. People who are used to reporting progress through standardized project management methodology (e.g. PMBOK, or Project Management Body of Knowledge) will not be able to demonstrate meaningful progress for the change initiative beyond the completion of tasks. The members of the team, including specialists, should be well-versed in the methodology through training and roll-out. Standards for change documentation in all work streams of the project must be understood and enforced, and managed through an integrated methodology. Progress demonstrated through the advancement of change solutions described in the methodology should be measured, and incorporated into the balanced scorecard for the initiative.

Possible pre-existing contributors to lack of demonstrated evidence for change progress include:

- lack of experience using change management methodologies and tools
- historically change management has largely been an afterthought. The change activities were treated as a separate work stream that was not tightly integrated into the overall solution
- lack of competence in project management.

Address lack of demonstrated evidence for change progress through these BCM best practices:

- develop a balanced scorecard and cascade it
- use a structured change management methodology with supporting tools and templates
- create a change road map and master plan
- manage the white space.

10. Poor understanding of the change road map, roles, and dependencies

Members of the change initiative may be diligently and efficiently performing their tasks but not collectively advancing the change. This is called the "fox-hole" effect. When queried about the bigger picture of how what they are doing needs to support higher levels of the change solution or big picture, team members operating in this type of paradigm will not be able to explain it. They will point out that they are doing their jobs and satisfying the needs of their immediate team leader. When it is time to deliver integrated change solutions, however, this tactical focus will come back to roost in the form of non-integrated and ineffective change solutions.

Change management is a cross-functional endeavor. On many projects, staying busy and keeping heads down may be a blessing, but in a change management initiative an understanding of the bigger picture is essential. Transforming an organization to a new state is not about discrete elements but about the white space and subtexts for which a high state of awareness is required. For example, a team creating technical solutions ignorant of how the new end-to-end processes must work puts the overall change solution at risk. Similarly, changes in culture must be carried through from the organizational development specialists to the process designers to achieve a sufficient solution. A clearly communicated change road map, a change master plan with specific responsibilities, clear communication on expectations for team members to work collaboratively, management of the white space, and regular assessment of team member understanding are needed to ensure that change team members have the required focus.

Possible pre-existing contributors to confusion or lack of focus regarding change direction and/or initiative include:

- communication is not a strong suit of leadership in the existing culture
- strategic or big picture focus is not articulated for initiatives and projects
- change initiatives are tactical in nature, or provide support to other larger projects.

Address confusion or lack of focus regarding change direction and/or initiative through these BCM best practices:

- make the vision for change clear, compelling, and credible
- consistently communicate to reinforce the change

- assess readiness and surface inhibitors early and often
- recognize and reward change progress regularly and consistently
- support the transition through the change wilderness
- develop a balanced scorecard and cascade it
- create a change road map and master plan.

Business Change Management best practices

In this section we present thirteen BCM Best Practices that can be used to address the common change management risks and issues discussed above. Change Levers are high-impact focal points for change leaders to reduce risk and optimize results for a change initiative. Accordingly, Change Levers can be measured and incorporated into a balanced scorecard. Best Practices are the means for ensuring that the Change Levers are sufficiently applied and are driving the change initiative forward. While they may support multiple Change Levers, Best Practices can be categorized by the Change Lever they most predominantly serve. Best Practices should be applied during planning and throughout the change initiative. Change Levers are described in detail in Chapter three: Change Leadership and Management.

The BCM Best Practices, grouped by Change Levers, are:

Decisive Leadership
1. Make the vision for change clear, compelling, and credible
2. Identify the problems and probe the causes
3. Make the tough calls.

Engagement
4. Model the change
5. Make the change personal and accountable.

Organization Alignment
6. Clarify boundaries between the old and new states
7. Consistently communicate to reinforce the change.

Culture Alignment
8. Assess readiness and surface inhibitors early and often
9. Recognize and reward change progress regularly and consistently
10. Support the transition through the change wilderness.

Balanced Measurement
11. Develop a balanced scorecard and cascade it.

Program Management and Change Integration
12. Create a change road map and master plan
13. Manage the white space.

Decisive Leadership

1. Make the change vision clear, compelling, and credible

The "pull" for change direction must be strong enough to engage, galvanize and sustain the teams and individuals dedicated to realizing the goals of the change initiative. The vision for change is the magnet around which all elements, creativity, and persistence of the change initiative momentum revolve. If the content of the change vision, the ultimate target, is not well-defined, poorly-defined or inconceivable, it will not matter that your communications are consistent, your stakeholders are aligned with the plan, or that a rewards and recognition program is in place. Processes are only as good as the content that moves within them. And in the case of business change, a strategic vision with substantive content is everything.

The vision for the change must include the full context surrounding it, which answers the implied questions associated with a vision. When developing your vision for change, consider these factors:

- **Provide the rationale and alignment of the change vision to business strategy.** The change vision is not the organization's overall business strategy, but it must derive from it. It should not be created independently. There is always a business driver, or set of business drivers, behind the need the change, which if explained honestly and justified in a business context, will ground the vision for change in realism and rationality which will enable people to understand and connect with it. Leaving it to their imaginations or not stating the real reasons or direction for the change can lead to distrust. Transformational change happens for reasons that are not small, but strategic. Business drivers can include:
  - market or competitive pressures
  - growth or expansion needs (e.g. acquisition)
  - consolidation (e.g. merger)
  - customer-driven needs for new products and services.

  Emphasize the positive drivers and goals but do not hide the ones that are negative (e.g. consolidation or efficiency improvement) which may result in job losses or changes.

- **Create a transformational vision for change.** The vision for change paints a picture that describes the future state that the transformed organization will look like. It should provide a viable, customer-oriented, longer-term target (e.g. five or more years out) of what the organization will become in its future state. The vision should include measurable goals. The shift to desired values and principles should be evident. Additionally, the vision should be strategic, aspirational, and extensive, projecting from and building upon the organization's strengths, including its history, culture, and assets.

Change team members and employees of the organization must be able to imagine this new, transformed state for the organization and believe in it. Consequently, the change vision cannot be so far-reaching that it strains credibility by ignoring the value of the current organization and cultural fit. For example, Steve Jobs envisioned Apple becoming a music provider rather than just a purveyor of computers and smart phones. Apple employees were inspired because they could see the picture Jobs was painting of how the Apple's iPhone presence provided a ready platform for digital music delivery.

A compelling vision for change embodies meaningful humanistic themes, in which employees strive for excellence and a higher purpose in meeting the needs of their customers as well as enriching each other. Such themes exert a much stronger motivational pull than a change vision directed primarily at financial goals, or at an empty abstraction such as an organizational entity. A good example of this powerful theme of meaningfulness is Mayo Clinic's Model of Care, which incorporates as its primary focus meeting the healthcare needs of the patient, supported by excellence in integrated care delivery and academic research.[6] Change initiatives at Mayo align with the framework and provide inspiration for team members.

A vision for change should not be mixed or confused with large-scale initiatives supported by change management activities, or an effort that exists with a change initiative such as implementing an enterprise-wide system. A vision for change must transform the organization in a broader and deeper context.

- **Establish a sense of urgency.** A strong vision for change and a good business rationale are still not enough by themselves. The change vision remains an ideal or a "nice-to-have" until a cogent answer to this implicit question can be supplied: "Why do we need to do it *now*?"

  The vision for change and key messages surrounding it must explain:
  - **The business consequences of not moving forward with the change towards the vision.** These could include losing an opportunity to seize leadership or growth, or losing out to more nimble and innovative competitors. Often referred to as the "burning platform," this perspective expresses the adverse consequences of not acting on the change now. These consequences must be credibly tied to real-time external events and not just assumed.
  - **WIIFM** (What's In It for Me?). Explain the benefits individuals will gain from the change, not just the general organization, investors or senior management. This could include future opportunities in the organization resulting from an individual's work on the change initiative or training and learning to boost their capabilities and market power. It could also include the chance to be recognized and rewarded for playing a role in the organization's historic moment.

A compelling case for change includes a sound business rationale, a clear vision, and a strong sense of urgency.

2. Identify the problems, and probe the causes

High risk is inherent in change initiatives, and problems will threaten to stall change progress at every turn. Change leaders must proactively find those problems (i.e. roadblocks), determine their root causes and address them. Is there an underlying problem with specific areas of the change not being addressed, such as cultural readiness? Are there sacred cows that no one wants to go near for fear of retribution? Are there key stakeholders who are either unwilling or unable to support the change who need additional intervention, such as coaching, education, or as a last resort, removal?

Such actions by leaders will not only keep the initiative from being stifled, but they will also build the change team members' and stakeholders' confidence in the leadership. Team members will be encouraged by their change leaders to model and follow them to surface problems, pinpoint their causes, and provide solutions.

Change leaders should apply the following in identifying problems and causes:

- **Make risk management a priority.** Change leaders should actively monitor risk as a core responsibility, and work to prevent risks from becoming problems and issues.
- **Put in place an effective process for issues identification and escalation.** As part of the change initiative infrastructure, leaders should set expectations for members of the change team to use these processes, and hold them accountable.
- **Encourage reception of difficult news.** Leaders can better identify patterns and related causes if their change team members are providing them with information on what is not working, reasons for such and suggestions for overcoming issues. Wanting to hear only good news or confirmation will convey the message that the change leader does not really care about removing roadblocks, and morale will quickly begin to falter.

3. Make the tough calls

Change leaders exist in name only unless they are taking on the big issues that impede the change. Those who avoid conflict or cannot say no to resisting political pressures to preserve the status quo when the stakes are high will diminish faith in the change initiative, thereby slowing if not reversing momentum. Authenticity is central to leadership, and actions must follow words. Leaders who ask their teams to give their time and effort to advancing change must be willing to walk the talk when much is on the line. This could involve publicly dismantling a sacred cow, removing a member of the team who is countering the change and affecting morale, confronting a stonewalling stakeholder, or reallocating resources to the highest priority issues, among other things.

The reluctance of some leaders to make tough calls required for change may be rooted in organizational culture. In our consulting experience, we have observed that middle management appears to be soft in taking on important issues in organizations where upper management operates in a command-and-control model. Middle management may not feel confident or empowered. This problem of avoiding conflict when it is most needed seems also to be more prevalent among managers in organization whose work is heavily data-dependent, such as IT and R&D.

Sooner or later the change leaders will be confronted with big-impact issues and roadblocks that must be removed in order to progress the change initiative. All eyes will be on the change leaders to clear the path.

4. Model the change

A change initiative may look good on paper and sound strong when articulated through the communications program. However, the plan, readiness survey and change team feedback may indicate that progress is in the red or yellow stages, not moving forward, and at risk of reversing momentum.

Behavior in an organization is largely dictated from above, in a cascading fashion. Why? Individuals in organizations emulate the behavior of the person to whom they report, and their superiors above them. Authenticity and consistency are core aspects of leadership. Subversive, conflict-oriented, or disengaged behavior among those on the change team and throughout organization often arises from the fact that the leaders of the change are not "walking the change talk" that they are articulating and asking others to follow. People are observant, and leaders must go beyond paying lip service to the change and demonstrating the desired values themselves.

When modeling the change, consider the following:

- **"Be" the change.** Exhibit the desired behaviors outlined in the change initiative that are reflective of those in the future transformed organization.
- **Avoiding responsibility is as bad as antagonistic behavior.** Don't be passive on the things that matter: accept responsibility and accountability, take initiative to advance the change, and resist adherence to the existing hierarchy and the old system when they inhibit change.
- **Support, encourage, and protect those working to move the change forward.** Publicly recognize those who are working hard and making sacrifices on behalf of the change initiative, and stand up for those who are being attacked for their efforts to change the status quo.
- **Demonstrate courage in taking on tough challenges.** Make the hard choices and take a stand for doing the right thing rather than the most expedient, including politically unpopular decisions in support of the change. These may include things like making tough calls and crossing organizational boundaries.

- **Make change a priority and demonstrate the commitment needed to promote it.** Shift priorities, rebalance your day job responsibilities, and make the time required to advance the change effort.
- **Be authentic.** Leaders must be honest, empathetic, and transparent with themselves as well as other individuals, not just excited about the cause for change. Motives matter. Inconsistent behavior breaks down trust.

Engagement

5. Make the change personal and accountable

Making change stick means making people feel that they own the change, connected to it in both an emotional and a cognitive work sense. In order for people to feel like they own the change they must be made responsible and accountable for making it happen. This means more than assigning them to activities in the change plan.

To build engagement, the following are useful:

- **Embed change goals in performance appraisals.** Incorporate responsibilities for the change initiative, along with the desired behaviors for change, into performance appraisals. Change will move from a "nice-to-do" (when I have time) to a "must do" priority.
- **Make line or reporting managers accountable for supporting the change through their people.** In order to meet the change-related requirements on a performance appraisal, a person needs support from their supervisor to reprioritize or balance day job requirements. If the supervisor is involved in the change initiative enlisting their support will be easier, but if the change is an executive priority, support requirements will trickle down.
- **Provide concrete behavior models and examples.** Values, principles, and charters go a long way towards a new culture, but desired behaviors are elusive. Idealistic "motherhood and apple pie" language built from generic and abstract aphorisms may have some initial appeal, but down deep humans respond to specificity. Convert "be open and accessible," or "take initiative" to particular examples such as: "Make time to talk with my team members one-on-one each week to understand their feelings about the progress of the change;" and "Generate at least three areas of improvement or reinforcement to share at the weekly update meeting."
- **Call the fouls.** Publicly but politely confront those who violate the goals for changed culture and/or behavior (e.g. being defensive, supporting the old system, reverting to a command-and-control leadership style when the organization is not in crisis-mode).

The level of engagement surrounding a change initiative is largely dependent on how well aligned the leaders are. As Dean and Linda Anderson describe it:

"Building leadership alignment up-front sets the ideal conditions for positive employee involvement throughout the change."[7]

Organization Alignment

6. Clarify boundaries between the old and new states

Anxiety about change is significantly influenced by uncertainty. Specifically, the more people feel they cannot control something that may negatively impact them, the more anxious they will be. Reducing anxiety about what will change will help to increase initiative and problem solving within the change teams, stakeholders, and impacted employees. Paradoxically, focusing peoples' concentration on what needs to change also requires specifying what will *not* change. Similarly, constraints are known to foster creativity in many disciplines. Providing specific constraints, or boundaries, will provide focus for what really will change.

Removing unnecessary uncertainty by clarifying what is in and out of the scope of change is also helpful in quelling rumors and gossip (i.e. the "swirl") which inevitably float around the change effort affecting morale and confidence among the troops. This also builds a level of trust in that change leaders are being square with those being asked to carry out and support the change.

Delineate the boundaries of the change by:

- **Specifying what is "off the table"** – what we won't change (what people don't have to think about).
- **Specifying what is "on the table"** – what we will change but don't know how yet (what people need to focus on).
- **Identifying why things "on the table" need to change** – old ways of doing things or sacred cows that are no longer relevant or useful to the future state (what people need to let go of).

These include cultural attributes as well as structural ones. Invite team members to participate in this exercise. What is on the table may grow as the transformation begins to take hold in the organization and change is seen as an agent of progress. This fluidity needs to be anchored. Knowing what aspects of the organization's values, structure, processes and culture won't change in the short term, and what will be preserved gives people something to hold onto while they focus their attention and creativity on areas that matter.

An example of describing the boundaries of change can be seen in this informal management communication:

What we won't change in our organization are our longstanding commitment to quality and investment in our people and our products. We have no plans to downsize the organization. What is likely to change are our processes and, potentially, our working relationships, in order to achieve and advance our goals for quality and excellence – because we do need to become more agile and adaptive in responding to our customers' needs and the competitive market. This will require some changes in our culture as well, and some things we are not used to. While we are preserving the important aspects of our culture, we need to transition to a new mindset of openness, bringing ideas and problems to the surface quickly.

Part of alignment also revolves around proactively understanding the ripple effects of change. Although we will discuss organization architecture in greater detail later on in the book, all organizations are comprised of an architecture that consists of Technology, Organization, and Process. We call this our TOPS model. The Technology architecture is comprised of the technology used to deliver the core products and services, applications, IT hardware, and databases (information needed to run the business of the organization). The Organization architecture is comprised of HR practices (i.e. rewards, performance management), culture, competencies, business model/structure, and administrative policies. The Process architecture is comprised of physical infrastructure (the location, number, age of the offices/plants), the physical layout of offices, and core and supporting processes. Each element of architecture must be aligned to the business strategy that is linked to the change vision or target. Additionally, each element of architecture is interdependent so when you change one element of architecture it will cause gaps that must be aligned for change to be successfully implemented.

7. Consistently communicate to reinforce the change

Having a clearly defined, compelling, and credible vision for the change is necessary, but not sufficient for the change to take hold. Even your most proficient, exemplary performers on the change initiative will be faced with competing priorities and pressures, distractions from their day jobs, overload, and natural temptations to fall back into the old ways of doing things which the change initiative is seeking to transform. To counter these change inhibitors, ongoing communication from the change leadership is essential.

Communication on the change initiative must:

- **Articulate the future state and the path to get there.** The change vision, the case for change, the change road map, and the plan and expectations for performance must be laid out clearly in language that everyone can understand and act upon.

- **Leverage the voice of authority**. Organizations are hierarchical by design, and individuals are more attuned to what the higher level members in the organization are saying about the change, and what they expect. Communication from senior members of the organization, including the change sponsor, will carry more weight than a flurry of communications at lower levels.
- **Encourage and support the change in a timely manner.** Highlight milestones achieved. Share examples or stories of where individuals and teams have demonstrated the desired values of the change. Commend effort and learning as well as results. Do not wait to the end of the initiative to justify the hard-earned efforts made along the way and the positive values demonstrated.
- **Provide new and substantive information.** Principles and bromides only go so far, as do pep talks and cheerleading. People are looking for information that will impact them or the change, such as progress updates, changes in the initiative approach, or revelations and findings which could impact the course of change.
- **Acknowledge and share what people are saying or experiencing during the change.** Relating to the people in the trenches who are trying to make change happen means allowing them to communicate their challenges – how they have overcome them, and how they have learned and grown whilst undertaking them. Incorporate their experiences into your communication for credibility, recognition, and opportunity.
- **Mix the media, but keep it concise.** Different modes of communication are stimulating, such as video, blogs, news clips, email, but they can be overwhelming. Remember that people have day jobs and may already be experiencing information overload.
- **Balance face-to-face with electronic communication methods**. Physical human-to-human interaction still carries the most impact. Include town hall meetings and spontaneous meetings with change team members (e.g. coffee breaks, lunches) to make it more personal.

Culture Alignment

8. Assess readiness and surface inhibitors early and often

A change initiative may appear to be on plan. There is no perceived confusion, conflict, disgruntlement, or disengagement among the ranks. People may not look or sound unhappy. But that does not mean they are embracing the change and prepared to take it forward. Do not wait for dissension and concerns about the change to emerge.

Change readiness is the degree to which people understand and are prepared to advance and implement change. Inhibitors are those things which affect people's readiness, such as confidence in the success of the change. Collective readiness for change, especially the lack thereof, can make, break, or stall a change initiative. There are often hidden concerns or inhibitors about the change which can surface unexpectedly and create risk for the change if not identified early and addressed. Assessing organizational readiness for change via secured surveys is a useful method. Force field analysis is another technique used in teams to engage members in uncovering inhibitors to the change and outlining ways to address them.

It is important to assess readiness for change and surface inhibitors continuously throughout the change initiative by doing the following.

- **Take the organization's pulse for change to establish a readiness benchmark.** Reassess readiness throughout the initiative as a measure of change progress.
- **Apply multiple methods to understand readiness and inhibitors**. In addition to the use of survey instruments, walk the halls, have conversations over breakfast and lunch, and solicit real input around what is – and what is not – working for the change.
- **Look for qualitative input on ideas on how to make the change work.** Do not just perform quantitative reads and statistics. What measures of change would employees like to see that demonstrate change is taking hold?
- **Assure safety and support for candor.** Authentically communicate that anything said to you or the change leaders by team members about the change will not be held against them. Though remember, like everyone else, you will be accountable for the new standards of change behavior.

9. Recognize and reward change progress regularly and consistently

Much money has been spent on celebrating change initiatives in public venues, and rewards given out to commemorate achievers and inspire others who are members of change initiatives. Often, however, within a short time people are reverting to the old culture and behaviors that the change was supposed to get rid of (e.g. closed doors, heads down, linear focus). Why does this happen?

Old habits die hard. Carrots and sticks are both needed, but their staying power is temporary if not reinforced. The following actions are useful:

- **Embed rewards and recognition into work practice, rather than just high-profile events.** Team members keep each other honest, and they know who is doing the heavy lifting, who is pushing the group to a new level, and who deserves commendation. Encourage them to vote for change leaders.
- **Reward cross-change initiative support.** Since much of the value of change initiatives can be found in the white space between dimensions of the change solution, look for behaviors and individuals that exemplify tapping this resource, and reward them. For example, technologists who work closely with the process and organization specialists to develop integrated solutions which support the new organization.
- **Celebrate incremental successes, as well as effort.** It's not always a "big result" that deserves recognition, but the hard-earned effort along the way.

Take time out to recognize and point out the "little things" that lead to the outcomes, including learning.

- **Align the rewards and recognition to fit the change.** Flashy award ceremonies, big parties, and expensive gifts may have been de rigueur in many change initiatives past, but they may not be representative of the kind of culture the new organization is heading towards. Reward and recognize behaviors and accomplishments which are consistent with the values and behaviors identified in the target culture.
- **Consider the audience: one size does *not* fit all.** Assess what matters to the teams and individuals in terms of reward and recognition. Different types of people, groups, and age bands may appreciate rewards and recognition for their change efforts in unique ways. Customize accordingly. Consider intangible rewards like time earned with family (life/work balance), investment in learning and growth vehicles, and exciting role or assignment opportunities related to the change initiative.

10. Support the transition through the change wilderness

The leaders of a change initiative may have performed readiness assessments, applied the necessary interventions, rewarded positive change behavior, and kept the teams on plan. The change initiative is well into the later stages, but people seem more anxious and concerned than ever. What happened?

There is an inherent cycle to change that applies to all types of human endeavors, especially change initiatives. There are moments of enthusiasm, trepidation, and outright fear. However, there is never a straight linear path which leads from unease to comfort. The deeper the venture into change, the less familiar the terrain becomes and the harder it is to let go of the old ways. Organizational psychologists have noted the psychological, mental, and emotional stresses, which must work themselves out over the course of the change "journey." This is a period of exploration of finding new boundaries and identities which cannot be controlled or directed externally. William Bridges called this transitional period of letting go of the old before claiming the new, the "wilderness."[8]

Even though it is impossible to externally expedite this transition state in others, there are things that should be done:

- **Encourage the transition.** Explain that the discomfort during transition is natural, anticipated, and importantly, encouraged. Allow people to express their real feelings, not just what they think management wants to hear them say.
- **Acknowledge what is going away.** Similar to what was described in change boundary definition, but with an emphasis on cultural and personal dimensions, try to identify and express what people are struggling to let go of (e.g. position, security, identity).
- **Share your feelings about change and how you are dealing with it.** Be honest and vulnerable in describing your experience from the perspective of a fellow participant in the organizational change, not just as a change leader

charged with driving the initiative forward. This will help build trust with change team members and stakeholders. Discuss suggestions from your own experience of how you have overcome fear and managed change to give them confidence.

- **Be patient and account for support.** While moving forward with the work of the change initiative, keep in mind that raw emotions must take their course, be expressed, listened to, and responded to. This is not a once-and-done effort. Encourage change participants to come back to you, express their challenges, and offer ideas that you will do your best to support, where feasible.

Balanced Measurement

11. Develop a balanced scorecard and cascade it

A change initiative may be running according to plan. However, it may not be making much of a business impact. What could be missing?

"You get what you measure" is a well-known saying. And what gets measured is often what is easiest to measure, for example, whether project plan dates were met. Schedule deadlines are important, but a business change initiative, in particular, needs measures that are comprehensive, addressing what is important to the change initiative across multiple domains. Beyond the change initiative itself, it is also important to measure the business impacts that the change is intended to bring about. These measures need to be cascaded from the top to subsequent levels of the organization to ensure consistency.

It is important to put clear measures in place and assess throughout the change initiative in the form of a balanced scorecard which addresses measures such as:

Quantitative progress indicators, target-based
- plan milestone dates
- deliverable targets (various elements of the change solution)
- activity completion dates
- budget level (variance over projected).

Qualitative change indicators, content-based
- change readiness (collective organizational mindset)
- commitment and initiative (advancement and support behaviors)
- change enablement impact (progress in specific areas of desired change)
- lessons learned (what knowledge was gained which resulted in improvements to the change effort).

Business outcomes, what is important to the organization
- business impact (how changes in culture and/or structure are impacting overall performance)
- customer satisfaction
- financial goals.

Program Management and Change Integration

12. Create a change road map and master plan

One of the things that differentiate a business change initiative from most other projects is the breadth of its scope, in addition to its depth. It is important to use a wide-angle lens to identify where change needs to take place, what organizational impacts must be addressed, where the dependencies and relationships are that need to be managed, and what corresponding actions must be incorporated into the change master plan. These change dimensions should include:

- people
- organizational structure
- technology
- change capability (methodology, tools, competencies)
- management and integration.

These dimensions, and their components, may end up as work streams in the overall master plan. A master plan will pay special attention to integrating change components. Change management should never be treated as a subordinate work stream to other initiatives (e.g. IT system implementations), but should subsume other work streams which support the change.

To effectively manage the white space and ensure integration across the change initiative:

- **Appoint a strategic business change leader to whom other functional leads on the change initiative report.** Allowing a particular operational function to lead the effort, e.g. IT, HR or Finance is too myopic, and will impart a biased flavor and lose strategic impact quickly. It is preferable to appoint someone respected from the executive ranks experienced in both strategic planning and change management.
- **Create a change road map.** Provide a conceptual path forward for the change which people can readily understand. Show how multiple work streams address specific areas of change, with specific accountabilities. Include an overarching work stream that manages and integrates the multiple areas of change associated with the sub-work streams, with overall accountability.
- **Align the plan work streams to the overall target and milestones in a master plan.** Pay specific attention as to what is needed from the work streams and when to produce holistic or integrated sets of changes (i.e. change releases).
- **Invite "bad news" to recalibrate your plan.** Getting "no news" is not really "good news." Seek input from those in the trenches of the change to augment the plan and reduce risk (e.g. activities to increase specific interventions where people need help with carrying out aspects of the change).

13. Manage the white space

Change initiatives by nature embody a number of interdependent components that need to be managed in an integrated manner for the change to succeed and take hold. "White space" refers to the relationships, dependencies and impacts between the change target/solution components, as well as between the work streams focused on completing them.

Within the white space are opportunities to reduce the considerable risk of the change initiative as well as to expand the impact of the change solution and make the change stick. For example, creating a target culture that possesses attributes like openness will impact the formality and degree of control inherent in business processes as well as management procedures and oversight in the future organization. Culture and business process design are often separate projects, or work streams, within a change initiative due to their distinct focus and skills required. Working closely across these disciplines to understand the impacts and addressing them as part of the overall change solution will promote integration, consistency, and effectiveness in the final result. Additionally, insights achieved in one work stream may be valuable learning for use in another work stream. For example, business rules created during the organizational design work can often be implanted in the process and technology solution designs, such as procedures.

Managing the white space across a change initiative starts with a master plan for change, which addresses the multiple dimensions of the change in a holistic manner, backed by a conceptual change road map. It is also critical to have an overall change solution architecture on which the technology, organization, and processes need to work together. Leadership for the business change solution architecture should reside with a business architect who can set the design guidelines and constraints, identify the integration needs between change domains, and manage completion of the various design elements. The program manager can address white space from the logistics aspect by ensuring frequent and accountable communication between the work stream project team.

Case study

Applying best practices in Business Change Management: How Quintiles navigated the change process to implement a global performance management process

Quintiles is an integrated biopharmaceutical services company offering clinical, commercial, consulting, and capital solutions worldwide. There are 25,000 Quintiles employees across 60 countries in technical and professional roles that help biopharmaceutical companies develop and commercialize products to improve and lengthen patients' lives. Patient health, safety and ethics are top priorities for Quintiles in their work with biopharmaceutical companies to navigate risk and seize opportunities in a constantly changing environment.

The catalyst for change

Since Quintiles is a service organization, the importance of earning and maintaining customer loyalty is well understood by its senior management. In recent years, customer loyalty had become an even bigger challenge. Intensifying competition among biopharmaceutical services vendors had made it more attractive and easier than ever before for customers to switch vendors or search for better deals. As a result, enhancing the loyalty of the Quintiles customer base was a high-priority strategic imperative.

For Quintiles, the most critical factor in maintaining and building customer loyalty had always been engaged employees who were motivated by skilled managers to consistently exceed customer expectations. A formula that Quintiles managers and most employees knew by heart was:

> customer loyalty = manager effectiveness + employee engagement

To ensure that the organization successfully delivered on this critical formula, Quintiles annually conducted a survey of its employees. This survey measured a variety of management factors that drive employee engagement.

An employee survey indicated that, due primarily to the multiple systems and approaches to performance management at the time, less than half of the respondents agreed with the statement, "My performance has been evaluated fairly." Whether perception or reality, this was a clear red flag with strategic implications for customer loyalty. Since employee engagement is linked tightly to being treated fairly in terms of performance, the potential implication was that a large number of potentially disengaged Quintiles employees created a risk for impacting customer loyalty.

From the survey results it quickly became clear that performance management was a top area of concern for employees which needed to be addressed. Analysis of the survey results revealed that employee engagement was being adversely impacted by the lack of consistent performance management processes across the company. The quantitative data from the survey results reinforced the anecdotal evidence that the existing performance management processes were in significant need of improvement.

Having identified an area of critical business need via their employee engagement survey, Quintiles senior management initiated a comprehensive change management effort to create global consistency in and enhance the effectiveness of its performance management process.

Defining the scope of the business change need

Senior management deployed an organizational design team to conduct a series of focus groups with employees and managers across multiple levels across the organization. Focus group participants communicated that the current performance management processes and systems were "too time intensive and complicated." The performance management process was at times circumvented, leaving employees with "performance ratings with no written review." Participants also indicated that the current process made it difficult for leaders to drive managerial accountability for conducting reviews, accurately differentiate performance, and align related processes like compensation and development planning.

The leadership defined the problem scope in terms of breadth and depth. Across the company, Quintiles had multiple approaches to managing performance. Some areas of the organization used homegrown processes and systems while others had no formal process. Quintiles also lacked:

- a shared approach for selecting and measuring competencies
- a process for designing and capturing SMART (specific, measurable, attainable, relevant, timely) goals
- a method of cascading goals and linking them to corporate strategy.

Taking action to address these performance management problems would make a positive impact on employee engagement, retention, and effectiveness that aligned with the strategic business direction of the organization and the imperative to improve and maximize customer loyalty.

In response to these business needs, the goal of Quintiles' change initiative was to improve their employee engagement by transforming performance management into a globally consistent, effective, and integrated process. A secondary goal of this project was to advance Quintile's capability as a performance-focused organization that routinely recognized, rewarded, and retained top talent. An effective global performance management process would shift the employee performance curve by helping "B" players reach their potential while assisting employees who already exceeded expectations to find the next level of performance.

Creating the change target and making the case for change

Senior management and the organizational design experts defined the current state of performance management at Quintiles and contrasted it with the desired future state target, the impact expected from the change initiative, as shown in Table 2.2.

TABLE 2.2 Expected impact of change from current to future state

Performance Management Change Target	
Current state	Future state (Expected impact of change)
• Little tie to corporate objectives	• Provide clarity of and alignment to corporate objectives
• Unable to align goals across the organization	• Drive shared ownership and accountability of key priorities
• Exit surveys cite unclear performance ratings as reason for departure	• Reduce turnover (increase retention) due to increase focus on performance management
• Unable to differentiate top performers	• Increase ability to manage performance and help "raise the bar"
• Current forms time consuming and cumbersome	• Reduce billable manager time in preparing performance appraisals
• Little tie to compensation planning	• Provide linkage to differentiation of ratings to insure people are rewarded for their contribution
• Multiple systems and approaches	• Eliminate multiple systems and duplicative costs (direct cost saving)
• Unable to include customer-managed populations	• Provide external customers with a "global process" to ensure adequate management of their projects
• Development efforts separate from performance inputs	• Refocus training/development on workplace performance and away from just attending courses

A business case was developed to gain support for the global performance management change project. The benefits of a global, consistent, and effective performance management process were specified, as shown in Figure 2.1, which was supplemented with supporting data and ROI metrics. The business case also incorporated the change target contrasted with current state weaknesses to give stakeholders, employees, and the change team a clear focus on what was going to change and why.

FIGURE 2.1 The benefits of changing to a global performance management process

Identifying change risks and applying best practices on the change initiative

The organizational change experts assessed the risks inherent in transitioning the organization from the current state to the future state target. Comparing the scope of the business change with current culture resulted in identifying key risks:

- potential resistance on the part of managers and departments to giving up their accustomed informal ways of managing performance in the form of lack of urgency, inertia or other means
- roadblocks to collaboration where managers want different things and customized elements in the performance management process and system that are inconsistent with a common global solution
- limited understanding of the big picture of the change and a tendency to focus on provincial needs or small details that could impede completion of the change project.

In addition to the change risks, there was a schedule project constraint that had to be taken into account. Senior management needed this change project to be completed within 3.5 months so that the global performance management process would be operational for the next performance management cycle.

A change project team was assembled with change leadership, project management, HR, organizational change, and experts in process and systems design. Stakeholders were identified. A staged approach from design through implementation was developed and turned into a change plan. The approach focused on a change solution that would embody multiple dimensions:

- process – design common workflows with business rules for performance management
- technology – use performance management software to enable the process and procedures
- organization – implement roles, empowerment and accountability for manager and employee use and adherence to the new process and procedures.

These change best practices were incorporated into the change approach and applied during the project.

Define the business problem, its causes and the change impact

The situation needed to be fully understood before embarking on the change project. The severity and urgency of the business need to make the change to a global performance management process had to link to the company's strategic direction as well as the specific problems that were impeding it. Quintiles had a deeper issue than that which could be addressed by some system tweaks or added functionality. After impact analysis, it became clear that a more holistic change was required.

This clarity around the situation helped focus the approach, create realistic estimates of the change effort, and identify the change risks that needed to be managed. The realistic baseline could be weighed against corporate strategy, business need, and stakeholder interest to justify the change project's relative importance and strategic priority in the company's change project evaluation cycle.

Set clear expectations

Securing early buy-in for the change was critical to managing the expectations of stakeholders. Change leaders used a before-and-after change target, a compelling business case supported by ROI and a cascading change project scorecard. A change road map and detailed plan with clear milestones were also reviewed with stakeholders for their input on how to make the change succeed.

Engage stakeholders in the change through custom communication

To expedite the project timeline, initial communications focused on communicating specific "what's in it for me?" messages for each stakeholder group. This soft-sell strategy facilitated the launching of formal communication and plans as soon as the project was kicked-off. Influential members of each stakeholder group on the RFP team also helped to earn manager buy-in and drive support for the program.

Table 2.3 provides a summary of key points that resonated with each audience.

TABLE 2.3 Segmented stakeholder change engagement benefits

Benefits of the New Global Performance Management Process *What's in it for me?*	
Employees	**Managers**
• Maximum input to goal-setting with alignment to senior level goals	• Provides a concise, automated, web-based review process, significantly reducing time spent on reviews
• Year-round input into performance and accomplishments	
• Timely mid- and end-of-year reviews	• Drives execution of key initiatives by clarifying/aligning business goals
• Encourages a culture of consistent coaching and feedback to avoid "surprises" at review time	• Retains top talent by highlighting and rewarding superior performance
• Increases focus on the performance discussion rather than forms	
Human Resources	**Senior Management**
• Robust reporting feature that allows HR to identify bottlenecks and report on results	• Eliminates multiple systems and duplicative costs
• Links with current compensation tool and HRIS system	• Increases our ability to manage performance
• Automates much of the workflow process with auto form generation and email prompts to managers and employees	• Provides clarity and alignment around corporate objectives
	• Drives shared ownership and accountability of key priorities
	• Engages employees throughout the organization by furnishing them with relevant, timely coaching and feedback to secure personal success

The change team spent considerable time engaging broad-based stakeholders to identify their concerns and identify the sources or causes of their resistance. This included HR business partners who would work with managers on employee performance and IT staff who would have to support the project from an end user standpoint. One of the biggest challenges was getting the HR community to disengage from past practices. Through careful dialogue, issues were surfaced and resolved.

The time change leadership invested in spending with stakeholders helped build alliances with them and created advocates for informal networks that were leveraged for employee communication. Personally addressing the concerns of influential naysayers also helped the change team limit the negative impact of their point of view on the change project.

Anticipate and mitigate resistance

Resistance was planned on given the nature of the change and the challenging transition that was required for the organization to embrace a common, global performance management process. Identifying, prioritizing, and managing risks through a risk management plan was vital in managing resistance during the change effort, ensuring the project met quality standards for impact, delivery, schedule and budget. A stakeholder assessment was an important tool for locating and measuring resistance in the form of things such as concerns about the change, lack of knowledge, misunderstanding, or skepticism. Assessments were performed at the beginning of the change project stage and periodically updated throughout the project life cycle. This received input was valuable for addressing the needs concerning the change and tuning the plan.

Select a technology approach that best suits the business change priorities

An important early decision on the change project was whether to build or buy the software platform that would enable the new global performance management process. Given the accelerated project timeline, the visibility of the effort, and its direct impact on customer loyalty the change team decided to partner with a vendor respected for its performance management software which ran a disciplined process. From a culture standpoint this situation had to be carefully managed.

Quintiles' highly educated workforce possessed considerable expertise in data analysis, technology management and related disciplines which installed pride of ownership and reliance on internally-developed solutions. The change leadership team had to overcome the "not invented here" objection and address the reality that while the company potentially could build a performance management system, it was not their core business and would exceed the project timeline.

A cross-functional selection committee (comprised of learning and development, HR business partners, HR systems professionals, IT, end users, strategic sourcing, and senior leadership) crafted an RFP with desired system specifications. Examples of the specifications included ease of use, rapid implementation, global capacity, ability to link with other internal systems, and ongoing training and support.

Collaboratively design the target solution (process)

To address the challenge of getting a global organization to adhere to a new global performance management process (which included goal-setting, interim reviews, informal coaching, year-end evaluations, and development discussions), stakeholder user representatives were engaged as active participants in designing the solution.

HR formed a cross-functional team to redesign the process. The change project lead and a subset of the RFP team remained to ensure continuity, while other members rotated, based on required expertise and stage of the project. Senior leadership was engaged at the outset of process redesign in developing performance management guiding principles.

Using a solution design lab approach, the principles along with business rules were incorporated into the sub-processes. A consistent, globally sensitive process for managing employee performance was designed which included:

- clear cascading goals aligned with business strategy and strategic priorities
- well-defined metrics for measuring organizational and individual success
- continuous feedback and coaching with a formal review at least twice annually
- honest and objective ratings that differentiate performance and clearly communicate value and contribution to the organization
- a consistent rating scale globally
- performance appraisals with a strong linkage to individual compensation and development actions
- development planning focused on improving performance in the workplace during the course of normal work
- integration of expected behaviors consistent with the culture and values of Quintiles
- on-going training and coaching to enable managers to effectively manage performance
- clear accountability in terms of management ownership of the process and guidance and employee ownership of the results for performance and development.

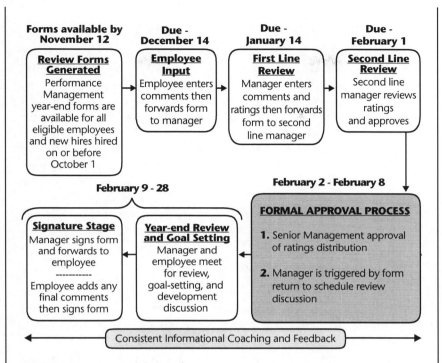

FIGURE 2.2 Designed global performance management procedures

The design team aligned parties on the same page and set realistic expectations that enhancements would evolve over time. Given the importance of the initiative to employees and the tie to customer loyalty, delivery of core functionality was paramount. Figure 2.2 outlines an example of the redesigned year-end workflow.

Respect the local dynamic

Change leadership recognized that global change initiatives must take into consideration international cross-cultural issues and differences in business requirements. The era of the United States being the "center of the universe" is over. Global change requires actively engaging global stakeholders throughout the project life cycle in ways that are relevant to their situation.

During the change project, change champions in the internal network were used to overcome legitimate global stakeholder concerns like local data protection laws and work council inquires. They were also vital in challenging stakeholder posturing in the form of statements such as "this won't work here."

Pick the right battles and apply decisive leadership

Change leadership recognized and respected that there were strong personalities with clear opinions on the "right way" to do things. HR practitioners and business managers had strong views on everything from leadership competencies and performance philosophy to rating scales and form workflow. In one instance the project was almost derailed over the number of decimal places in the performance rating. The passion was healthy as long as it was channeled into problem-solving to meet the overall goals of the change and the business. What was important was that change leadership not only encouraged strong voices to be heard, but they provided ground rules for discussion and getting to closure. In the event that differences of opinion could not be reconciled, change leadership made decisions to move the project forward in a timely manner.

Leverage training as a key change enabler

The change leadership team recognized the importance of training on the global management process to make the change work in practice. Investments were made up front in training that was customized to different user segments and aligned with the roll out.

Live and virtual instructor-led training was provided for system administrators and HR generalists while broad-based recorded webinars were employed to walk employees through the new process. Managers received online tools and live, open sessions to answer questions. Desktop job aids were also created to help impacted stakeholders manage their respective learning curves.

Delivering results with business impact

The scale of the project and compressed timeline for delivery resulted in an accelerated staged rollout approach to implementation. The purpose of this approach was to secure a proof-of-concept for the new process as well as to capitalize on "early wins."

- **Phase 1 – Employees in the US, Canada, Latin America, UK, and Ireland**

  The first phase tested core system functionality and piloted language capability (Spanish) in a controlled setting. The standard approach training was redesigned to incorporate web-based modules, audio distance solutions, and manager-led development to spread the message and ensure understanding. The change was well-received and paved the way for additional uses of these mediums in future projects.

- **Phase 2 – Employees in Asia and 36 countries throughout Europe**

  The second phase was completed in time for mid-year reviews the following year. Language capabilities were expanded within the system and training was customized for cultural nuances and various work council issues that arose in several countries. Employees were seeing the benefit of the new approach and year-end satisfaction surveys were providing the first signs of expected ROI.

- **Phase 3 – Rounding out the initiative**

  The third phase was completed in time for year-end reviews with the system expanded to the entire employee population. The functionality of the product was enhanced to set the groundwork for ties with future systems such as the learning management. Phase three also ushered in approval for the implementation of a succession planning and talent review module that would complement and formalize the existing paper-based approach.

The results of the change project were clear from the conclusion of Phase 1 (three months after the project start date). The following benefits were achieved:

- average 97 percent compliance with year-end performance reviews
- average 75 percent compliance with optional mid-year reviews
- 45 percent of managers noted a reduction in time to complete, even in year end rollout
- increased quality of reviews for employees, attributing the extra time to thoughtful conversations with managers.

The most compelling impact, however, came from the following year's employee engagement survey which highlighted performance management as a top area of improvement for employees at Quintiles. The organization reported an 18 percent improvement (3 percent is statistically significant) in the number of respondents who "agreed" or "strongly agreed" with the statement, "My performance has been evaluated fairly." This dramatic improvement in associated engagement scores, which resulted from the change effort, ultimately surpassed survey benchmarks for employee engagement.

In addition to the quantitative results, the work team also captured qualitative input from managers and employees across the organization, including:

- "More consistency of processes across regions and managers."
- "Encourages employees to take ownership of managing their own performance."

> • "Concise, intuitive system that shortened time for managers to complete appraisals."
>
> Managers and employees also viewed the performance management change project as not driven and owned by HR, which potentially would have diminished its credibility and adherence in embracing the new process. The change addressed a strategic business need which managers and employees recognized and produced tangible results in a reasonable amount of time.

Notes

1   Cited in Bradford, Gamaliel (1930). *Daughters of Eve*. Every effort was made to contact the publisher to use this quote.

2   Aiken C. & Keller S. "The Irrational Side of Change Management." *The McKinsey Quarterly*. April 2009.

3   IBM News Room. (News Release, IBM Media Relations). IBM Global Study: Majority of Organizational Change Projects Fail: Changing Mindsets and Culture Continue to Be Major Obstacles. 14 October 2008.

4   Amabile, T. & Kramer, S. "How Leaders Kill Meaning at Work." *The McKinsey Quarterly*. January 2012.

5   de Bono, E. (1985) *The Six Thinking Hats*. USA: MICA Management Resources.

6   Berry, L. & Seltman, D. (2008). *Management lessons from Mayo clinic: Inside one of the world's most admired service organizations*. US. McGraw Hill.

7   Anderson, D. & Anderson L. (2001). *Beyond change management: Advanced Strategies for transformational leaders*. San Francisco. Jossey-Bass/Pfeiffer. 166.

8   Bridges, W. (2003). *Managing transitions: Making the most of change*. 2nd ed. Reading, MA. Addison-Wesley.

3

CHANGE LEADERSHIP AND MANAGEMENT

"Leaders must encourage their organizations to dance to forms of music yet to be heard."[1]

Warren Bennis

SITUATIONAL CONTEXT FOR CHANGE LEADERSHIP

You have a team in place, drawn from members of the organization, to lead the change initiatives. The team members are well-respected and experienced in achieving the organization's business performance goals over time and in driving successful projects. Well into the first phase of the change initiative, you observe that the teams are busy. After some questions, however, you find that the teams are not aligned around an overarching change solution which will move the organization towards the change vision. Further probing reveals that the team members are uncomfortable moving out of the paradigm of the organization's current state. The leaders are defending their teams' progress because the detailed plan schedule dates are being met, but that is not substantively moving the change forward. You have an issue with change leadership.

The right leadership is essential to change initiatives

Leadership can make – or break – a change initiative. Everything depends on the quality of leadership. The degree of change capabilities of the leaders will directly influence the change teams' ability to create substantive change. People who have leadership or management positions in the organization and successful track records are not automatically a good fit for leadership roles on a change initiative. Change

ire not synonymous with well-oiled machines. Change initiatives
amic, well-rounded leaders who can meet the unique combination of
hat change initiatives provide.
initiatives pose specific demands on leadership.

- **Change initiatives require leadership which transforms the status quo.** Most projects that organizations perform are not aimed at fundamentally changing the organization. They are intended to improve what is already in place or make more efficient use of existing resources. Standardization and improvement of processes and systems are common examples. Change initiative leaders must have the solid project management skills required of these common tactical projects, but they need much more. Disrupting the status quo and aligning the organization and culture to new models will test leadership abilities to manage a wide variety of issues, especially resistance.

  When the status quo is attacked, resistance flourishes. Tight project planning, execution and control will not take the place of leadership fortitude, courage and persistence. After establishing and communicating direction for the change initiative and engaging stakeholders, one of the change leader's key responsibilities is to manage resistance. The change leader must cross silos, persuade stakeholders, remove roadblocks, and make tough decisions. Managers who are vested in the current organization will be challenged when it comes to dismantling sacred cows and the old way of doing things, since these are key targets of change initiatives. Change initiatives are not about keeping the peace and protecting friendships. Change leaders must be able to transcend the natural discomfort and resistance of people by creating confidence and trust in the journey to a better future for the organization.

- **Change initiatives embrace ambiguity.** Uncertainty is what change is about, both in outcomes and in the processes for getting to the new target. Like other projects, change initiatives contain quantifiable goals and a disciplined plan. However, change initiatives are about *creating* unknown territory and aligning people around a conceptualized vision of the organization's future, not aligning people to something that is known in advance and spelled out. Most people are not comfortable with this level of ambiguity. People prefer predictability, which is inherent in the more linear, static models of the classic corporate organization. The change leader's job is to take people out of their comfort zones to creatively advance the organization to a new state.

  Ambiguity will prompt people to search for direction, boundaries and clarity. Change leaders must be top-flight communicators on these topics. But the most important handrail a change leader can provide to his or her teams for managing ambiguity is to instill confidence and trust in the change effort. Members of the organization and change team need to feel that their change leaders are capable of effectively guiding them through the uncertainty ahead. They also need to feel that the change leaders are fair in making decisions and ethical. Honesty is paramount. The change leader is a realist and an empathizer, not a cheerleader.

Part of overcoming the organization's negative view of ambiguity and change is for the change leaders to distinguish change initiatives from once-and-done projects. Change is a continuous process, which includes learning and opportunity. The change leader's passion for the change vision and his or her adaptability to change demonstrate comfort with ambiguity that team members will emulate. Change is an emotional journey. Thoughts raging inside people's minds such as, "We haven't gone this direction before," need to be recast as a positive adventure rather than a dangerous trail to be avoided.

- **Change initiatives are aligned with strategic business direction.** Efforts that are aimed at fundamentally changing the business, or that are linked to a longer-term fundamental imperative to transform the organization to a new state, are guided by a much different type of leadership than efforts with more tactical aims. While optimization, improvement, and support projects may embody some aspects of change management, we do not classify them as change initiatives. These types of initiatives are usually led by project managers seasoned in execution and focused on achieving results that satisfy the immediate requirements of a project. In contrast, change leaders have their sights on the direction of the organization and how it is being advanced by the change.

This dynamic relationship between the change initiative and overall strategic business direction means that the change initiative cannot be led independently of the big picture. Change leaders need to apply a well-rounded set of measures which reflect the change impact on the organization. These measures must cascade from the highest through the lowest levels so that the change initiative impact on the strategic direction is reinforced and the change initiative does not become tactical or an end in itself. Therefore, change leaders must remain externally focused on the business to steer the change initiative away from the gravitational forces of internally-driven focus.

- **Change initiatives require culture alignment.** Aligning an organization around a new structure is one thing; aligning it to a new culture is another. As described it Chapter 1, the postmortem on structure-oriented change initiatives in the 1990s by BPR thought leaders revealed that culture and human factors were ignored, or at best they were treated as add-on's or afterthoughts. The "soft" side of change is the "harder" side in creating effective, sustainable change, at the core of which is culture. Change leaders know how to balance the people-structure fulcrum of change, and provide the necessary focus on culture.

Being successful as a manager in an organization requires embracing and leveraging the existing culture (i.e. the patterns of how the organization values, thinks, and behaves) to get things done. In a change initiative, however, the existing culture is a barrier to change in many ways. The intangible aspects of culture, such as changed values, attitudes and behavior, are as important as hard metrics are to a change initiative. Change leaders understand these dynamics of culture, as they sensitively and skillfully guide change teams to define the gaps between the old and desired culture and transition the organization.

- **Change initiatives embody high complexity in approach.** All projects require focus, a well-defined plan, and solid execution. This is a simple formula that successful managers know by heart. However, by their very nature change initiatives are much more complex than other projects in how they are focused, planned, and managed. Change initiatives require leaders to see the big picture, a strategic perspective that aligns with the organization's future. Change leaders must also think and coordinate broadly in terms of change scope and impact, across multiple dimensions of change at the same time. Leaders need to be able to coordinate multiple work streams, especially the white space between them. This includes integrating the various architectural components of change into a unified solution.

  Change initiatives demand that change leaders be more horizontal than vertical, as well as less linear, than project managers. There is a critical path for a change initiative, but not a singular track or point of focus. The boundaries of a change initiative are fluid and fluctuate with those of the organization, requiring change leaders to engage change champions and missionaries who do not formally report to the change initiative. There are lots of tricky stakeholders to manage constantly. Unlike other projects, proactive risk surfacing and making the tough decisions needed to remove roadblocks are not emergency or contingency actions on change initiatives. Change plans are dynamic. They must be re-evaluated in real time, and recalibrated as necessary. Effective change leaders are those who are capable and motivated to deal with these high amounts of initiative complexity.

Change leaders possess fundamental management capabilities, but they transcend the typical role and capabilities of a project manager. Table 3.1 shows key contrasting differences in terms of perspective between a change leader and a project manager.

In response to the challenging needs of change initiatives, change leaders must first inspire confidence in the change team, and in the organization's employees, that they will achieve the vision and goals for change as they traverse unknown territory. This confidence is built on the change leader's ability to simultaneously comprehend the big picture as well as what is happening on the ground of the change initiative. In this way, the change leader is a field general rather than an ivory-tower operator. Making difficult, high-impact decisions in a timely manner and removing roadblocks send strong positive signals to the change initiative and the organization. Additionally, providing support and equipping the troops to carry out the change will create confidence.

TABLE 3.1 How a change leader differs from a project manager

A project manager...	A change leader...
Administers	Guides
Completes tasks	Inspires and develops people to transform the organization
Focuses on structure	Balances focus on people and structure
Leverages control	Influences via trust, empowerment and collaboration
Has a short-range view, satisfies expectations through meeting plan measures	Embodies a long-term view, exceeds expectations by delivering high business impact
Asks how and when	Asks why and what do people feel
Stresses quantitative results	Applies qualitative and quantitative measures, to process as well as results
Seeks to build organizational conformance and/or optimize the status quo	Aims to transform the organization and culture to think and operate in a new, strategic context
Does things right	Does the right thing(s)
Relies on power base through hierarchy, chain-of-command and top-down communication	Leverages multiple power sources and spheres of influence, multi-directional and personal

Change leaders must also inspire trust that they (and the overall change initiative) are acting in the best interests of the organization and its people. Trust is built on a number of core factors. Having credibility in terms of previously advancing the organization's business performance is important but it is not a substitute for authentic leadership; change leaders must model the desired behaviors for change. Leaders must be straight talkers and not sugarcoat, underestimate, or fabricate information about the change. Trust requires that leaders will not only avoid sacrificing people's careers or credibility for the sake of business and political aims, but that they will address the tough issues, sacred cows, and elephants in the room that are holding people back. Leaders cannot remain, as Martin Luther King said, "...silent about the things that matter."[2]

Leaders must also reward and recognize the effort and results of those working for them in advancing the change. Professor and business psychology author Mihaly Csikszentmihalyi notes, "It is part of management's function to recognize and reward the performance and the attitude of employees, and not just their success, which may be due entirely to fortuitous circumstances."[3]

Table 3.2 describes key traits embodied in change leaders which inspire confidence and trust.

TABLE 3.2 Change leader traits which inspire confidence and trust

Change leader trait	Examples
Credibility and personal commitment	• Demonstrates passion for the change, displays dynamic energy working on the initiative • Walks the talk – models the behavior, attitude, and thinking embodied in the change vision • Demonstrates the hard work and sacrifices expected of others • Is honest in presenting information and news
Emotional intelligence	• Understands the importance of self-management and people-management, and where stress flares up during change • Is intuitive and "senses" human issues and concerns and provides interventions in response to them • Shepherds others through emotional challenges of transition
Understands culture	• Respects where the organization has come from – leverages the organization's strengths and enduring legacies where appropriate (i.e. does not throw the baby out with the bathwater) • Understands the importance of organization values, mindset, and behaviors and how to transition to them • Knows how people are differently motivated, and not solely by the obvious (e.g. compensation and position)
Does not confuse leadership with management	• Keeps people focused on the target • Knows how to cascade and delegate, avoids micromanaging • Holds managers accountable
Excellent communication skills	• Knows how to customize messages to each audience (i.e. segments) • Communicates substance and credibility • Is comfortable communicating regularly, in a timely manner • Employs two-way communication and listening

As shown in Table 3.2, an understanding of culture is uniquely important to change leaders. A change leader who understands the importance of culture and knows how to align the organization to it will promote investment in the cultural dimension in addition to the structural dimension. Many studies have supported the positive link between an organization's culture and its financial performance. As discussed in Chapter 5, changing culture requires a concerted, ongoing effort by change leaders rather than sidebar or periodic activities with symbolic intent.

Leaders need to understand that significant culture change will take a lot more disruption to the status quo than facilitating a few seminars and displaying a new vision statement. Studies suggest that organizations that tightly align their culture in support of a business strategy outperform their competitors in both the short and long term.[4]

An important role of change leadership is to act as shock absorbers and facilitators for the inevitable anxiety that will arise as the change initiative moves forward and the change starts to feel "real." In this respect, change leaders must apply emotionally-intelligent skills and patience in listening, encouraging, supporting, and guiding those involved in carrying out the change or affected by it. Change leaders cannot and should not supply all the answers, but instead should view their role as process facilitators. This requires surfacing the implicit anxieties around the change, identifying the root causes and working with employees and stakeholders to overcome the inhibitors to change.

> Leadership is needed to help the group identify issues and deal with them… the leaders must often absorb and contain the anxiety that is unleashed when things do not work as they should. Leaders may not have the answer, but they provide the temporary stability and emotional reassurance while the answer is being worked out.[5]

Communication is the backbone of effective change leadership capability. Strong communications skills are often confused with the ability to deliver polished rhetoric to a captive audience. But for change leaders, communication embodies a number of characteristics which create substantive impact. Developing messages targeted to the perspectives and needs of particular stakeholders is one important characteristic, in contrast to one-size-fits-all messaging, which will quickly erode communications' credibility. Communication in the change leadership context is also two-way. Effective communication elicits valuable input from change stakeholders while building the trust, credibility and influence of the change leader. Effective communication provided by change leaders is multi-dimensional:

> Leaders who communicate effectively listen actively, write and speak clearly and concisely to stakeholder groups within and outside of the organization, develop and maintain long-term business relationships, uncover and resolve conflict, provide candid feedback, influence others and build cross-functional collaboration, and seek and use feedback to improve individual and organizational performance.[6]

Leadership is integral to engaging people in the change effort

Arguably, engagement is the most fundamental aspect of change leadership. Without engaged members of the organization, substantive and sustainable change will not happen. The high levels of performance demanded by a change initiative are fueled by engaged teams, which leaders guide. Motivation, self-initiative and a solution-oriented mindset are indicators that people are engaged in moving the change forward. Even if a leader does everything else right, such as change direction, discipline and communication, the initiative will fail without the personal commitment of the change teams and stakeholders.

Engaging the necessary people to advance the change is a core reason for the existence of change leadership. Leadership cannot exist without engaged stakeholders and employees, who in turn cannot be engaged without effective leadership. Business Process Reengineering (BPR) postmortems often cite lack of leadership as the common point of failure. The people-structure fulcrum of change (described in Chapter 1) must be balanced, with engagement as the foundation of the people dimension.

The complexity of modern-day organizational change is so high that leadership which substitutes compliance for engagement, for example, command-and-control, is insufficient to transform today's organizations. Such compliance-oriented or other similar leadership approaches will stifle the critical bottom-up aspect of change that springs from personally committed participants. Engaged employees and stakeholders are an important source of information for leaders to understanding how the change initiative is performing and registering impact, as well as what needs to be done to get the initiative on track or improve it. Two important competencies for change, learning and problem-solving, are also fueled by the sense of engagement leaders instill in people.

Change leaders who sufficiently engage people in the change foster the necessary cooperation and collaboration across organizational boundaries. Cross-functional interdependencies are a way of life in the modern organization. While hierarchies and silos remain the dominant form of structural reporting in large organizations, they are transcended through leadership that is influential and engaging. This is how change is achieved.

What exactly does engagement look like on a change initiative? Engaged change initiative team members, stakeholders, and others in the organization feel connected to the change in a positive sense and want to see it happen. They display initiative and energy in helping move the change forward. They convey a sense of urgency: the change is their priority, and they are willing to put the effort in and make sacrifices. They trust the change leaders and other members of the team to support them. In turn, their commitment motivates others, and their drive for creative problem-solving overcomes resistance and attempts by others to thwart the change momentum.

Change leaders influence engagement in a number of ways. First and foremost, they are personally connected to the change and those participating in it. Change leaders are highly visible and interactive throughout the change initiative and with its stakeholders. They demonstrate passion and energy for the change. They pay attention to the people side of change by actively sensing, observing, and responding to peoples' attitudes, perspectives, and behaviors. They learn by connecting at all levels, by actively soliciting input, feedback, and ideas from all members of the change team and not just their direct reports.

Leadership alignment around the change is important in creating engagement with members of the change team and stakeholders in the organization. Dean and Linda Anderson stress the need for leaders to commit themselves fully to the change before aligning others around it: "...part of upstream change is the leaders' opportunity to get their heads, hearts, and hands aligned before engaging the rest of the organization in the change...Building leadership alignment up-front sets the ideal conditions for positive employee involvement throughout the change."[7]

Change leaders also remove barriers to engagement by actively surfacing emerging concerns and potential conflict to prevent them from materializing. John Kotter emphasizes the importance of this responsibility: "The big [obstacles] must be confronted and removed...Action is essential, both to empower others and to maintain the credibility of the change effort as a whole."[8]

Change leaders also build engagement by modeling the change. They are consistent with the values embodied in the change vision and goals. As Margaret Wheatley points out "...the behaviors reflected throughout an organization are, in effect, modeling on the behaviors and values of those at higher levels."[9] As change leaders consistently collaborate, provide support, and empower people, for example, engagement builds as these behaviors ripple through the organization.

The Change Leadership Team (CLT)

Change leadership in terms of a change initiative is not a single person, but a team of change leaders who have overall responsibility for the initiative, called the Change Leadership Team. These roles are distinct as they represent unique perspectives, specialized competencies and different motivations. People in these leadership roles must work collaboratively, as a synergistic unit, as they all provide complementary elements to leading the change initiative.

The number of leadership roles required varies with the complexity of the change initiative. Although these roles represent distinct responsibilities, they may not all be performed by separate individuals on a smaller, less complex project. In instances in which the degree of architectural and cultural change is limited, qualified change team leaders (or "project leaders") may be able to fulfill specialized aspects of the change architecture work (e.g. technology, organization, or process design) and qualified program managers may act as the overall integrator of the change architecture. The important word here is "qualified." The leadership responsibilities and competencies discussed in this section are not easy-to-acquire skills that can be learned in real-time on the initiative. These leadership characteristics must be developed prior to the change initiative and then brought into it, in order to supply the needed traction for change.

Collectively, the Change Leadership Team:

- **Sets the change target, direction, and scope of change.** The CLT provides the "what" for change, which is the change vision, business case, goals (both qualitative and quantitative) and boundaries for change. The members of the organization are empowered to supply the "how" for the change, which are the tactics for achieving the goals of the business change.
- **Establishes Change Program Management Organization (C-PMO) processes by which the change initiative operates.** These processes include: governance, team chartering, project planning, risk management, issue tracking and resolution, reporting, communications, measurement, and change architecture integration. Staffing, tools, and training are included with these processes.
- **Manages stakeholders and removes roadblocks.** This is a primary day-to-day responsibility for the CLT once the change vision, processes, and plans are in place.
- **Holds people accountable for delivering as well as modeling the change**. Creates individual performance expectations along with cascading, balancing metrics for the overall change initiative.
- **Manages the white space and change integration.** Defines the dependencies and critical path across the change master plan. Facilitates cross-work stream collaboration to get work done, ensure alignment, and integrate the change solution.
- **Delivers frequent and substantive communications regarding the change initiative**. These include communicating:
  - Direction, including the big picture, target and expectations
  - Updates on change progress, or changes in initiative approach
  - Encouragement and recognition for the progress of the change team, stakeholders and other members of the organization involved in the change
  - Two-way communications between management and the field
- **Balances the needs of business performance with the change initiative.** Demonstrates progress to senior management in not only whether the change initiative is on track, but how it is improving the performance of the organization in real-time.

As shown in Figure 3.1, the CLT includes these roles:

- Change Initiative Sponsor
- Change Program Manager
- Business Change Architect
- Change Team (Project) Leaders.

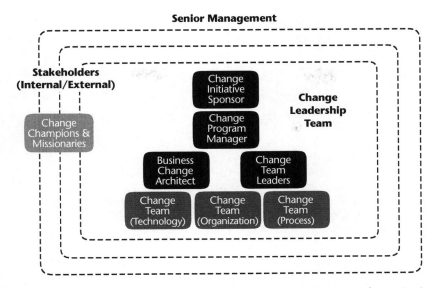

FIGURE 3.1 The change leadership team in the context of the initiative and organization

As depicted in Figure 3.1, the CLT reports to senior management. The CLT manages the change teams, each of which addresses a particular work stream or discipline on the change initiative. The CLT also engages Change Champions and Change Missionaries who do not formally report to the change initiative but support it through their influence. They are important to managing stakeholders as they operate in areas of the organization affected by the change.

The CLT is responsible for the Change Program Management Organization (C-PMO) which is the centralized function that manages the change initiative. Specifically, the C-PMO is concerned with scope definition, process infrastructure, staffing, project planning, execution, monitoring, integration and communications of the change initiative. Members of the Change Leadership Team have specific responsibilities for aspects of the C-PMO. For example, on the logistical side the Program Manager is responsible for defining the change initiative, putting in place the process infrastructure, creating the master plan and coordinating resources across the initiative, while the Change Team Leads plan and manage work stream projects on a day-to-day basis. On the content side, the Executive Sponsor addresses communications and manages stakeholders, while the Business Change Architect leads and integrates the development of the change solution architecture.

Table 3.3 describes the key competencies that each of the four roles of the CLT needs to bring to the change initiative and the degree to which they are applied (High, Medium, Low, or not used). The bold cell values denote which of the four roles is primarily responsible for exercising each competency on the initiative.

TABLE 3.3 Change leadership team competencies by role

Cell values

High, Medium, Low values express the recommended level of competence and experience in this area for participation on a change initiative. These competencies must be correspondingly demonstrated throughout the change initiative by the roles.

***Bold text** values denote primary role responsibility for each competency area*

Competency & experience areas	Change initiative sponsor	Change program manager	Business change architect	Change team (project) leader	Change champion or missionary
Crafting and articulating change vision (including aligned team charters)	**H**	M	M	L	M
Aligning change team, organization members, stakeholders and senior management around the change initiative	**H**	H	M	L	H
Framing and specifying the change initiative including requirements for processes, resources, budget and dependencies	H	**H**	M		
Procuring organizational resources and funding	**H**	H			M
Developing and managing the master change program plan (initiative level)		**H**	H		
Developing and managing detailed project plans (workstream level)		H	H	**H**	L
Developing and implementing a cascading balanced scorecard (measures)	H	H	M	L	H
Managing and motivating change initiative personnel	H	**H**	M	M	M
Managing stakeholders and removing roadblocks	**H**	H	M	M	M
Making strategic or directional decisions on behalf of the change initiative	**H**	**H**	H	L	L
Process management (including managing the workstream whitespace)	H	L	H	L	L
Change model development and integration (managing the solution architecture and white space)			**H**		
Solution design and conceptual change scenario development			**H**	L	
Management of technical specialists (towards integrated solution architecture)		M	**H**		
Change management methodology development, customization and roll-out		M	**H**		
Change impact analysis	H	H	**H**	M	M
Surfacing issues on the change initiative and identifying interventions	**H**	H	H	M	H

The **Change Initiative Sponsor** is the highest level of change leader, and consequently has the largest influence on the outcome of a change initiative. When identifying candidates and selecting a change sponsor, consider these competencies and characteristics:

- **Understands change and is experienced in change management.** The sponsor should be grounded in the concepts of change management, including the human dynamics of change beyond the structural and quantitative aspects. This includes an understanding of the change life cycle (phases) and the importance of methodology. The sponsor should think broadly as well as deeply (i.e. sees and manages the white space). This sponsor should not think in a linear way or like a micromanager.
- **Operates like a field general.** The sponsor should be motivated to be hands-on in the field in addition to providing high-level direction. He or she must think strategically and know how to align the change initiative with higher-level organization direction. Sensing (i.e. actively trying to identify understand the attitudes, mood, feelings, and other characteristics present in people in any environment) and objective inquiry should be strengths for the sponsor. Zoom-in/zoom-out capability (i.e. going from big picture to change initiative specifics and back again at any time) should also be a core strength.
- **Has a high-level position in the organization but is also an authentic leader.** The sponsor naturally leads by influence (e.g. trust, credibility and competence).
- **Possesses a track record of diligence and excellence in cross-functional business performance, particularly with strategic business impact** (not just efficiency and "lean" projects).
- **Is a strong communicator.** The sponsor is articulate, clear, confident, inspiring, and credible.
- **Is seen by members of the organization as dynamic and progressive.** The sponsor is not viewed as a keeper of the old ways.
- **Is respected by members of the organization as trustworthy, hard-working, fair and consistent.**
- **Is known for representing the people of the organization and not just the interests of senior management.**
- **Is seen as courageous and willing to make tough calls.** The sponsor is experienced in removing roadblocks and dismantling sacred cows. He or she is not afraid to surface conflict and taboo subjects and address them.
- **Is regarded as emotionally intelligent.**
- **Is collaborative.** The sponsor works well with others and stimulates thinking.
- **Is open to feedback and willing to adapt to needed course changes for the initiative.**
- **Is objective and comprehensive.** The sponsor knows how to apply multiple "hats" at the appropriate times (e.g. Edward de Bono's green hat [opportunities], red hat [instinct], black hat [risks], and so on).[10]

- **Is comfortable delegating and holding subordinates and stakeholders accountable for high levels of performance.**

The **Change Initiative Sponsor** is selected by senior management and is the ultimate authority for the change initiative. He or she is the face of the change initiative as seen by the change team, stakeholders and the organization. The Sponsor's role is strategic. He or she ensures the change initiative is aligned with the organization's strategic direction. The Sponsor appoints other Change Leadership Team members and team leads, sets expectations, and holds people accountable for performance.

A key responsibility for the Sponsor is managing stakeholders at the executive level, which includes selling across silos and removing roadblocks. The sponsor makes the tough calls and high-impact decisions for the change initiative. He or she approves significant changes to the initiative, including funding. Delivering high-impact communications to the change team, stakeholders, and the organization as well as to senior management is an important responsibility of the Sponsor.

The **Change Program Manager** (CPM) works closely with the Sponsor but he or she is primarily responsible for the structure, logistics and performance of the change initiative on a day-to-day basis. The CPM establishes and runs the Change Program Management Organization office. The CPM implements the charter for the initiative, with input from the Sponsor. The CPM establishes the overall change initiative process infrastructure (governance, risk management, issue tracking, communications, etc.) and tools, rolls out training, and ensures compliance.

The CPM also leads planning and execution for the change initiative as well as the work streams. He or she creates the overall approach for the change initiative, including the high-level change plan with milestones and schedule. Along with the sponsor, the CPM selects the change team (project) leaders and team members. The CPM guides and monitors not only the work streams in the change initiative portfolio, but also the white space between them.

The CPM is responsible for defining measures for the change using a balanced scorecard and cascading them through levels of the initiative and organization. He or she manages expectations of the team leaders and holds them accountable for performance.

An important responsibility of the CPM is managing risk and addressing escalated issues surfaced by the change teams. Any changes to the plan, including new work streams or interventions, must be authorized by the CPM. The CPM also assists the Sponsor in preparing and delivering high-level communications and updates to senior management, as well as in managing stakeholders.

The **Business Change Architect** has the important responsibility of creating and managing the integrated change model (i.e. the change solution architecture) in accordance with the overall change vision. He or she assists the Sponsor and CPM in defining the change initiative approach and master plans. Guidance to the team on change management methodology usage is supplied by the Business Change Architect.

The Business Change Architect guides Change Team Leads in work stream plan development. He or she leads the design, development, and implementation teams across the change architecture dimensions and their respective components (the solution white space), which include:

- technology
- organization
- process.

Design teams have a dotted-line report to the Business Change Architect.

The Business Change Architect identifies and addresses issues relating to the change architecture solution and its integration. He or she also assists the Sponsor and CPM in managing stakeholders and providing senior management updates.

The **Change Team (Project) Leads** are officially part of the Change Leadership Team but their focus is more tactical than that of the other roles. The Change Team Leads report to the CPM and have a peer relationship with the Business Change Architect. The Change Team Leads' primary responsibilities are to plan and manage the work streams of the change initiative (e.g. change architecture, implementation, and transition). Team Leads set performance expectations for their team members and report plan progress.

In addition to their team responsibilities, Change Team Leads also provide cross-functional assistance to the C-PMO and Change Leadership Team in helping to construct the change master plan, identify dependencies, specify requirements, and develop estimates. They also assist in team training, risk surfacing, and applying interventions. Because of the Change Team Leads' involvement with the C-PMO and the Change Leadership Team, they have a wider perspective and more responsibility than that of a typical Project Manager.

The role of a Change Lead is sometimes confused with the more tactical role of a Project Manager. Project Management is necessary to change initiatives but it is not where a Change Lead should be applying most of his or her effort. Management is tactical, concerned with meeting project plan schedules and driving the day-to-day work. Because of this narrower scope, conventional Project Managers cannot easily see across the change initiative program and solution white space like Change Leads.

Change Champions and **Missionaries** are respected and influential members of the organization who work on behalf of the Change Leadership Team to advance the initiative across the organization. Champions and Missionaries are not full-time members of the change team; although they have some change team responsibilities their primary responsibilities remain with their operational day-jobs. Champions have higher formal levels of authority, while Missionaries are respected for their hands-on skills. The primary responsibilities of both Champions and Missionaries are to align members of the organization around the change, motivate them, collect information and impressions for progress measurement, and monitor risks. Their most valuable contributions are in the form of surfacing risks and removing roadblocks.

Their "insider" status gives the Champions and Missionaries power to leverage in performing these actions unlike other members of the Change Leadership Team. Their position supplies credibility to members of the organization who are more strongly influenced by the organization rather than the change initiative itself. Additionally, the more independent nature of the Change Champions and Missionaries enables them to retain a level of objectivity on the change initiative, which provides real-time input to the initiative plans and execution.

The importance of stakeholder management

One of the most important responsibilities of the Change Leadership Team is to manage stakeholders surrounding the change initiative. The quality, level of integration, and ultimate impact from a change initiative depends on how well stakeholders are managed.

Change leadership should engage not only the functions of the organization, but also its partners, suppliers and customers who have an impact on the change, or will be affected by it. Their buy-in, as well as their input to designing an effective change model, is essential.

Cascading engagement is an important aspect of stakeholder management. Leveraging Change Champions and Missionaries at each level of the organization that is impacted by the change extends and strengthens the influence of the Sponsor and Change Leadership Team. Cascading engagement includes:

- communicating the change vision, goals, and benefits to stakeholders and the need for their support
- providing stakeholder orientation and training on the change initiative plan and change management concepts
- enrolling the stakeholders in problem-solving and roadblock removal
- incorporating change support measures into the organization, such as performance expectations, rewards, and recognition and change training programs.

Stakeholder segmentation is another key component of stakeholder management. Individual stakeholders must be targeted and addressed in response to their specific issues, needs and communication styles. One size does not fit all. For example, one stakeholder may be concerned with a lack of resources to support her organization's future commitment to the change vision. Another stakeholder may be a change advocate but is burdened with old technology that enforces the existing paradigm. These situations must be thought through carefully for each stakeholder. From a communication standpoint, some stakeholders may prefer receiving more detail on the change initiative to support their decisions, others may prefer a summary of the issues and actions required of them.

Change Champions and Missionaries are important in extending the reach of the change initiative to necessary stakeholders in the change who operate in multiple

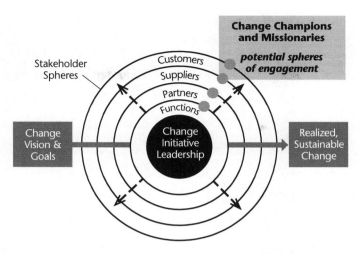

FIGURE 3.2 Change leadership engages stakeholders surrounding the change initiative

spheres. Stakeholders who may interact with Change Champions and Missionaries exist not only within organizational functions, but externally, as partners, suppliers and customers. Figure 3.2 demonstrates how important it is for the Change Leadership Team to reach stakeholders in order to realize the change vision and goals.

Change Levers: the "hot spots" for leadership in a change initiative

Change Leaders can leverage their influence for the greatest impact during the change initiative life cycle through Change Levers. Change Levers emphasize Change Leader actions across the BCM life cycle methodology phases, which are manifested in work streams and task plans.

In addition to their use as a tool for change leaders to focus their actions, Change Levers:

- function like critical success factors for the change initiative
- can serve as areas for measure to support a balanced scorecard
- are a quick, intuitive way of getting to understand the business change methodology before diving fully into the end-to-end life cycle and tasks
- provide a handy reminder or checklist of the most critical actions in each phase of the methodology.

The Change Levers are shown in Figure 3.3. They span the Business Change Management life cycle.

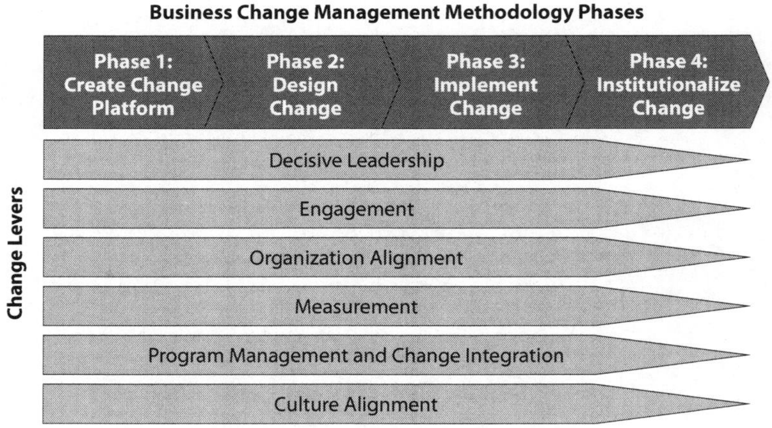

Business Change Management Methodology Phases

FIGURE 3.3 Change Levers in the context of the Business Change Management lifecycle

In Tables 3.4, 3.5, 3.6, 3.7, 3.8, and 3.9, the leadership actions within each Change Lever are organized by the phase of the BCM methodology life cycle in which they are performed. The life cycle phases are:

1. Create Change Platform
2. Design Change
3. Implement Change
4. Institutionalize Change.

For reference purposes, at the bottom of each Change Lever table are the BCM tools used during the phases. This is to assist with applying the Change Levers. The BCM methodology phase tasks and the tools are described in the appendices.

Change Lever # 1: Decisive Leadership

The focus of this Change Lever is building change, championing, and visible commitment of managers and influencers at all levels of the organization to assertively advance the change initiative. Of high importance for change leaders are identifying, surfacing and removing change risks and roadblocks. Table 3.4 shows the key change leader actions regarding the Decisive Leadership Change Lever.

Change Lever # 2: Engagement

The focus of this Change Lever is identifying, prioritizing and motivating stakeholder groups and participants relative to the change, both internally and externally. It is important for Change Leaders to identify actionable events to ensure cascading commitment and to link engagement to change initiative communications. Table 3.5 shows the key change leader actions regarding the Engagement Change Lever.

TABLE 3.4 Change Lever #1: Decisive Leadership

Phase	Create Change Platform	Design Change	Implement Change	Institutionalize Change
Key Change Leader Actions	Develop and communicate a change vision that includes: • What is broken • Business case • Timelines • WIIFM Substantiation for the change in the form of customer input, environmental scan, performance data, strengths and gaps Define goals, both quantitative and qualitative, for the change for the short and long term Define performance expectations	Ensure there are enough managers/ influencers at each level in the organization to ensure cascading commitment Provide coaching to ensure manager/influencer effectiveness Proactively and consistently provide change communications Model desired behavior change Recognize and respond favorably to individuals, particularly direct reports and line management who demonstrate desired behaviors	Apply a formal conflict management process to identify issues and remove barriers Coach managers/ influencers in behaviors and language needed to support endeavor Demonstrate support to ongoing efforts, reinforce the direction, discuss progress, and communicate wins Help managers/ influencers recognize and reward role models Assertively disarm, and if necessary, remove "blockers" Hold leaders accountable for achieving desired results	Encourage managers/ influencers to keep organization focused on results and the promise of the desired future while managing the transition to change Help managers/ influencers identify and engage other areas of the business ready for the change (next wave of change) Sustain energy, engagement, and commitment by challenging employees to identify new opportunities for change Publicly recognize change team, supporters, and individual contributions for meeting goals
Supporting BCM Tools	• Business Case Template • Risk Assessment Instrument	• Communication Planning Template • Communication Assessment Pulse Survey • Risk Management Tool • Meeting Management Template	• Issue Escalation Template	

TABLE 3.5 Change Lever # 2: Engagement

Phase	Create Change Platform	Design Change	Implement Change	Institutionalize Change
Key Change Leader Actions	Identify and prioritize all stakeholders into winners, losers, and unaffected groups	Provide coaching to Change Champions and Missionaries	Integrate learnings from sensing to update risk management and overall project plan	Continue to develop messages and cascade throughout organization about future, successes and progress of change efforts
	Identify opinion and informal group leaders	Ensure initiative is properly resourced	Assess engagement efforts and broaden efforts to address trouble spots	Define, approach and launch future initiatives aligned with the rationale and vision of recently completed change initiatives
	Determine how the change initiative will impact each key stakeholder and solicit their concerns and input	Design and complete "sensing" efforts to collect intelligence on change initiative: • Level of commitment • Level of change impact • Potential resistance and concerns, drivers and benefits	Work closely with PMO to determine scope of change introduction (simulation, pilot, full implementation) and speed	Continue to solicit feedback and input
	Perform change readiness assessment and take necessary steps to promote readiness for change		Apply new experiences to educate, engage, and gain support of additional opinion leaders and the broader population to mobilize further activity	Identify individuals to continue to lead/ manage change efforts (e.g. change agents) in the business
	Develop actionable recommendations for optimizing the support of each stakeholder group	Tightly integrate learnings from sensing to target communication events: • Analyze audience to ensure coverage and minimize overload • Link all messages to the goal and desired future state • Leverage multiple communication channels		Develop lessons learned, and best practices, and share with team, sponsors, and relevant audiences
	Develop communication strategy and execute initial messaging			Help team members train and oversee planning of subsequent project team(s)
	Test and validate messages with employees	Tailor messages to audience		
	Integrate key influencers into the initiative team through creating and communicating the business rationale for change and the ideal future state			
Supporting BCM Tools	• Executive Sponsor Assessment Instrument • Backwards Imaging • Chartering Template • Stakeholder Assessment and Commitment Planning	• Elevator Speech • Interview Primer • Missionary Assessment Instrument • Champion Assessment Instrument • Commitment Planning Primer		

Change Lever # 3: Organization Alignment

The focus of this Change Lever is ensuring that the elements of the change solution or target model are developed in alignment with both the business strategy and integrated change architecture. Table 3.6 shows the key Change Leader actions regarding the Organization Alignment Change Lever.

Change Lever # 4: Measurement

The focus of this Change Lever is creating balanced measurement and cascading it through the organization and change initiative (at team, process, and individual levels). Table 3.7 shows the key Change Leader actions regarding the Measurement Change Lever.

Change Lever # 5: Program Management and Change Integration

The focus of this Change Lever is establishing and rolling out the formal processes and tools by which the change initiative will operate and be managed. This includes coordinating and monitoring the change initiative projects to perform in alignment with the program goals, and deliver integrated change results. Table 3.8 shows the key change leader actions regarding the Program Management and Change Integration Change Lever.

Change Lever # 6: Culture Alignment

The focus of this Change Lever is ensuring that the organization's culture is aligned with, and effectively transitioned to, the change vision or target. This includes laying the groundwork for and assisting the members of the organization in learning, embracing, and enforcing the desired values, mindset, and behaviors of the new organization. Table 3.9 shows the key Change Leader actions regarding the Culture Alignment Change Lever.

TABLE 3.6 Change Lever # 3: Organization Alignment

Phase	Create Change Platform	Design Change	Implement Change	Institutionalize Change
Key Change Leader Actions	Define how the change initiative will impact each element of architecture: • Identify impacts to technology and architecture including hardware, applications, and data • Identify impacts to organization architecture including organization design, HR practices, administrative policies, etc. • Identify impacts to process architecture including physical layout and infrastructure, core and support processes, and business rules Integrate actions to address architecture impacts into change management plan	Perform gap analysis to assess distance between current and desired future state architecture Determine specific change requirements Design appropriate changes to technology, organization, and process architecture Identify transition requirements resulting from design changes to architecture Identify potential organizational enablers and barriers to change	Clarify roles for transition as well as desired future state and develop plans to close capability gaps, such as training Prioritize implementation tasks, identify interdependencies and schedule for highest and best use of resources	Assess alignment of new architecture with change vision, identify any unanticipated ripple effects, and address any new issues Continue to capture learnings, roadblocks, best practices, and critical success factors for future change efforts Capture and develop guidance and templates for new tools created during change initiative for future use/training and change methodology augmentation
Supporting BCM Tools	• Change Process Primer • Impact Analysis Template	• Design Implementation Challenge Questions • Competency Gap Tool • Business Rules Tool		

TABLE 3.7 Change Lever # 4: Measurement

Phase	Create Change Platform	Design Change	Implement Change	Institutionalize Change
Key Change Leader Actions	Develop metrics for the business change that can be cascaded through management levels from top to bottom	Document key responsibilities and overall leadership for the change initiative	Measure, monitor and report progress to further refine change plan and execution	Continue to report measurement results to change leadership team for guidance in refining and executing the initiative
	Identify which metrics need to be closely aligned with related business processes such as balanced scorecards, management and project reporting, performance management, and compensation	Identify audiences who require progress reports and type of report required	Complete cause analysis when performance gaps arise	
		Develop metrics for the overall change initiative and for each work stream, ensuring they are closely aligned with the business change metrics	Discuss learnings with PMO and the change leadership team	
	Ensure metrics are a consistent part of stakeholder communications	Design changes to organizational and process metrics		
	Focus on importance of sustaining current operations performance while embarking upon changes	Link metrics to goal-setting and the performance management system for team leader and members		
Supporting BCM Tools	• Change Scorecard Tool		• Project Team Assessment Survey	

TABLE 3.8 Change Lever # 5: Program Management and Change Integration

Phase	Create Change Platform	Design Change	Implement Change	Institutionalize Change
Key Change Leader Actions	Develop processes to address the following: • Team chartering • Project definition, planning, and management • Risk management • Performance reporting • Cross-team integration • Project portfolio management • Issue escalation and resolution • Business case development • Scope change control Develop tools and templates for performing each PMO activity Develop the critical path across all change initiatives Define key change master plan dependencies and white space Share change master plan with stakeholders	Provide education and coaching on processes and tools Ensure compliance on processes and tools Create linkage to performance management process so team leaders and members are held accountable for results Develop monitoring strategy, accountabilities and procedures Identify and address white space dependencies and integration issues	Periodically evaluate planned vs. actual results Define key change project status and business performance metrics Complete cause analysis when key variances occur Refine change plan accordingly Ensure cross-team coordination	Continue to report measurement results to change leadership for guidance in refining and evolving the initiative Capture learnings Update PMO processes and tools for subsequent initiatives
Supporting BCM Tools	• PMO Best Practice Assessment	• Cross Project Coordination Template • Project Management Pulse Survey	• Quick Wins Tool • Scope Change Request	• Individual Progress Reporting Template • Project Close-Out and Lessons Learned

TABLE 3.9 Change Lever # 6: Culture Alignment

Phase	Create Change Platform	Design Change	Implement Change	Institutionalize Change
Key Change Leader Actions	Identify target culture characteristics for the organization, including values, mindset, and behaviors which will enable the change vision and strategy Determine where the change initiative requires culture change to align with the change vision Identify the new behaviors that stakeholders must model Perform a gap analysis between current and future state culture characteristics Identify the technology, organization, and process architecture changes that will result from the culture change Integrate culture changes into the change plan	Incorporate the principles and design impacts from the culture change target into the architecture change design: • Technology • Organization • Process Develop transition plan, including interventions to transition organization to new culture	Implement the culture changes in the architecture: • Technology • Organization • Process Develop monitoring strategy, accountabilities, and procedures Facilitate behavior change through performance metrics, performance management, compensation, recognition, and employee selection processes	Continue to report measurement results to change leadership for guidance in refining and evolving the initiative
Supporting BCM Tools	• Culture Mapping Tool • Readiness Assessment Instrument	• Focus Group Primer		

Notes

1 http://www.brainyquote.com/quotes/quotes/w/warrengbe121710.html
2 Boone, E.L. (1992). *Quotable business*. Random House. Quote from Reverend Dr. Martin Luther King.
3 Csikszentmihalyi, M. (2003). *Good business: Leadership, flow and the making of meaning*. Penguin. 105.
4 Recardo, R. "Taking a Fast-Cycle Approach to Align Organizational Culture With Business Plans" March/April 2011, *Global Business and Organizational Excellence*. Wiley Online Library.
5 Schein, E.H. (1992). *Organizational culture and leadership*. 2nd ed. San Francisco. Jossey-Bass. 375.
6 Recardo, R. (2000). *Best Practices in Organizations Experiencing Extensive and Rapid Change*, John Wiley and Sons., Inc.
7 Anderson, D. & Anderson, L. (2001). *Beyond change management: Advanced strategies for transformational leaders*. San Francisco. Jossey-Bass/Pfeiffer. 166
8 Kotter, J. (2006) "Leading Change: Why Transformation Efforts Fail", HBR OnPoint,
9 Wheatley, M.J. (2006). *Leadership and the new science*. San Francisco: Berrett-Koehler Publishers.
10 de Bono, E. (1985). *The Six Thinking Hats*. USA. MICA Management Resources.

4

CHANGE RESISTANCE

"A new philosophy, a new way of life, is not given for nothing. It has to be paid for and only acquired with much patience and great effort."[1]

Fyodor Dostoevsky

SITUATIONAL CONTEXT FOR CHANGE RESISTANCE

Your change initiative has been rolled out. The change master plan is in place and the change vision, goals, and benefits have been thoughtfully crafted and communicated at a town hall meeting by the change leadership team. Things should be progressing, and you expect to find an abundance of uplifting energy across the initiative. But as you walk the halls, pop in to teamwork sessions, and listen in on candid conversations between your leaders, it becomes clear that people are holding back. Attitudes, behavior, and energy are not flowing in a unified, positive direction. Resistance is impeding your organizational change initiative. You need to get the resistance out on the table, find out what is causing it, and implement actions to address it.

Resistance is a high risk for change initiatives

On a change initiative, leaders need to identify resistance, surface its underlying causes, and address the causes efficiently and effectively. This cycle of *identify-surface-address* resistance should be performed at the outset of the change initiative and continued periodically throughout its duration. If resistance is not sufficiently addressed, the minds and hearts of those in the organization will not transition to the desired state of change. When implementing change stakeholders' hearts and minds have to be aligned. Individuals may understand the business case for change but still need time for their emotions to catch up before they can embrace change.

Why do stakeholders and other members of the organization resist change?

• **People are afraid of uncertainty and the unknown, including what they perceive they might lose.** Natural human anxieties and concerns about change, as described in Chapter 1, are organic and common to individuals. These concerns collect, grow, and intensify around efforts to change the organization. This resistance can negatively impact and disable change initiatives, as described in the IBM study on the causes of organizational change initiative failure cited in Chapter two which highlights the failure to address human factors.

• **The stakes are higher on change initiatives than other types of initiatives or projects whose focus is not organizational transformation.** Organizational change will disrupt the status quo, in contrast to projects which seek to improve an aspect of the existing environment (e.g. efficiency optimization, process improvement, or system implementation), which minimally alter how people work, and do not require a substantive shift in thinking, attitude or behavior. Resistance naturally increases when people know that the status quo will change and that the predictable systems that they were used to and comfortable with will not return. On change initiatives, people are naturally more sensitive and will be quick to take defensive positions in order to protect themselves from what they perceive are threats to their entrenched self interests.

• **Culture does not change easily.** Making the "soft" or human side of change stick is more difficult than making the "hard" side of change stick (e.g. an organization's structural aspects, like processes and technology). Change initiatives do not start with a blank slate when it comes to culture. There is strong resistance to overcome the unwritten as well as stated ways an organization thinks and behaves, as discussed in Chapter 5. The deep roots of a culture cannot simply be pulled out because they have evolved from the organization's history, its management styles, personalities, and proclivities of its work force. Research into the links between neuroscience and change are finding that there is even a physiological basis for resistance to "unlearning" old ways. "Learning to do something differently is a far greater challenge than simply having to learn something new. You already have a developed synaptic superhighway."[2]

• **Managing resistance is difficult because it is centered on human factors, for which skills and experience in organizations are in limited supply**. Most managers and business professionals are products of the prevailing management paradigm, one that has not significantly evolved since the beginning of the twentieth century. This mindset emphasizes the financial and structural aspects of organizations over the human aspects and is therefore ill-equipped to deal with human resistance. Reactive, hierarchical interactions promote conformity over change rather than overcoming resistance to it. Forced compliance or simplistic training and communications cannot overcome resistance. Most leaders and managers are not used to looking for resistance, addressing it, or preventing it.

Resistance to change is clearly a difficult nut to crack. However, resistance should not be viewed only as a problem. It is also a positive contributor to a change initiative. If properly harnessed, resistance:

- **Provides an indicator that the change is starting to take effect**. If there is no resistance, then people are not feeling the change, or taking it seriously enough, since change is a legitimate threat to the status quo and to the human condition.
- **Gets people out of their comfort zone, if properly channeled.** Fear often underlies resistance, and fear can be a motivator for change. When people realize there is no turning back, their fear can be channeled into problem solving and creative solutions.
- **Provides input to how the change initiative is going and where change leaders need to allocate resources to address people's concerns** (i.e. an early warning system).

Indicators of resistance

If you look for resistance you will find that it varies in form and intensity, which will help you understand to what degree it is impacting the change initiative. Resistance can be classified as active and passive. These are the things that people do, or don't do, which impede the change effort. Active forms are more obvious; they can be seen by the untrained eye. Passive forms are more difficult to detect, and because they are below the radar they can cause more damage if not surfaced.

- **Active forms**
  - conflict between members, teams, and leaders of the change initiative
  - sabotage and attempts to derail or damage the change initiative
  - rumor spreading and gossip which attacks the credibility of the change initiative
  - public power plays or exertion of influence which undermine the change.
- **Passive forms**
  - exhibiting behaviors and ways of thinking of the old culture instead of the desired change
  - avoidance of responsibilities on the change initiative
  - disconnection or apathy towards the change

-   being inauthentic, including exhibiting behaviors not consistent with the stated commitment to the change
-   not supporting those trying to move the change forward
-   reluctance to express honest feelings about the change, including ideas that could help move it forward
-   not stepping up to the tough issues, or addressing the elephants in the room.

Resistance can be deliberate or done out of a lack of understanding about change. Intention is not important, however. What is critical is getting resistance out on the table so that its change initiative-related causes can be diagnosed and addressed. Resistance that is not exposed or surfaced will not go away by itself, but will grow stronger and even migrate to different forms. For example, if passive resistance by key influencers – in the form of apathetic attitudes or withholding behaviors towards the change – is not addressed early by the change initiative leadership, resistance across the change team can lead to supporting the old culture, spreading rumors, and side-stepping responsibilities for the change initiative.

How resistance evolves on change initiatives

You cannot stamp out resistance on the change initiative (nor should you), but it can be prevented and mitigated like other forms of risk. In essence you *control* resistance and prevent it from evolving into issues that can damage the change initiative and therefore the prospects of realizing the benefits of the change. This requires first identifying the *intrinsic sources* of resistance before they turn into risk. Resistance is rooted in people's anxieties and concerns about the change, which are present at the start of the change initiative. In contrast to *extrinsic causes* of resistance related to actions or lack of action on the change initiative which will be described later in this chapter, these intrinsic sources lie below the surface of common interaction and communications.

By identifying and acknowledging these intrinsic sources of resistance you help people understand that they are not alone. Their anxieties about change are legitimate feelings, even if their conscious perceptions of what is causing, contributing to or increasing these anxieties in terms of organizational factors are not entirely accurate. Anxiety associated with the peaks and valleys of change initiatives are well known. A seminal BPR consulting company once highlighted 20 stress points on the journey of reengineering initiatives.[3]

Change leaders should encourage people to express their feelings about the change, especially the anxieties. Once these change anxieties (unrealized resistance) are acknowledged people can talk through them and interventions can be applied. This open discussion about people's change anxiety will also help build self-awareness in individuals when their natural resistance to change emerges, causing them to reflect on resistance before automatically succumbing to it.

Intrinsic sources of resistance are shown in Table 4.1.

TABLE 4.1 Types of intrinsic sources of unrealized change resistance

Type of intrinsic sources	Example
Fundamental fear of the unknown	Discomfort with uncertainty and not knowing how things will turn out after the change, including how to adapt to a new environment
Overwhelmed	Things moving too fast on the change initiative (in contrast to the milder pace of routine operations)
Impatience	Things not moving fast enough towards a conclusion in a linear, predictable manner
Information overload	Too much information and unfamiliar detail outside of existing roles to process in a short period of time
Fear of loss	• **Work-related.** Do I have the resources and power that I will need to get my job done in the changed environment? Will I have a job? • **Relational.** Will I lose my colleagues and allies I was comfortable working with? • **Personal.** What will my identity become once the change is over?

Tangible and intangible fear

Fear of loss can be broken down further into forms that are tangible and intangible. Tangible fears are those that are real, and need material solutions or offsets. They will require definitive answers at some point in or after the change initiative since they provide the rules and boundaries for each employee in the changed environment. These include fears of loss or downgrades in: position, rank, compensation, job security, work/life balance, and career path. The answers may not always be quantifiably "better" than before the change, but they will require change leaders to provide positive solutions in a qualitative sense. For example, though specific roles and responsibilities after the change will be less hierarchical in terms of scope of authority, the new environment will be more empowering, flexible and supportive in enabling employees to achieve higher levels of business performance. There will be greater opportunities for individual growth and achievement which should be specified.

Intangible fears are those which are perceived losses. Intangible fears will require time, support, and navigation (handholding) through the transition by change leaders and those skilled in process interventions. Intangible fears of loss include: identity and status, relationships and old ways of doing things. There are no definitive answers that change leaders can provide to these feelings. The goal here is changing perspective, to help people to think more clearly, realistically, and proactively rather than worst-case scenario planning or slipping into the old mindset. For example, formal working relationships may change, but in the new open environment interaction with a broad range of people will be encouraged and rewarded. Likewise, the new culture will provide opportunities for personal growth, change mastery, and relationships which did not exist previously.

Whether dealing with employee fears that are tangible or intangible, it is always best to be honest. During the transition definitive answers and solutions will take a while to emerge.

Risk and resistance

As depicted in Figure 4.1, anxieties are a form of unrealized risk. It is not enough to acknowledge and encourage awareness of unrealized resistance. Resistance will evolve into risk and as such must be *anticipated* and planned for as an integral part of the master change plan. Like other forms of risk, if properly managed resistance can be prevented from emerging into issues (i.e. *realized resistance*) which will adversely impact the change and initiative.

Resistance is different and more volatile than most other types of risk. It requires interventions that are proactive as well as responsive to specific manifestations of resistance in order to keep resistance in check. Resistance will not go away if just carefully watched, but will erupt at some point in potentially damaging ways to the change initiative. The goal is for *prevention* first: don't let risk evolve into an issue. Surface unrealized resistance risk as early and quickly as possible.

Figure 4.1 expresses key principles involved in change resistance:

- The impact severity of unaddressed resistance on a change initiative (i.e. disengagement, potential change initiative derailment or failure) increases over the timeline and in relation to the surface-level at which resistance is addressed (i.e. at realization, the impact is greater than at inception).
- Resistance that is addressed early in the change initiative timeline is more effective and less expensive than if addressed later.
- Manage risk and unrealized resistance before they progress to issues. Anxiety that people have about the change is resistance that has not yet been realized; if not managed as a risk it becomes an issue.

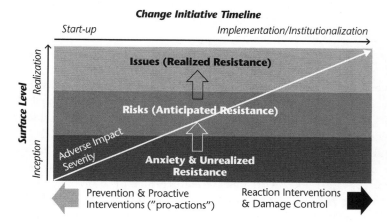

FIGURE 4.1 Addressing resistance at its inception and earlier in the change initiative reduces negative impact

Managing resistance risk

The goal of managing resistance risk on the change initiative is to identify resistance and keep it in, or move it to, a controlled state. Resistance cannot be eliminated completely, but it can be kept from becoming persistent or pervasive. Managing resistance requires:

- identifying and assessing resistance
- surfacing extrinsic causes of resistance (resulting from the change initiative)
- addressing the resistance (proactively, and if required, reactively).

Figure 4.2 provides a model for managing resistance risk on a change initiative.

Resistance that is unexposed can be plotted on the bottom two quadrants of the grid. These are manifestations of resistance that have been sensed, observed, or communicated, but their causes have not been systematically surfaced through the change initiative. Unexposed resistance can be identified in the form of behaviors, attitudes, cultural patterns, communications, and team dynamics which are in opposition to, or not supportive of, the change. Quantifiable data is also an important indicator of potential resistance, such as missed plan deadlines or failure to complete assigned work.

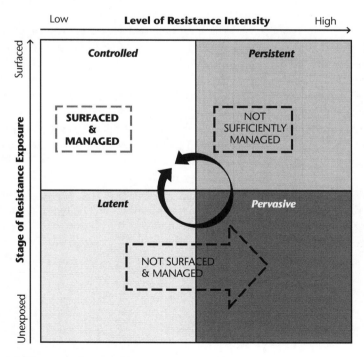

FIGURE 4.2 Change resistance risk management grid

Unexposed resistance should be plotted in the *Latent* quadrant if the resistance is present or potential, but not fully active or widespread across the change initiative and the target organization. At this stage latent resistance is considered a low level of resistance intensity impacting the change initiative. However, if unexposed resistance is observed in larger numbers of people with greater frequency, it is considered a high level of resistance intensity, and should be plotted in the *Pervasive* quadrant. Latent risk that remains unexposed will ultimately migrate and expand to the Pervasive quadrant. Symbolic of the quadrant colors used in management dashboard tools, resistance will move from light gray (caution) to dark gray (danger/stop) if it is not surfaced and managed in a timely and effective way. Pervasive resistance is the most dangerous type because it is risk that is not surfaced or managed and has spread.

Previously unexposed risk that has been systematically surfaced through diagnostic methods, tools, and interventions should be plotted in one of the top two quadrants. This means that the causes have been revealed from the resistance observed in the bottom two quadrants. As alluded to earlier in this chapter, these are *extrinsic* causes of resistance: what the change initiative is or is not doing that is contributing to the resistance. In other words, the intrinsic sources of resistance that people naturally bring with them to the change are either growing or they are being alleviated and controlled by how the change initiative is being managed.

Resistance causes which are specifically being addressed on the change initiative should be plotted in the *Controlled* quadrant. This is the most desirable position for resistance to be in, reflective of the white neutral shade (maintain). Although resistance is dynamic, it is being contained proactively through systematic measurement, applied interventions and adjustments to the change initiative where needed.

Resistance that has been systematically surfaced, but has not been sufficiently managed and contained, should be plotted in the *Persistent* quadrant. Persistence means continuance of specific resistance after the cause has been initially addressed, which has a greater intensity on the change initiative. It may be that the interventions have not been effective or frequent enough in addressing the causes of resistance or that more substantive change on the initiative is needed. The medium gray shade symbolizes that although the causes are known, more effort from the change initiative is needed to counter them.

Figure 4.3 provides an example of plotting resistance risk.

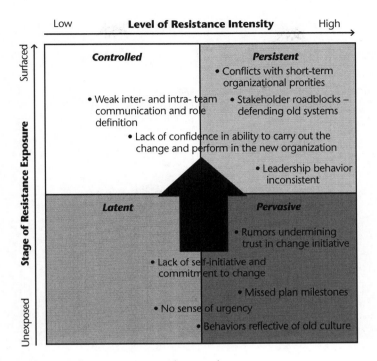

FIGURE 4.3 Plotting change resistance risk example

Surfacing and countering resistance

Your identification of resistance through sensing, observing, or having people communicate what is holding them back is an important first step, but it does not substitute for the need to systematically surface the causes of resistance. Surfacing is the process of exposing "what" the specific resistance is that has been observed or reported to determine "why" it is occurring (i.e. causes). This sets the groundwork for addressing the causes through specific interventions.

Figure 4.4 depicts the process of surfacing resistance.

There may be a common cause contributing to multiple types of resistance on the change initiative, which, if isolated and addressed on the change initiative, would mitigate much risk (e.g. inconsistent anti-change leadership behavior). There may also be multiple causes affecting a recurring type of resistance. Surfacing tools, especially diagnostics, are useful for these analytical purposes (e.g. lack of directional clarity and boundaries, poor communications).

Diagnostic and assessment tools are classified in this book broadly under interventions, since they provide results which explain resistance. This promotes self-awareness which may encourage individuals to modify their own resistance. Diagnostic tools and methods, however, are not a substitute for providing specific actions to counter the resistance, which may include altering aspects of the change initiative itself (e.g. new performance models and behavior standards for change leadership).

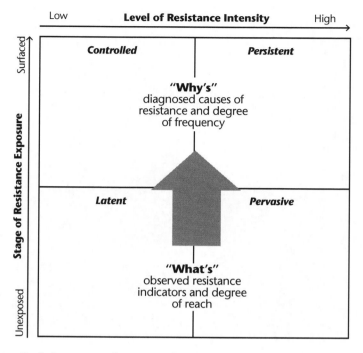

FIGURE 4.4 Surfacing causes of resistance from "what's" to "why's"

The process of surfacing cannot be separated from the results. Surfacing has impacts on those who are providing input on resistance as well as those leading the surfacing activities and must be applied thoughtfully. The Hawthorne effect is a form of reactivity whereby subjects improve or modify an aspect of their behavior being measured simply in response to the fact that they know they are being studied.[4] Even the acts of sensing or observing resistance in an attempt to identify it and its impact can be intrusive. If you are a change leader or an authority figure for the change initiative you are subject to the Hawthorne effect: your presence or your participation in resistance identification and surfacing will affect the behaviors of those you are attempting to measure. This can be a positive. In this sense clarity, consistency and authenticity in leadership behavior modeling have additional impacts when identifying or observing resistance among members of the change initiative and target population. Honest and open surfacing of resistance with clear, timely reporting of results and follow-up actions goes a long way to building trust in a change initiative.

Be cognizant that what you measure and how you measure it will shape the results, as Heisenberg famously theorized from his work in quantum mechanics measurement.[5] To this end, surfacing resistance should seek a broad and deep range of input regarding peoples' perception of the change and without presumption that the causes are known in advance and are just being validated. Surfacing should be performed interactively with members of the change initiative and organization, for purposes of empowerment, accountability and problem solving (e.g. assessments, facilitated inquiry, team exercises). It is not an independent behind-the-scenes analytical exercise.

It is important to use a combination of surfacing methods which are:

- **Formalized** – repeatable, verifiable and rooted in change management practice
- **Measureable** – in a quantifiable sense, progress can be tracked over time
- **Qualitative** – in terms of respondent input, e.g. thoughts, perceptions, feelings, and suggestions
- **Safeguarding** of individuals – encourages honest, unrestricted expression by assuring anonymity, confidence, and/or immunity from retribution for their views
- **Empowering** – enables the respondents to see themselves as responsible for acting on some of the data they provide, not just to identify actions change leadership needs to take
- **Applicable to change initiative leadership** – not just staff and employees
- **Preventative as well as repair-oriented** – addresses both types of instances.

A strategy for resistance surfacing and countering should address interpersonal dynamics as well as individual needs. Aspects of personal and group dynamics which surfacing and countering tools should seek to assess and address include respondents' perceptions and feelings regarding:

- **Personal**
  - purpose/passion alignment with the change
  - role on the change initiative
  - support/capabilities confidence level they have to perform the change work
  - WIIFM regarding the change
  - goals for personal and career growth in relation to the change
  - understanding of what is expected of respondent on the change initiative
  - difficulties with change.
- **Inter-personal (within and across teams, as well as interaction with change leadership)**
  - authentic interaction, trust and credibility
  - openness to ideas
  - fairness/rules/guidelines
  - communication
  - effectiveness, especially regarding decision-making, action, closure.

Figure 4.5 depicts a range of interventions which can be used to surface and counter resistance.

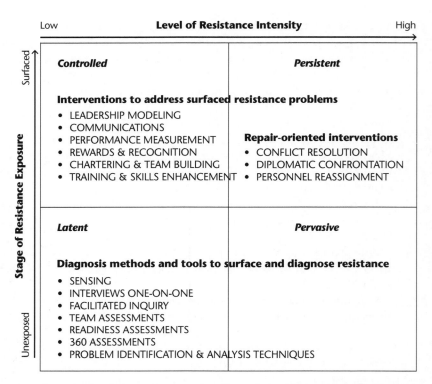

FIGURE 4.5 Organizational change interventions for surfacing, diagnosing and addressing resistance

As shown in the bottom half of Figure 4.5, latent or pervasive resistance should be surfaced via one or more methods. Sensing is considered here in the list as the least intrusive method of surfacing, but it is not completely passive. The manner in which sensing is performed will reveal more or less candid and useful impressions of potential causes that can be used to frame probing in subsequent diagnostic activities. Interviews, facilitated inquiries, and assessments follow in order of intervention depth and complexity. These will be examined in a table later in this section.

The top half of the diagram contains types of interventions which can be applied to the surfaced causes of resistance in order to prevent and control them. Although many of the interventions listed can be applied in a proactive manner to prevent or mitigate causes of resistance, persistent causes of resistance may require a more reactive stance through repair-oriented interventions, like conflict resolution or personnel reassignment. Structural interventions, such as performance measurement and rewards and recognition, should consider the kinds of resistance likely to persist in the existing culture, lilke for example, lack of accountability, weak self-motivation, inefficient decision making, and not thinking outside the box.

Surfacing may reveal, for example, that rumors running wild around the change initiative's "hidden goal to streamline operations and cut employees" are being caused by a lack of clarity around change boundaries, the business rationale for the change, as well as communications clarity and frequency. Additional reinforcing causes of resistance may include change leadership's:

- failure to prevent stakeholders and team members from blocking or undercutting change initiative activities
- absence of participation and input to important change tasks
- not making resources available.

Table 4.2 examines when and where these interventions can be applied on a change initiative to prevent, surface and address resistance.

Addressing resistance at the organizational level

Interventions and changes for addressing resistance are largely focused at the *individual* and *group* levels, since that is where the source of resistance ultimately lies. If resistance at those levels is not managed effectively and in a timely manner it grows in scale to a level where larger-scale or macro organizational solutions are required. To prevent and control resistance from escalating to a persistent or pervasive state, as shown in the right-hand quadrants of the resistance matrices discussed earlier in this chapter, it is important to implement *organization* level interventions and changes. These may be permanent or semi-permanent changes reflective of the ultimate change solution, like new or redesigned roles and measures in contrast to temporary "project-level" adjustments that are intended to keep the change initiative on track. While resistance must be addressed at the individual and group levels, applying the necessary organization-level interventions and changes will also help keep resistance in check by encouraging support for and reinforcing adherence to the change target.

Organization-level interventions and changes include:

- **Business alignment.** Aligning or redesigning the business model or architecture (e.g. technology, organization, and process dimensions) and roles to the change target.
- **Process and system enablement.** Updating the policies and procedures, including embedding new business rules into the processes to reflect the changed environment.
- **Expanded performance measures and accountability.** Defining and applying metrics for organization and team performance in addition to individual performance, and incorporating change requirements.
- **People management augmentation.** Updating human resources practices and systems, rewards and recognition (e.g. compensation), competencies, hiring criteria, succession planning, and training and development programs to reflect the goals of the changed environment.

Organization-level interventions and changes play a key role in institutionalizing change in the culture, which are discussed in Chapter 5.

TABLE 4.2 Intervention types and how they can be used for change resistance

Intervention type	Identifying resistance	Preventing resistance	Surfacing resistance causes	Addressing causes and issues	Useful for resistance in these areas	Intervention examples
Diagnosis methods and tools to surface resistance						
Sensing	H	L	L		Engagement, urgency, mindset, behavior, culture	Random walks through the change initiative; meeting participation
Interviews (one-on-one)	H	L	H		Engagement, trust, understanding, probing concerns	Structured interviews with wide range of participants
Facilitated inquiry			H		All – root causes	Group sessions to probe known resistance areas and problem-solve
Team assessments	H	M	M		Communications, collaboration, work styles, roles, trust, goal-setting, productivity, support	Personality inventories and work style assessments (e.g. Myers Briggs)
Readiness assessments	H	M	H		All – especially roadblocks, trust and change capabilities	Survey questionnaires, anonymous
360 Assessments	M	H	H		Trust, authenticity, quality of communications, competency	Surveys or interviews at all levels
Problem identification and analysis techniques		L	H	M	Root causes, including needed adjustments in design and implementation	Force field analysis; fishbone, inhibitors/enablers

Intervention type	Identifying resistance	Preventing resistance	Surfacing resistance causes	Addressing causes and issues	Useful for resistance in these areas	Intervention examples
Interventions to address surfaced resistance causes and issues						
Leadership modeling		H		H	Engagement, culture	Pro-change attitude and behavior, authenticity, team member support
Communications		M		H	Engagement, understanding, performance	Regular messages providing clarity in direction, boundaries, and expectations, progress
Performance measurement		H		H	Performance, productivity	Desired change values and behaviors embedded in appraisals
Rewards and recognition		H		M	Engagement, productivity	Awards, bonuses, opportunities, time off
Chartering and team building		H		M	Collaboration, performance, productivity, integration	Facilitated exercises, chartering
Training and skills enhancement		H		M	Confidence, performance, productivity	Leadership training; change management training
Repair-oriented interventions						
Conflict resolution				H	Roadblocks	Structured sessions to work around entrenched issues
Diplomatic confrontation				H	Stakeholder support, roadblocks, culture	Providing consequences to stone-walling stakeholders
Personnel reassignment				H	Engagement, culture	Addressing lack of fit for change with a less influential role

Readiness: a critical aspect of surfacing change resistance

Change resistance is correlated with readiness. Resistance is higher when people feel less ready or prepared for change, and vice versa. In terms of organizational change, readiness refers to how prepared people feel in regard to the change as it has been defined and communicated in the change initiative. Specifically, for members of the organization at large who will be targeted or affected by the change, readiness refers to how they feel regarding accepting and embracing the change. If they are members of the change initiative, readiness goes further to include how capable they feel to actively move the change forward.

The level of readiness for change which people feel depends on the cognitive as well as emotional mindset of the respondents. Readiness is perception-based, which means that how people feel and think regarding the change may or may not be rooted in reality. Even if their perception of their readiness for change is unrealistic (e.g. too negative or overly optimistic) it must be surfaced and addressed. Perceptions accumulate and create a collective force which can infect many members of the change initiative and those surrounding it, leading to slowing or derailment of the initiative.

Readiness assessment should determine if and how strongly those participating in the change, supporting it or affected by it:

- are clear on the vision and the business reasons for the change
- understand the benefits of the change to organization as well as the consequences of failing to change
- are clear on expectations for their role in the change
- understand their personal benefits from the change (i.e. WIIFM)
- have confidence in leadership's capability to make the change successful
- trust their leaders
- trust their team members
- are realistic about the work required and letting go of the old ways of doing things
- are accepting of the fact that the change will require hard work and sacrifice
- are being asked for their input and ideas, not just conformance
- feel empowered to make the change happen.

Readiness assessments work well because they:

- possess a formalized, quantitative rigor, which is useful in measuring progress
- retain respondent confidence through anonymity
- capture qualitative input, and invite thoughtful reflection and ideas
- foster public sharing of collective results, thereby creating accountability to address them (by change leaders as well as empowered team members).

Change readiness assessments are most often provided in the form of surveys (usually online). Surveys protect respondent identity and encourage openness and authenticity in responses, as well as encourage flow of input. They are easier for sorting and analyzing results, looking for patterns, and evaluating progress against prior benchmarks. A Resistance Readiness tool is provided in Appendix B.

Case Study

Addressing change resistance: **Overcoming resistance at Easter Seals to embrace change and a new model for growth**

The need for business change and a reluctance to embrace it

Creating sustained business growth and a management team capable of driving it had been a long-standing challenge for Easter Seals. Operating much like a small business with 45 employees and an annual revenue base of $4 million, Easter Seals Capital Region of Eastern Connecticut possessed limited administrative and logistical infrastructure and was run by a senior management team selected primarily for their ability to deliver consistent, quality services. As a result, the organization was nimble from a tactical standpoint but not sufficiently equipped to take advantage of opportunities for growth and change.

The Easter Seals' regional executive director was aware that small businesses and organizations with less than $5 million in revenues tended to grow primarily through the efforts of their top executive. As with many other organizations of this size, the senior managers reporting to the executive director had little capability or incentive to create needed models for meaningful business growth and facilitate the corresponding business change required to make that happen. The inherent strength of the management team had embedded in it the seeds of complacency. The managers believed that quality was achieved through doing whatever it takes to create a positive outcome for the patient, client, or customer, approaching work, "the way that a professional would recognize as the highest standard of service." While this was philosophy was laudable in terms of meeting current customer needs, it did not address the need to proactively understand customer market potential in a "big-picture" context, devise new strategies for expanding Easter Seals' customer base and apply analysis-backed forecasting and budget planning. Neither did it address the important need to develop models to support the new growth opportunities once identified.

The executive director had privately and publicly communicated his expectations of the managers, who were in positions of strategic leadership for Easter Seals, to adopt a growth-oriented mentality and the enabling capability to begin creating models for new business growth. However, within a short period of time after each attempt to communicate the importance of this management responsibility the managers' focus and behavior defaulted to the day-to-day delivery of service to customers, responsibilities which could have been delegated to their more tactical subordinates.

In response to the managers' reluctance to move beyond a narrowly-defined delivery mentality and embrace the need for changing to a growth-oriented mindset, the executive director began taking management responsibility for everything in the company besides delivery of services. Other than a nominal level of staffing for accounting and billing, most of the infrastructure support and planning remained within the executive director's domain of responsibility. The time, effort, and energy required to develop growth strategies for Easter Seals was consumed by immediate priorities.

Despite its limitations, the short-term delivery-dominated model practiced by the management team fueled Easter Seals' success for a number of years in terms of earning the organization a strong reputation for quality and internal stability. But when the reputation, quality, and stability gave rise to growth opportunities, the executive director encountered problems with Easter Seals' ability to capitalize on and sustain the growth because he was stretched to drive the line-level business planning and reallocate administrative infrastructure resources by himself. To transfer and stabilize a service line innovation or expansion to an existing manager who was focused on maintaining his or her existing business was a nearly impossible task.

Probing the sources of resistance to the change

Over time, a clear pattern emerged:

- The executive director identified and championed an emerging growth opportunity for Easter Seals to act on and around which to create a new service or business line.
- Expectations were communicated to a manager or managers to embrace the opportunity and implement the necessary changes to support the new service or line of business.
- Resistance arose in terms of the reluctance of the managers to embrace change and address the growth opportunity (e.g. by putting in place the necessary business planning process elements and creating or reallocating the infrastructure resources to provide the needed innovation solutions to support the new business).

The issue ultimately was perceived within the organization as a "disconnect" between the executive director and the managers. The impression also of a shared lack of ability and confidence in Easter Seals' leadership to create business change began to form.

When queried by business change consultants who assisted Easter Seals with its transition to a growth-oriented model, the executive director explained that he was perplexed by the reluctance of the organization to embrace this opportunity for changing to a more dynamic business model. He had assumed that managers and their respective staff would be motivated to engage in the change by the prospect of seeing their programs grow, expanding their mission to a larger scale, and achieving commensurate financial rewards.

When that belief had proved ill-founded, it was assumed that only a lack of resources would prevent otherwise intelligent, capable managers from embracing the change. But a wealth of supportive resources still did not elicit change in the managers in the direction of a growth-oriented mindset and business model.

The executive director wondered if a reluctance to embrace change was the absence of the managers feeling the change need, because it was the executive director who "owned" the responsibility to change the organization. However, no combination of carrots, sticks, or support proved effective in delegating responsibility to or creating ownership for the change in the managers. The organization continued to deliver its quality services, but it would not grow or demonstrate impetus to change in that direction.

This situation grew even more difficult as the executive director stretched himself increasingly thin to pursue his goal of change and growth for Easter Seals, without getting closer to achieving it. Realizing that he needed help, the executive director called in business change consultants to diagnose the problem.

Using the results of the organizational and leadership change assessment, the consultants conducted in-depth interviews with the executive director, the management team, and representative members of the staff to objectively understand the barriers that were causing the resistance to change. In summary, the analysis revealed that sources of resistance were mainly passive but deeply rooted:

* The managers and their respective staff perceived the change solely being the executive director's personal agenda.
* The executive director was doing little to create a culture of change and address the root causes of the resistance. In fact, by not empowering his managers and instead continually throwing out growth opportunities without engaging his managers in realistic dialogue about the process of change, the executive director was creating a contradictory role model that enforced the managers' dependence on him.

- The "pull" of the existing culture was strong. The managers were proud of what they were achieving in terms of consistent delivery. They had difficulty seeing what was in it for them to change (WIIFM), the benefits as well as the consequences of failing to change.
- By virtue of what had made them successful in their roles for so long, the managers lacked change experience and the ability to conceive of significant change from their insider perspective.

Analysis of these surfaced issues resulted in a plan of action for the change. The approach would need to include a status quo-destabilizing "business trigger" for change that came from outside the organization, rather than another imperative from the executive director. Managers would need to immerse themselves in substantive change and see concrete examples of the new growth-oriented organizational culture and business model that Easter Seals needed to build. The approach would need to include senior-level individuals who were experienced and successful in managing the change process, and who could serve as role models for the managers ensconced in the existing culture. Additionally, clear rewards and consequences regarding embracing change and the new growth-oriented direction would also have to be put into place.

Stage 1: Creating the external impetus for change

The change plan was initiated around a growth opportunity which arose in the form of a failing competitor that was servicing a slightly different customer base in an adjoining region. The competitor company was preparing to shed most of its business lines that it had been unable to transform into viability and were now dragging the company into insolvency.

The Easter Seals executive director identified three particular lines within the failing company that were compatible with Easter Seals' mission and service lines, and complementary to its operational expertise. If the company's business lines were acquired, the annual revenues and employee population of Easter Seals would both double in size. The management of the competitor organization's business lines understood that if Easter Seals decided not to take on the dying business lines their jobs would disappear. This potential for job liquidation provided incentive for the senior manager and his staff to be open-minded about change should they be acquired by Easter Seals.

If exercised, this would be an ideal scenario to apply the change strategy for Easter Seals by demonstrating a model for growth through acquisition and addressing its culture's internal resistance to change. Integrating the company's business lines into Easter Seals' existing operation would engage 55 new employees in the change process, which could be tested and refined before applying it to the current management culture of Easter Seals.

In the absence of meaningful data to support a decision on acquiring the three business lines of the failing competitor, the executive director built his pro forma business analysis around the issues and risks that potentially contributed to the business lines' financial misfortunes. But rather than simply base the Easter Seals' decision on whether or not to acquire the new business lines on the analysis results, the executive director asked the senior business manager of those business lines for a business case as to why and how the business lines could be brought to a point of viability if Easter Seals acquired them. This method demonstrated how the risks and issues might adversely impact the organization's business performance and it became the responsibility of the senior business manager and his team to convince the executive director that the risks carried less impact than the analysis would suggest, and that the risk could be prevented, reduced or mitigated. In their efforts to sell the Easter Seals executive director on the value of acquiring them, the senior manager and his team were selling themselves on the process of change.

While making most of the decisions for the Easter Seals organization and centralized leadership, rather than delegating to his managers, had been counterproductive to a culture of change and growth, the executive director's directive style could be leveraged to foster the new business line manager's and staff's confidence in the executive director as the champion of change they needed. What had previously been a barrier to change for the Easter Seals managers could now be a catalyst for a motivated group that had suffered through a leadership void.

In contrast to the situation which existed within the Easter Seals' current culture, resistance on the part of the new managers was anticipated and mitigated before the change unfolded, to reduce the risk of the organizational change failure. The first step in addressing potential resistance was understanding the change concerns and needs of both parties (i.e. the executive director and the potential new members of the organization) and working together to address them.

As the impending acquisition started to take real form and the likelihood of execution grew, the executive director met with the management of the to-be-acquired business lines, presenting and collaboratively fine-tuning the plan for change required to effectively integrate the new business lines into Easter Seals' operation. They agreed on three core thrusts needed to drive and sustain the effort:

- a vision for business line viability aligned with Easter Seals' overall vision and mission
- an affirmation of the new management team's belief in their capacity to achieve that vision

- a guarantee that upon execution of the acquisition that individuals currently working within the business lines would be employed without suffering a decrease in hours, wages, benefits or position.

The executive director communicated his expectations around the change. He would supply the "what" and the new senior manager and team would deliver the "how" in terms of realizing the change. As their champion of change, the executive director would supply the target for the change, the change road map, and support for helping the new members navigate through the change wilderness while they brought their business lines up to financial viability. Having previously gone through multiple iterations of unmanaged change, the new managers eagerly embraced the "offer" and the change leadership the executive director presented.

Once the acquisition was completed the real work of bringing on the new businesses and creating a unified organization began. The executive director modeled the change by making himself a highly visible and accessible business change manager, frequently shifting his work location to the "new" service sites. His words, actions, and presence communicated that the needs and interests of new staff were his priority and that there would be no favorites in this blended organization.

The executive director kept his word that he would retain all of the acquired managers and staff, but he knew that previously burned employees would test the gray areas of preserving their employment status and compensation before they could fully embrace the change. As a result, those initial tests were resolved in the employees' favor wherever possible and the strongly communicated decisions quickly built acceptance and buy-in to the executive director's plan for change.

This building sense of buy-in paved the way to begin the shifting of operations and procedures in accordance with the executive director's growth-oriented vision for the future of Easter Seals. Though the new employees knew that they had to change to embrace many procedures of the acquiring Easter Seals organization, the executive director's readiness to support their interests spurred the employees' trust and readiness to accept that the evolving changes.

Since they were engaged in discussion of the pro forma statements before the acquisition was executed, the new senior business line manager and his team were already comfortable with the language and focus of the potential changes. The key now was to create assessment and monitoring tools that incorporated these factors and evaluated their impact on attainment of the goals established in the projections of financial viability. These tools would track the factors that were positively or negatively impacting business line viability.

The executive director had created similar tools for managers of the Easter Seals' business lines, but adoption of those types of tools had been weak because those managers never internalized or owned the impetus for change. The managers correctly assumed that if their individual line was underperforming, the executive director would take the steps needed either within their line or elsewhere in the organization to make things work out.

In the acquired lines, however, the executive director had managers and staff who realized that their sustained employment was still ultimately dependent on financial viability, which was a motivator for change, and adoption of the tools that monitor changes and their impact. Scorecards were created to monitor daily operations around the possible causes of those services' previous failure.

It became clear that the identified operational and logistical issues incorporated into the pro forma statements and monitoring tools were accurate and improvement was on track. The focus of the business change process shifted from the newly acquired operations to the entire organization or, more precisely, the "original" management team that had been reticent or unable to embrace change.

Stage 2: Addressing resistance to change in the expanded organization

Stage 1 was a change process in and of itself that set the groundwork for overcoming the resistance of the original team of managers who were comfortable with the Easter Seals culture and the executive director's owning responsibility for change. Within that culture, the de facto norm was to leave change to a supervisor, which was ultimately the executive director. In contrast to the complacent style of the original managers, the newly acquired business lines had a manager who readily took responsibility for initiating change when the executive director communicated his expectations for change and was thus demonstrating measurable success. Then the question became, "Would the behavior of the original managers emulate the new manager's embracing of change as the new management model, or resist it?"

The change consultants established a group process to: (1) systematically evaluate the integration of old and new into a unified organization relative to the recent acquisition and (2) plan for the migration of the original business lines (which provided different services to a different customer base in a different region) into the territory of the acquired operation. Both the senior manager of the new business lines and the original managers were brought together into a work group that would be reporting to the executive director and his board of directors. The group was given its charter and then the executive director carefully stepped away from the process, leaving the managers to find their collective way without him.

The senior business line manager was cut from the same cloth as the other managers, believing, "I'm a program person who knows how to deliver consistently and with quality," but having no more skill or experience in business analysis, planning, or marketing required for the growth-oriented business model the change was aimed at. However, during the negotiation, execution, and implementation of the acquisition, the senior manager had learned the tools of how to effectively manage change and growth. The new business line manager acquired the change skills and unwittingly became the model to show the original managers the mindset and behaviors required of the change.

Since they were not used to these tasks and tools associated with growth-oriented business models, the original managers initially struggled while they watched the new senior manager systematically document projections for profitability and growth with quantitative rigor and assemble detailed forecasts and plans to support their attainment. The new business line manager was not intentionally looking to show up his peers. He was following the normative approaches from his work with the executive director and assumed that everyone else would be doing the same.

The executive director strategically reinserted himself to provide feedback on the group's intermediate progress. While the senior business line manager's efforts didn't necessarily reflect mastery of the new process and tools, they set an example for learning and a willingness to work at change. Well-timed and repeated praise for the business line manager's efforts focused on his having brought a new level of analysis and perspective to the process. The sharply contrasting feedback to the original managers ("I am unclear as to what you are planning to do or what impact this strategy may have") made clear that they would have to bring greater thinking and value to the table in order to compare favorably to the senior business line manager when a final product was presented to the board of directors.

In contrast to the method for countering resistance applied before and during the acquisition, this method effectively employed role modeling to help managers see the change in terms of concrete behaviors, attitude and mindset. Additionally, the new behavior model for change provided a baseline for setting expectations, and building rewards and consequences around it.

Realizing the change and achieving business impact

Over the latter period of the change effort, most of the managers began stepping up to embrace the desired behavior model for change and the business target: the growth-focused, analytical, and plan-based approach in contrast to the informal process and the documentation of status quo that had been previously been accepted as sufficient for business planning.

The resulting output of the change effort and the implementation of the new planning model were useful in communicating the value and efficacy of the post-acquisition efforts and pave a clear path to the future. What was even more striking was the direct impact on the business performance of the Easter Seals organization after the executive director and the board of directors proclaimed the efforts of the work group to be complete. The managers:

- embraced annual budget development with a degree of analysis and planning not previously observed
- for the first time in years, managers initiated budget proposals for significant growth within their departments, in one case as much as a 60 percent increase
- started developing business and operational plans on their own, without request or spurring from the executive director or the board
- personally initiated use of monitoring tools that the executive director had previously provided
- started bringing in sustained growth 20-30 percent over the ambitious growth goals that were now being set
- for the first time in years, brought in new large accounts without losing existing accounts
- for the first time in years, successfully introduced service and product lines without losing others.

A management development program centered on building change capabilities was instituted to support ongoing needs for change required of the new growth-oriented organizational model.

Managers and employees of both the original and the acquired organizations of Easter Seals had overcome their resistance and embraced the change. Culture and behavioral measurement showed that the existing norms upholding the status quo and creating inertia had been displaced in favor of new norms which encouraged dynamic, disciplined planning supportive of growth for the organization.

Notes

1 See http://livebyquotes.com/2012. Every endeavor has been made to locate the copyright holder and if anyone has reason to question the usage of this quote then please contact the publisher, Routledge.

2 Collins, John. W., "The Neuroscience of Learning and Change." 39(5):305-310, October 2007, *Journal of Neuroscience Nursing*.

3 Mangurian Glen. & Cohen Allen. "Reengineering Stress Points: The Race to Results." Vol 7, No.1 Spring 1995. *Insights Quarterly: The Journal of Strategy and Reengineering*.

4 Adair, G., "The Hawthorne Effect: A Reconsideration of the Methodological Artifact". *Journal of Applied Psychology* 69 (2): 334–345, 1984 and Bramel, D. & Friend, R. "Hawthorne, the Myth of the Docile Worker, and Class Bias in Psychology". *American Psychologist* 36 (8): 867–878, 1981.

5 PBS. "People and Discoveries: Heisenberg states the Uncertainty Principle." Available at: http://www.pbs.org/wgbh/aso/databank/entries/dp27un.html

5

CREATING AND SUSTAINING CULTURE CHANGE

"The thing I have learned at IBM is that culture is everything."[1]
Louis Gerstner, former IBM CEO

SITUATIONAL CONTEXT FOR CULTURE CHANGE

Your change initiative has completed the implementation stage. Despite some peaks and valleys, the initiative seems to have gone well. The change vision and new statement of values proudly adorn the walls of offices and cubicles throughout the organization. The newly designed processes, technology and organizational architecture are in place. Training has been performed. Your leadership team is ready to pop the champagne and celebrate. However, a quick glance down the halls reveals that not much has changed other than employees are playing with some new computer applications. People have reverted to the old ways of operating in silos, withholding information, and suppressing difficult news. The latest change assessment and interviews confirm that people have not embraced the new mindset and desired values. You have a problem with culture change.

Organizational transformation depends on changing culture

Change management is aimed at changing organizations. Culture change is what makes change management transformational. Transformation requires that members of the organization think and act in ways which represent the new change vision and goals. The desired mindset and accompanying behaviors must shift to a culture different from the ones that existed previously. The 2008 landmark IBM study on why change projects fail points out: "The most significant challenges when implementing change projects are people-oriented – topping the list are *changing mindsets* and *corporate culture.*"[2] Change initiatives cannot claim success without transitioning the hearts and minds of an organization's members to a new culture.

Despite its recognized importance to business change, the concept of culture is not simple to grasp. Culture represents the essence of the organization. It is more easily sensed and expressed by outsiders to the organization than by its members who operate automatically within the culture. Our research indicates that no common definition of organizational culture exists across change management thought leaders. Definitions of culture often include an organization's values, how members see themselves and how they interact with each other, how work gets done, the acceptable boundaries for behavior, and what gets rewarded or punished. We define culture as the cultural characteristics, values, and behaviors that are resident in the organization.

What makes culture so powerful and gives it such lasting impact? Culture embodies shared assumptions that explicitly and implicitly guide how members of the organization behave in work situations. These assumptions would have been formed early in an organization's history when its leaders and members successfully worked through challenges together. Organizational culture pioneer Edgar Schein describes the motivation for creating these shared assumptions as a form of survival and adaptation that becomes embedded in the organization. These shared assumptions then get passed down to new employees as the organization evolves. He formally defines culture as:

> A pattern of shared basic assumptions that the group learned as it solved its problems of external adaptation and internal integration, that has worked well enough to be considered valid, and, therefore, to be taught to new members as the correct way to perceive, think, and feel in relation to those problems.[3]

These cultural assumptions provided the organization's members with needed stability and predictability as they initially worked through the organization's challenges. As the organization grows the formative culture remains largely intact. Old habits die hard. Even as the business landscape outside the organization and the needs of its customers change around them, the organization's values, leadership style, ways of communicating, and other facets of culture often prevail. Throughout the organization's history, though, significant events and changes will impact the culture. Organizational members will be forced to adapt to these impacts, causing some changes in the predominant culture while reinforcing others.

Culture is intertwined with the business of the organization. It is not a distinct, separate entity as previous change management trends like BPR had treated it, described in Chapter 1. Schein provides perspective: "We tend to think we can separate strategy from culture, but we fail to notice that in most organizations strategic thinking is deeply colored by tacit assumptions about who they are and what their mission is."[4]

What influences culture? There are a number of factors:

- **Roots of the organization.** Where the organization started from and what it prides itself on (e.g. family founded, community-oriented, high quality products, customer service) will provide the underpinnings of the culture.
- **Learning during length of time working together.** Cultural patterns form and are reinforced when groups of people work together and repeat what works for them,
- **High impact events in the organization's history.** Mergers, acquisitions, consolidations, and restructurings challenge the existing culture, requiring people to reevaluate aspects of the culture in order to reestablish stability and predictability (e.g. what behaviors during and after downsizing are rewarded for survival and promotion?).
- **New beliefs, values, and assumptions brought in to the organization.** New members, and particularly new leaders, influence the existing culture through their ideas, experience, and behavior.
- **Structural factors.** The structure and systems of the organization embed values in work practice which influence the culture (e.g. technology procedures, controls and communication, rewards and punishment, performance management, reporting hierarchy).
- **Leadership and management.** The most powerful determinant of culture is the organization's leadership, which sets the tone for, shapes, and models the culture (e.g. what beliefs and values are espoused, what gets supported, what gets rewarded and punished). Schein summarizes leadership's role with regard to organizational culture: "…one of the most decisive functions of leadership is the creation, the management, and sometimes even the destruction of culture."[5]

Cultural paradigms exist at multiple tiers and inform the overall organization culture. These tiers are not in perfect alignment in terms of values, mindset, and behavior style. Specific elements dominate, subordinate, or blend in response to environmental and group pressures. These tiers are:

- **Individual.** Each person brings with them a cultural paradigm to the organization based on their prior experience and values.
- **Group.** Teams, departments, and functions subsume individual paradigms into the pre-existing group paradigm (unless a particular individual tends to have authority or leadership), which can be adjusted by group consensus to meet its needs. Note that functional groups may also share additional aspects of a subculture based on their discipline or specialty (e.g. IT, research, and scientific areas tend to be more data-driven and focus less on people elements than marketing, sales, and HR).
- **Organization.** The organization's cultural paradigm represented by senior management shapes and controls group culture. The organization's

pre-existing culture exerts the most powerful influence through leadership, structure, reward and punishment and other factors, informing and often overriding group and individual paradigms.

In culture change, it is important to keep in mind the variances between and across these tiers. It is likely that sub-paradigms among members or groups within the organization that are useful to change are being suppressed by the dominant cultural paradigm. It is useful to surface and examine paradigms across the organization for potential leverage and influence for the change initiative.

Culture exists at two levels. The *explicit* level can be observed, verified, and measured. This level describes "what" an organizational culture consists of on the surface. Dean and Linda Anderson call these observable manifestations "indicators of culture."[6] In contrast, the *implicit* level of culture is tacit, providing the underlying assumptions or cultural drivers beneath the explicit level of culture. This level describes "why" the observable culture exists and continues to persist.

In Figure 5.1 below we provide a model for understanding the explicit and implicit aspects of culture and how they are related.

The implicit assumptions for the explicit values, norms, language, rules, symbols, and so on are rarely examined by an organization. In a change initiative, however, these assumptions underlying accepted beliefs, feelings, and perceptions must be challenged in order to transform the culture. These roots of culture, which may have once been useful to the organization, are often holding it back from positive change. Such assumptions must be brought to the surface, evaluated in terms of their helpfulness or hindrance to the change vision, and replaced where needed. The corresponding ideals and patterns that depend on these assumptions can then be changed. Conversely, directly changing the explicit aspects of culture such as espoused values and measures is also valuable. New values, systems, and models can be used to reverse-engineer and retire cultural assumptions that are no longer valid.

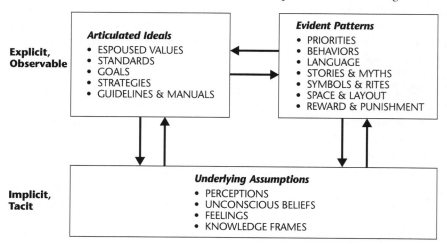

FIGURE 5.1 Explicit and implicit aspects of culture

Kurt Lewin, a social scientist and early pioneer of Organizational Development, described this as a three-step change model, i.e. unfreezing, moving, and refreezing.[7] Once existing cultural assumptions are publicly examined and evaluated, i.e. "unfrozen," the organization can then move to a new cultural model and embed it in practice.

The *explicit, observable* layer of the culture model in Figure 5.1 consists of Articulated Ideals and Evident Patterns. *Articulated Ideals* represent those aspects of culture that have been deliberately put into place by leadership to guide culture and direct priorities. These ideals have been formalized, documented, and communicated as a form of expectations. *Espoused values* and standards are a type of Articulated Ideal, found in mission statements, charters, credos, slogans, and standards for ethics and compliance. "Our customers always come first," "Our people are our greatest asset," or "Our purpose is to create healthier patients through caring people and innovative solutions," are examples of this type of values narrative. However formative these espoused values may have been earlier in establishing the roots of a culture, they may have lost their power over time as the organization evolved, new leaders arrived, and business priorities changed which were not consistent with the espoused values and their original intent.

Other Articulated Ideals put into place by an organization's leaders may be in the form of business direction. These ideals may not be expressed directly as values, beliefs, or attempts to change culture, but they inherently shape the culture. Specific business *goals* and *strategies* will force people to think and behave in certain ways and these become patterns. For example, implementing a strategy to become a "lean organization" or moving to a "customer intimate" business model will result in different implications for how people in the organization prioritize their work efforts, interact with each other, use information and make decisions. Processes and technologies in place also shape how people think and act. An organization that is more controlling or detailed in character will have more step-by-step procedures and compliance measures which can be verified through *guidelines* and *manuals*. In such cultures, patterns of, decision making, collaboration, and use of information will be much different from those that emphasize autonomy and empowerment.

Evident Patterns are the other half of the explicit, observable level of culture. They represent what people in the organization actually *do* rather than what they *should* do according to the organization's Articulated Ideals. Some of these patterns will be consistent with espoused values, business philosophy and systems, but many will not. These patterns can function like an "underground economy" to get things done by circumventing ineffectual standards and systems.

Priorities are a significant type of pattern that reveals what is important in a culture. Examples include where investments are made in the organization, who gets resources, which initiatives get launched and supported, and where people spend most of their time. Priorities are watched closely by members of the organization for consistency with espoused ideals and quickly copied.

Behaviors are another type of pattern. Behaviors range from leadership style to communication, decision making, information sharing, and collaboration. A type of leadership style that pervades this culture is "consensus-driven," soliciting more input into decisions but taking much longer to make them and take action. Other leadership patterns are more "command-and-control" with less delegation and empowerment. Some cultures have more face-to-face interaction while others predominantly rely on electronic communication, resulting in efficiencies but also creating more transactional relationships with reduced trust.

Language, stories and myths, and *symbols and rites* are types of patterns that have strong associations with identity. These are manifestations of how people view the organization and their relation to it. More formal language and exaltation of titles will convey a stricter, more authoritarian culture than one that uses more relaxed, casual language, and has more egalitarian interaction. The common use of "we" rather than "I" indicates more of a collaborative, sharing culture rather than one that is individualistic. The use of "us" and "them" registers an impression of a more competitive, adversarial culture than one that is unified. The content of language will also reveal things like how people view their role in the organization. For example, language will reveal whether people possess an assembly-line mentality or a caseworker mentality.

Stories and myths that are repeated in the organization can recall heroes as well as villains. A charismatic founder or influential leader of the organization can influence the culture long after their departure through commonly retold stories about them, for better or worse. Examples include Thomas Watson at IBM, Jack Welch at GE, Steve Jobs at Apple, and Al Dunlop at Sunbeam. Similarly, stories or myths about significant events in the company's history, including game-changing innovations, turnarounds and challenging moments reveal what members of the organization take pride and comfort in, or pay attention to. James Burke, former CEO at Johnson and Johnson, was revered through the culture in stories for decades after leading the company through his decisive, public action to remove one of the company's leading products, Tylenol, from all store shelves after reports of tampering in a store. The story reminded people of the importance of product safety and quality, as well as public initiative, which the company prided itself on.[8]

Symbols and rites are another type of pattern. Levels of classifications and privileges are revealed in who receives reserved parking spaces, larger offices, travel perks, and investment in training and coaching, among other things. Informal, regular gatherings where people from all levels celebrate progress over pizza and drinks convey a more down-to-earth culture than one in which leaders broadcast messages on business performance via video, email or town-hall meetings. Work ethic and commitment to balancing life priorities can be seen in when and how long people work, including use of flex-time and virtual collaboration. Space and layout forms such as shared offices and community spaces demonstrate a commitment to openness and sharing. Office and cubicle décor also reveal culture patterns. Personal artifacts and color in cube and office ornamentation reflect encouragement for self-expression and individuality.

How people are *rewarded and punished* is a highly observable and influential pattern in culture. The "rules" and criteria for compensation and promotion indicate what is truly valued. For example, management promotions may be based on technical achievement with limited regard for business acumen and leadership capabilities. Common traits in leaders or new hires are also indicative. Managers and new hires may exhibit a high regard for quality and confronting issues in one culture but in another culture they may exalt speedy execution and passive obedience to hierarchy. Performance may be rewarded in one organization for completing task plans and meeting the numbers, but in another delivering business impact and customer satisfaction are rewarded. A culture is which the ends were not justified by the means was exemplified by a common phrase: "Leaving dead bodies behind will keep you from advancing in this organization." How the consequences of failure are treated is also revealing. An organization that encourages informed risk and rewards effort and learning sets a cultural tone different from the organization that rewards only successful results.

The *implicit* level of culture is made up of underlying assumptions for why the explicit elements of culture need to exist as they do. These assumptions are shared and mutually reinforced. Some assumptions carry over from when the original culture was formed; other assumptions are formed with the addition of new leadership, structures, and systems. Because these assumptions provide cognitive stability and continue to benefit certain members of the organization, they are unconsciously assumed and not confronted or debated.

Assumptions provide people with a rationale for the status quo, which enables them to make sense of and live with the culture's outdated, illogical, and ineffective aspects. This provides justification for not changing culture. "Because that's the way we do things around here" is a refrain often heard in a culture that is fighting change. These assumptions are no longer logical or justifiable when assessed in light of the organization's current and future needs. Surfacing and testing the logic that supports anti-change assumptions will invalidate them. The business environment and the organization evolve over time even if the culture remains largely unchanged. Doing the same things from the past quickly degrades an organization's competitiveness.

As shown in Figure 5.1, assumptions are rooted in *perceptions*, *unconscious beliefs*, and *feelings*, which are often not grounded in reality. For example, the existence of erroneous beliefs that the people at the top of the organization have all the answers or that management will always protect the people in the organization result in passive behaviors such as lack of initiative and dependence on the organization for learning and development. Another misperception may be that loyalty to "one's tribe" or business department is the key to individual success in the organization. This outdated belief is often manifested in lack of collaboration across silos and even turf wars. Another assumption may be that speed is more important than quality, which can always be addressed later, resulting in a culture that lacks discipline. These examples of faulty assumptions are enemies of modern, competitive, change-driven organizations.

ther area where outdated, change-impeding assumptions flourish is that of *e frames*. Avoiding or filtering out new knowledge about customers, tors, and the business landscape allows the old assumptions to remain intact. For example, an assumption may be that customers will always buy the organization's products and services because the organization was a pioneer in the field with a reputation for elegant technology solutions. If performed, market research would reveal that customers are seeking more custom solutions rather than supplier-driven one-size-fits-all offerings, and are less loyal to brands than they once were. By ignoring the changing expectations of the customers and not allowing them to disconfirm old assumptions, a culture of complacency thrives.

A closed or limited knowledge frame in terms of methods for organizational change is another example of an area where faulty assumptions can inhibit progress. This is an assumption that favors reusing simple, linear methods to drive transformational change but it will result in misplaced priorities, which are costly and demoralizing. Changing a culture is not a simple fix. Culture must be addressed as an integrated set of elements, as Steven Denning describes:

> The elements fit together as a mutually reinforcing system and combine to prevent any attempt to change it. That's why single-fix changes, such as the introduction of teams, or Lean, or Agile, or Scrum, or knowledge management, or some new process, may appear to make progress for a while, but eventually the interlocking elements of the organizational culture take over and the change is inexorably drawn back into the existing organizational culture.[9]

Exposing cultural assumptions and disconfirming them through logic unleashes considerable anxiety. The stability and predictability that held the culture together will be dismantled. This is where strong leadership is required for culture change. Schein describes it this way:

> Unfreezing the organization requires a creation of psychological safety, which means that the leader must have the emotional strength to absorb much of the anxiety that change brings with it and the ability to remain supportive to the organization through the transition phase even if group members become angry and obstructive.[10]

Culture will defend itself against change, so leaders must prepare for resistance. Resistance will arise from needs to protect the old culture where systems of survival, adaptation, stability, and predictability are anchored. Changing culture is more than pointing organizational members to the desired culture and setting expectations for them to learn it. Organizational learning and development pioneer Chris Argyris points out that, "A new culture requires not only learning, but unlearning as well. It requires changing the more stable portions of our structure."[11]

Change capability and culture

Surfacing and countering resistance as described in Chapter 4 are important to culture change, but the focus of culture change extends much wider. Culture change is also about implanting an environment with positive behaviors and mindsets to realize the change vision and continue to advance change. An overarching goal of culture change is to create a *change-capable* culture that is self-sustaining and progressive.

A change-capable organization is one whose members are continually engaged in building their knowledge of the challenges and opportunities of their industry in parallel with their change management skills. They actively explore the impact of change and possible improvements as part of their day-to-day work. A change capable-organization possesses a culture that sees change as vital to the health of the organization. Members are self-motivated to pursue value-adding opportunities for change.[12]

To this end, culture change is not value-neutral. *Culture* is a neutral term, representing the unique combination of characteristics that make up an organization's culture for better or for worse. *Culture change*, however, seeks to optimize certain characteristics of culture while eliminating others on the basis of their long-term value to organizational change.

The goal of culture change is not to make all cultures the same. There are aspects of culture in one organization that give it identity and strength, but that would not work in another organization. The creative, entrepreneurial cultures of Apple and Google are well respected, but they would not fly in traditional brick-and-mortar corporations that are more conservative. However, both of these distinct types of culture, as well as others, benefit from incorporating change-capable values and characteristics.

A change-capable culture embodies core themes, which include:

- **Culture change cascades from the strategic direction of the organization.** Culture change is grounded in the organization's business aspirations and the goals for the future. Culture evolves with the organization's business direction, not independently.
- **The people of an organization are its most important asset.** People are respected as owners of the organization's future and for the unique strengths they bring to the organization. They are entrusted with change and invested in it accordingly.
- **Empowered, motivated individuals create organizational change.** Leaders are their guides. Everyone is equipped and accountable for driving change. Without the engagement and commitment of the organization, change will not stick.
- **Work gets done through and across teams.** Teams are the fundamental working units and collaboration is the fuel they run on. Efficient and effective change performance is achieved through healthy interaction between and among teams at all levels.

- **Openness and transparency thrive in communication**. Honest, substantive information flows freely in all directions. Dialogue and diverse discussion are encouraged. Difficult and tough news are not withheld. People are comfortable voicing opinions, seeking clarity, and surfacing risk.
- **Trust, fairness, and objectivity are embedded in cultural systems and behavior.** People are treated, rewarded, and punished in ways that are consistent, predictable, and demonstrative of dignity. Everyone is held to the same standards for values and behavior regardless of rank. Leaders, teams, and individuals can be counted on to "walk the talk."
- **Culture change is recognized as a process with inputs and outputs.** Modifications to architecture will cause culture to evolve over time. For example, HR practices such as performance management, compensation, and recognition create incentives and consequences for enhancing the desired – and extinguishing the undesired – culture elements.
- **Continuous organizational learning is a constant goal.** People and organizations change when they make learning a priority. Actively learning what is working, and what is not, is followed by putting this learning into practice in real time. Informed risks are taken as opportunities to learn, and not treated as failures. Learning goals are set and acheivements are rewarded.
- **Change is rooted in business knowledge and reality.** Change is not done for its own sake, and it is more than just a set of principles. Change is anchored in the organization's strategic direction and long-term goals. Through research and knowledge exchange, people are well informed of up-to-date customer needs and the business landscape, which are used to drive the change, not just perception.

The value of these change-capable cultural themes to organizational performance is increasingly demonstrated and quantified in studies such as those by Towers Watson, Gallup, and others. For example, the value of "openness and transparency thrive in communication," is strikingly relevant to business performance. As reported in *Forbes*: "A recent survey by the Corporate Executive Board of more than 400,000 employees across various industries reveals that companies that break down two key barriers to honest feedback not only reduce fraud and misconduct, but also deliver peer-beating shareholder returns by a substantial margin."[13]

Success factors for culture change

There are seven key factors to consider when planning and executing culture change as part of a change initiative.

1. **Create and facilitate the environment for culture change through leadership.**
    Leaders create the conditions for culture change by prioritizing, supporting, and enforcing the new culture characteristics, values, and behaviors. They

embed them in performance expectations as well as reward systems. Leaders also model the desired behaviors themselves. They provide safety and support during the transition from the old to the new culture. Schein summarizes the important role of leaders in culture change: "One could argue that the only thing of real importance that leaders do is create and manage culture…and the unique talent of leaders is their ability to understand and work with culture."[14]

2. **Reexamine and challenge the driving cultural assumptions while managing resistance.**
    Long-held underlying cultural assumptions need to be surfaced, publicly challenged, and invalidated. Logic, environmental scans, market research and other data can be used to show how long-held assumptions are holding the organization back. Leaders must then address the ensuing resistance, as described in Chapter four. Schein makes the point:

    > Leadership is needed to help the group identify issues and deal with them… the leaders must often absorb and contain the anxiety that is unleashed when things do not work as they should. Leaders may not have the answer, but they provide the temporary stability and emotional reassurance while the answer is being worked out.[15]

3. **Create a new cultural paradigm that is credible and tightly aligned to the business strategy.**
    The new mindset, values, behaviors, symbols, work styles etc. should be carefully defined in light of the company's business plan. Culture forms the boundary to what kind of strategies will be successful. There have been many studies that have concluded that employee behavior drives customer satisfaction and ultimately organization performance. Consequently, culture must be tightly aligned and cascaded from the strategy.

    It needs to be clear what aspects of the organization's culture are going to be retained and which ones are not. The reasons for changing as well as retaining aspects of culture must be rooted in business reality. What is a source of pride and future use to the organization and of business value should be leveraged rather than thrown away. Conversely, cultures that are entirely foreign to an organization should not be thrust upon it.

    For example, take an organization with deep roots in science that is undergoing a change to become more customer-intimate. It has not been a marketing-driven company. Its research-based mindset and commitment to quality are aspects of the culture worth preserving. However, its lengthy decision-making, silo-defending, and foxhole behaviors are aspects of the culture that will need to be replaced with more efficient decision making, cross-functional cooperation and team collaboration.

4. **Establish clear guidelines and concrete examples for the new culture.**
    Values and principles set the high-level ideals for culture change, and they need to be "made real" through context in the work environment. Contrast the

before-and-after states that people will recognize and relate to in terms of behavior. The change-capable culture themes described earlier should be woven into situational examples. Behavior patterns from the existing culture that will enable the change should be flagged for leveraging, while patterns from the culture that will inhibit the change should be identified for elimination. New behaviors that need to be added for the new culture should also be captured. The members of the organization and the change team should perform this exercise so they can also own the results and be accountable and not just the change leaders.

Table 5.1 provides an example of an organizational culture diagnosis. It identifies patterns that enables the change that should be leveraged in the new desired culture, patterns that inhibit the change that should be eliminated, and new behaviors that need to be incorporated.

TABLE 5.1 Culture patterns: enabling, inhibiting, and needed

Patterns enabling the change vision (leverage)	*Patterns inhibiting the change vision (eliminate)*
Team members are dedicated to producing quality work for customers.	Tough decisions are avoided or if discussed, never resolved.
A collegial environment exists *within* teams where people share ideas, work hard, and enjoy each other's company.	People are not held accountable for violations of work standards and trust, especially when it comes to meeting timelines and stakeholder follow-through.
People are rewarded for finding better ways to use information technology.	People are punished for risk taking and new ideas that do not succeed.
There is a healthy respect for life/work balance that includes flextime, day care, and virtual working.	Management and leadership are passive or absent when it comes to demonstrating commitment to change
People provide honest, helpful feedback when they are asked for their opinions and assured safety (or anonymity as in a survey).	Suggestions for improvement are not encouraged or are tabled indefinitely in favor of short-term priorities.

New behaviors needed (add)

Conduct decision-making with a process that includes assignment and close-out.
Recognize and reward actions which help advance the change vision.
Perform leadership team modeling of the new cultural model and assess impact.
Identify priorities and ensure they are completed.
Champion new ideas and solution alternatives with key stakeholders.
Conduct lessons learned to improve team dynamics and project management.

5. **Empower people to build the new culture and hold everyone accountable.**

While leaders establish the "what" regarding direction and expectations for culture change, they must rely on team members for determining "how" to make it work. Team members as well as leaders must hold each other accountable for supporting the culture change. Members should be equipped and encouraged to use emotional intelligence, particularly in situations where there is a tendency for negative behaviors to flourish. "Inevitably, a team member will indulge in behavior that crosses the line, and the team must feel comfortable calling the foul."[16]

6. **Manage culture change as an iterative transition and learning process, not a linear project.**

    Change needs to be viewed and internalized by the organization as a constantly evolving process, not just a one-off, event-driven, or "big bang" project. The Cultural Transition Cycle depicts a four-step process in Figure 5.2.

FIGURE 5.2 The cultural transition cycle

Aligning culture to change in business direction

An important aspect of culture change is aligning culture to the organization's change vision and strategic business direction. We present a model for cultural alignment that has been successfully used in a cross-section of organizations to realize their desired culture change. In the context of describing this model, we present a real-life example.

1. **Obtain consensus on the organization's strategic direction that the business change will help realize.**

    In most environments there is a formal business or strategic planning document that exists, while in others you will need interviews with key members of the executive team to obtain the information required. Translate the strategy into three to five strategic thrusts that succinctly convey the new business focus of the organization.

2. **Identify the "future state" cultural characteristics, values, and employee behaviors that are critical to successfully executing the new or changed strategic direction.**

Cultural characteristics are general themes that provide the overarching frames for the values and behaviors as well other cultural ideals and patterns. Values and behaviors are the most observable aspects of culture and are specific. Relative to Figure 5.1 described earlier in this chapter, values represent articulated ideals and behaviors represent evident patterns. The identification of cultural characteristics, values, and behaviors should be facilitated by the change leadership team – with participation from all members of the change team. They represent the employees of the organization who will operate in the new culture. Similarly, stakeholders who have a clear understanding of business direction and who will be impacted by the change should also be involved. See Table 5.2 for an example.

3. **Collect data using a variety of sources (e.g. leadership interviews, project team input, culture mapping pulse survey).**

Blend and distill the data to come up with two different deliverables:

- An "as is" culture map (see the Culture Mapping Tool in Appendix B)
- A summary of five to ten "as is" values and their corresponding behaviors.

The completed culture map should clearly depict where the organization falls along the continuum of the desired cultural characteristics. Note areas of convergence and divergence between the "as is" and "future" cultural characteristics. Pay careful attention to areas of divergence that are material (i.e. what things must be addressed for the organization to achieve its key goals).

TABLE 5.2 Example of future state cultural characteristics and values needed for a business change

Cultural characteristics needed to execute a change vision or new strategic direction	*Value and behaviors needed to execute a change vision or new strategic direction*
• Customer-focused • Trust and respect • Unfiltered communications • Decentralized decision making, low bureaucracy • Calculated risk-taking	**Value**: Inspire others to take pride in the organization through dedication to excellence. **Behaviors**: • We hold ourselves and each other to high standards of excellence in our work results, means of achieving them and relationships. • We learn from our successes and mistakes by continually improving our methods and plans. • We are solution-driven, persistent, and resourceful in overcoming adversity. • We provide constructive and actionable feedback.

At the conclusion of this step it is necessary to develop a summary of the key cultural characteristics, values, and behaviors that are the most mission critical gaps. See Table 5.3 for an example.

TABLE 5.3 Example summary of key cultural characteristic, value, and behavior gaps

Key cultural characteristic gaps	Key value and behavior gaps
• Customer focus	• Trust
• Clarity around strategic direction	• Allowing people to do their jobs and delegate decision-making authority to the lowest level
• Clarity around roles and decision-making	
• Leadership alignment and behavior consistency	• Treating people with respect independent of their status
• Too reactive and tactical	
• Teamwork and cross-functional collaboration	

4. **Develop a plan for aligning the culture with the organization's business architecture.**

All organizations, whether Fortune 500 conglomerates, small cap companies, institutions, or government agencies, have three fundamental components of business architecture: *technology*, *organization*, and *process*. Business architecture is a *structural enabler* of change that embeds and reinforces desired cultural changes in practice. We view architecture in the "Driving/ Imposed" quadrant in the Culture Change Enablers grid, described in Figure 5.4 later in this chapter. In the opposite direction, business architecture changes create impacts on culture that must be evaluated and changed, if necessary.

We define the *technology architecture* as being comprised of the data employees need to make decisions, the IT hardware, the production, or operations technology that is instrumental in delivering your core product or service, and the software applications. The *organization architecture* is comprised of management systems (e.g. planning, budgeting); workforce enablement and support systems (e.g. recruiting and rewards, succession planning); developing the knowledge, skills, and abilities of the workforce; and the organization structure (e.g. job design, reporting relationships, staffing levels). The *process architecture* is composed of the business processes, physical layout of work areas, and the administrative policies and business rules that drive behavior.

Each dimension of business architecture is interdependent. Whenever any part of the architecture is "modified" it creates ripple effects in the other dimensions and elements. For example, if a process is modified it will likely impact such things as IT technology, management and workforce systems, performance metrics, job design, and physical layout.

Architecture is both an input to and output of culture change. Culture will evolve over time by embedding into work practice the identified cultural characteristics, values, and behaviors needed to realize the new direction and change vision. This is achieved by modifying the technology, organization, and process architecture to enable and reinforce the desired cultural targets. This will increase the likelihood that the desired culture will begin to institutionalize over time. Progress can be measured from the initial baseline using a maturity model as described in the next section on institutionalizing culture.

Figure 5.3 illustrates the model for cultural alignment using an example. Start by identifying five to seven strategic thrusts of the new business direction or change vision. In this example, these thrusts are intended to increase market share and customer retention. Then ask what type of cultural characteristics and employee behaviors are needed to achieve this strategy. Identify five to seven clear characteristics. Relative to desired cultural characteristics this can result in such things as low bureaucracy, high operational flexibility to respond quickly to market changes, and aggressive use of technology to enable the core processes. Managers and employees must also model behaviors such as: be willing to learn new skills, become facile at developing and maintaining customer relationships, and demonstrate flexibility regarding task and job assignments. Identify gaps in the current culture relative to these desired characteristics, values, and behaviors.

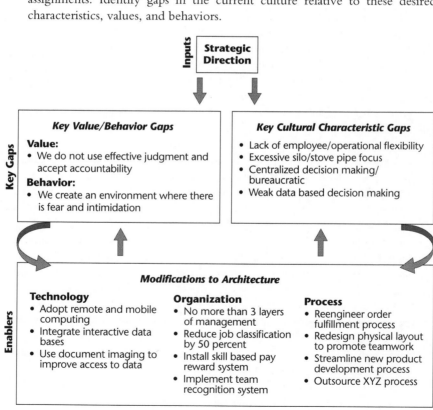

FIGURE 5.3 Cultural alignment model with example

The desired cultural characteristics and employee behaviors will evolve over time if the technology, organization, and process architecture is modified. This could include integrating relational data bases to ensure information is available to lower level personnel to enable decentralized decision making, adopting remote and mobile computing to enhance information availability, reducing the number of layers of management, implementing a skill-based pay reward system, redesigning the physical layout to promote cross functional teamwork, and reengineering the order entry process.

Crafting and executing a plan of action and paying careful attention to "cause and effect" will facilitate culture alignment over a moderate period of time.

Institutionalizing culture

Change does not end when the implementation phase of the change initiative is completed. In fact, culture change is the change initiative's strongest test. Will the new culture take root and continue to grow in strength once the major thrust of the change initiative subsides, or will people revert to the old culture?

Institutionalizing the new culture means embedding the desired mindset, behaviors, and competencies in work practice. These aspects of a change-capable culture should become nearly automatic. A change capability culture maturity model is a useful method for tracking where and how well the culture change is becoming embedded in work practice. Table 5.4 is an example of a Change Capability Maturity Model.

TABLE 5.4 Example of a Change Capability Maturity Model (culture) template

Change capability	1 Not practiced	2 Minimally practiced	3 Somewhat practiced	4 Embedded in practice	5 Advancing in practice
Leadership modeling					
Open, transparent communication					
Change commitment and focus					
Fairness and objectivity					
Collaboration					
Learning and adaptation					
Support					

The left column contains change-capable behavior patterns that could be targets for the culture change. The cells in the columns to the right of the capabilities are for plotting values as to the relative frequency of each capability in practice. The degree to which these patterns have been institutionalized in the organization's culture will be represented by the movement of the values from left to right columns. The value ratings are classified as:

1. **Not practiced.** The change capability or behavior pattern is not commonly demonstrated throughout the organization. The behavior appears in remote individuals or isolated circumstances, if at all.
2. **Minimally practiced.** The change capability or behavior pattern is randomly demonstrated throughout the organization's population.
3. **Somewhat practiced.** The change capability or behavior pattern is demonstrated throughout the population, but under *situations that do not involve stress*. The pattern is not demonstrated or weak when tested under pressure.
4. **Embedded in practice.** The change capability or behavior pattern is routinely demonstrated throughout the population. The pattern is usually automatic, performed without prompting, reminders, or much thinking. The pattern can be said to be fully "institutionalized" in the culture if it achieves this level.
5. **Advancing in practice.** The change capability or behavior pattern is being continually optimized through lessons learned, continuous improvement, and innovative ideas for application. There is a deliberate commitment and passion on the part of members in the organization to make the pattern even stronger in practice.

The maturity values collected for the culture patterns should include a wide sampling across the organization and levels to avoid distortion errors. Respondents should focus their assessment on the population at large that is exposed to the change based on their observations and experience. They can include their own behavior in demonstrating a value or behavior.

Online survey tools are useful for this work as they encourage candor and thoughtful responses. Questions regarding assessing the maturity of the behavior patterns should be clear and concise. For example:

> Leadership Modeling: "How strongly do leaders demonstrate the stated values of behaviors expected of the new culture?"

It is important to provide respondents with an open-field following each question to express their feelings, provide concrete examples of the behavior patterns and suggestions for improving their uptake in practice. Information collected from the respondents can be some of the most valuable information for tuning the change initiative as well as ongoing efforts to institutionalize the new culture model.

Table 5.5 depicts an example of a completed Change Capability Maturity Model.

TABLE 5.5 Example of Change Capability Maturity Model progression

Change capability	1 Not practiced	2 Minimally practiced	3 Somewhat practiced	4 Embedded in practice	5 Advancing in practice
Leadership modeling		t1 +3mo	t2 +12mo		
Open, transparent communication		t1 +3mo	t2 +12mo		
Change commitment and focus		t1 +3mo		t2 +12mo	
Fairness and objectivity		t1 +3mo t2 +12mo			
Collaboration		t1 +3mo	t2 +12mo		
Learning and adaptation		t1 +3mo		t2 +12mo	
Support		t1 +3mo	t2 +12mo		

t1 – Time Period one: three months after change implementation
t2 – Time Period two: one year after change implementation

The values in the Table 5.5 show progression of the change-capable behavior patterns across two time periods, identified as *t1* and *t2*. The t1 identifier in the cell values is the initial benchmark established when the maturity assessment was performed. The t2 identifier represents the follow-up maturity assessment taken a year after the change implementation. The time periods are arbitrary. However, it is important to establish a benchmark early after the initial change implementation from which to demonstrate progress. Ideally, subsequent assessments should not occur beyond six months to a year.

Interpreting results from the example shown in Table 5.5, several conclusions can be drawn. Organizational members collectively perceive that a solid progression from one category to another has occurred in all capabilities except one. Data behind each plotted *t* indicator in a column may reveal a stronger or weaker result based on the constellation of respondent data. This indicates that the enabling changes and interventions are taking root. The pattern for *fairness and objectivity* has not progressed substantially, requiring root cause analysis. It may be that there is a lingering perception of favoritism towards certain individuals, which has not been merited or supported by objective criteria. Potentially, there may be some breaches of desired behaviors and lapses in emotional intelligence for which some prominent individuals were not reprimanded or held accountable. These interpretations, among others, will have to be tested and substantiated through surfacing interventions.

A finer-grained look at the maturity data is useful as the type or level of respondent can influence perception. Different results can be revealing. Often people higher in rank in the organization register a different perception from those on the ground of a change initiative or whose work practices have been significantly impacted. In the desire to see the results of a hard-earned change effort, there is an inherent tendency to see things more optimistically than they actually are. Table 5.6 shows an example of how the results of a change capability maturity assessment have been segmented by the perspectives of change leaders, team members, and stakeholders.

It is useful to look for trends not only across time periods but between types of roles as well. In Table 5.6 the respondents are stratified by three levels. The *change leader* perceptions, identified by an "L", collectively include senior management, the initiative sponsor, change missionaries, and champions, and team leads of the change initiative. "T" includes team members of the change initiative carrying out the work as well as organizational members whose work is directly impacted by the change (these may be one and the same or different, depending on the change initiative). "S" collectively includes stakeholders such as managers who have functional responsibility within the organization and who are being affected by the target of the change effort. The identifiers show both the role type and time period, e.g. L2 = results of the second assessment period for the change leaders.

A cursory glance at the data in the table reveals that the change leaders hold a more optimistic view of the culture change than the team members and stakeholders. For example, the leadership modeling capability indicates that team members and stakeholders perceive that modeling of the desire culture changes by leaders does not progress as fast into practice as the change leaders would like to think. A

TABLE 5.6 Example of Change Capability Maturity Model results segmented

Change capability	1 Not practiced	2 Minimally practiced	3 Somewhat practiced	4 Embedded in practice	5 Advancing in practice
Leadership modeling		T1 S1 **S2**	**T2** L1	**L2**	
Open, transparent communication		T1 **T2** L1 S1	**S2**	**L2**	
Change commitment and focus		T1 S1	**S2** L1 **L2 T2**		
Fairness and objectivity		T1 **T2** L1 S1	**S2**	**L2**	
Collaboration		T1 L1 S1	**T2 L2 S2**		
Learning and adaptation		T1 L1 S1	**S2**	**T2 L2**	
Support		T1 S1	**S2** L1 **T2**	**L2**	

Perspective
L – Change leader
T – Change team or organizational member
S – Stakeholder

L1, T1, S1 – Time Period 1: 3 months after change implementation
L2, T2, S2 – Time Period 2: 1 year after change implementation

disconnect exists. Subjective bias may be present in that since leaders are the subjects of this behavior assessment they may tend to rate themselves higher than how they are perceived by others. Analysis may reveal that there are specific behaviors that are being omitted and need to be more clearly modeled. Mentoring and coaching may be an intervention.

The data suggest that stakeholders are registering positive responses to the progression of the change initiative. This is a very good sign. Team members are less optimistic, except for the change commitment and focus. Analysis may reveal that while the members are working hard and are committed, they do not feel the rewards and recognition are being provided commensurate with their investment of effort. Possible alterations in reward and recognition may need to be considered.

Once the underlying causes of the ratings are diagnosed, enablers of the culture change can be implemented or adjusted. These enablers can take the form of changes to the organization. Figure 5.4 depicts culture change enablers by type and impact.

As depicted in Figure 5.4, enablers for culture change can be classified into two dimensions. Change enablers can either be structural or behavioral. They can also be categorized in terms of higher or lower impact: driving or reinforcing the desired culture changes. Behavioral enablers are more powerful for shaping culture change than structural enablers because behaviors are personalized and demonstrated, they are actual evidence for the change. *Behavioral* enablers invite "pull" in contrast to structural enablers that create a "push."

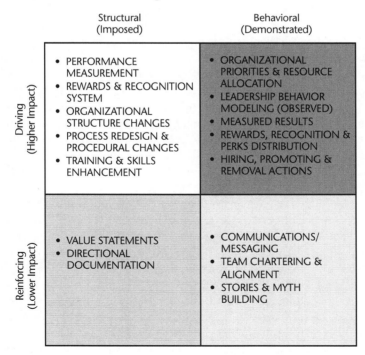

FIGURE 5.4 Culture change enablers

Driving enablers are those which are direct and actionable. They are substantive investments in change, which require a response from the organization. *Reinforcing* enablers may be symbolic and carry less power, but they are useful reminders to encourage and enforce adherence to the driving changes. The Behavioral/Driving Impact quadrant (dark shaded right corner) contains the most powerful shaping of culture change.

Structural enablers are imposed by leaders on the organization with the intention of guiding or facilitating members of the organization to act in specific ways. These are usually formalized, documented, and outward facing, i.e. they are designed to make others accountable for upholding them. Because of the investment they require, they demonstrate the organization's commitment to making the change work. For example, changes in processes and organizational structure design may intend to make members work more collaboratively, openly and innovatively in contrast to controlling and silo-defending behaviors inherent in the old process and organizational design.

Driving structural changes require adherence. Adherence is not the same as self-initiated engagement and therefore these changes will not stick unless behaviors in practice are consistent with them. Business architecture, as described in the preceding section on aligning culture, is a prime example of driving structural enablers. Value statements (e.g. credos) and directional business documentation are important reinforcements for the structural changes but by themselves they are not binding or specific enough to drive culture change.

Behavioral enablers are what is demonstrated and observed in practice. Members of the organization will look to driving behavioral enablers as evidence that the structural enablers are not just window-dressing. Leadership is under particular scrutiny for whether it is aligned and consistent with the change vision and expectations set for the organization. For example, leadership's priorities will indicate what it really cares about. Are significant time and resources being committed to the change vision for the long-term, or is it business as usual with a focus on other short-term non-change priorities? Are actual rewards and perks going to people who are advancing the change or entrenched insiders? Are the people being hired, promoted, or removed representative of the criteria for the new culture, or the old?

Leadership behavior modeling is the most direct and powerful enabler in the shaping of a new culture. Leaders are closely watched for their commitment to change, especially regarding making tough decisions, removing roadblocks and standing up for the change initiative when it inevitably encounters pressure from the old culture. How leaders react to difficult situations and organizational challenges is the supreme test of whether they are truly breaking with the old culture and guiding others to the new. Individuals will model their behavior on that of their superiors since their compensation, status, and security depend on it.

Communications, team building, and helping create new organizational stories are good reinforcements once the driving behaviors are being practiced. For example, there is power in communicating true stories of success (i.e. "wins") during the change initiative where a leader or team members took on tough, entrenched roadblocks and paved the way for the change. Where leaders or others demonstrated self-sacrifice and putting others first in support of the change will spread fast and resonate well as reinforcement for the change.

Case Study

Addressing culture change in alignment with strategic direction: **How a consumer marketing company realigned its culture around a new direction for the healthcare marketplace and the emerging healthcare consumer**

The case for business and culture change

Catalina Marketing is a global leader in consumer marketing solutions for brand manufacturers, retailers, and healthcare providers. The company's healthcare solutions business unit, Catalina Health™, had been a leading point-of-sale consumer marketer for pharmaceutical brands and prescription retailers using a unique, proprietary behavior-based data solution. However, the healthcare business unit's growth had begun tapering off as significant change was beginning to occur in the healthcare industry, which was also starting to impact the perception of Catalina Health™ in the marketplace.

The company's two key customer segments, the pharmaceutical industry and retail pharmacy chains, were undergoing changes in their businesses. Many of the top pharmaceutical brands with which Catalina Health™ was engaging in business were nearing the patent cliff, after which generic competition would significantly weaken the brands' positioning and reduce the need for marketing offerings that Catalina Health™ provided. At the same time, some of the retail pharmacy chains which provided consumer touch points were exploring equivalent systems of their own. Catalina Health™ could no longer count on their traditional business approach and customers to sustain its growth.

In 2010, a new president was brought in to Catalina Health™ to reinvigorate the business unit. The president's experience was useful in determining that significant change was needed to enable Catalina Health™ to address the changing marketplace. In order to reset the company's strategic direction on a competitive path toward growth in alignment with healthcare trends the company would require a different kind of organizational culture – one centered on the needs of healthcare consumers.

Challenges to change rooted in past success

Like many companies, Catalina Health™ was a victim of its own success. Its business challenges were reflective of a once highly effective culture that thrived in a different business environment, but was not evolving sufficiently to meet the needs of the changing and uncertain healthcare environment. The new leadership recognized that creating a new strategic direction would be necessary but not sufficient for business change. In addition to organizational structure changes, the underlying mindset, values, and behaviors would need to shift to meet the demands of a strategic direction centered on "the health consumer." This paradigm was becoming increasingly different from the business approach historically followed by the organization. A consultancy that specialized in strategic healthcare transformation and organizational culture change was brought in to assist the organization during this critical time.

Through observation and interviews with the new senior leadership team, the existing organizational culture was diagnosed and contrasted with the culture that would need to drive the emerging strategic redirection, as depicted in Table 5.7.

Overcoming culture challenges while crafting a new direction

To refocus and align the organization around a new strategic direction, a two-day work session was launched with the senior leadership team and cross-functional team members. Incorporated into the workshop design and activities were paradigms and behaviors emblematic of the target culture. For example, the work session operating guidelines specifically encouraged the participants to apply leadership characteristics of the culture change by "challenging current thinking" and "thinking long term." The president modeled these aspects of the culture change, including empowerment, by declaring at the outset and reinforcing throughout the work session that the team members take ownership of the change and work it out collaboratively.

The collaborative dimension of culture was exhibited through the leadership team members' development of a new company vision, mission, and strategic direction. This was achieved by leveraging materials provided by the strategic consultants such as a comprehensive overview of changing drivers in healthcare and appropriate strategic mapping templates. To stimulate thinking around the new direction and build a change-capable mindset, the team completed a "headline" exercise of how they would like Catalina Health™ to be publicly perceived three years from now, including the significant impacts it would make towards improving health consumer behavior. By creating the image of a new, leading-edge reputation for the company they would own it and take responsibility to build toward it.

TABLE 5.7 Current vs. future state culture mindset, values, and behaviors

Domain	Current culture	Target culture
Consumers	Commercial consumers. Focus on the consumer's prescription usage and purchase behavior using consumer demographics. Use mass-market communication.	Health consumer insights. Focus on the health consumer journey® and opportunities for better health through more effective care delivery, integration, maintenance and prevention. Use communications tailored to segmented patient populations.
Customers	Find new ways to help our customers increase product sales volume through customer purchases.	Focus on health outcomes. Engage different customers whose goals are to improve patient health and reduce costs to more effectively achieve them.
Innovation	Create customer offerings in functional silos and launch with limited input to get things out fast. Field will need to work harder to keep customers and get more of them.	Innovation focused on addressing consumer and healthcare need gaps. Collaborative development between marketing, research and field (sales) to test quality solutions with the end users in mind. Become healthcare research-oriented and leverage knowledge of health consumer needs.
Leadership	Top down. Catalina corporate executives and investors provide direction for the company's immediate priorities and revenue targets with narrowly focused scope of input from the Catalina Health™ leadership team and other resources.	Empowered. Catalina Health™ members educate corporate leaders and investors (and each other) on healthcare industry change and opportunities for Catalina Health™ with evidence from research, piloting, and business case scenario evaluation.
Solutions	Tweak the current systems and tools. Build rather than buy.	Rethink, reengineer, and acquire if necessary the systems and tools needed to support a new strategic direction.
Channels	Find better ways to leverage the existing point-of-sale retail channel and stave off competitors.	Go to where the healthcare patient is being treated, or could use help to stay healthy.

During the course of defining the company's new direction and how to get there, it was important to identify not just the inhibitors and limitations in the company's current situation but also strengths in order to leverage them in the new culture. Prominent among the strengths in the company's current culture were:

- strong commitment to delivering results and meeting partner/customer needs
- diligent execution in delivery of services
- dedication to quality and data integrity
- strong client relationships and capability for building them.

Not carrying these aspects forward to the new culture would also risk diminishing the pride members of the organization took in their work and the company's considerable accomplishments. Ignoring these strengths would leave Catalina Health™ nothing on which to anchor its new identity.

Through facilitated inquiry, cultural inhibitors and areas of resistance to change emerged and were put on the table for discussion. The consultants initiated the dialogue by challenging the team to confront the potential inhibitors in order to effectively address the necessary change: "Why can't we change? What's keeping us from moving to this new direction?"

In terms of articulated ideals, some members of the leadership held aspirations for Catalina Health™ to remain an innovator, though the company was largely riding the successes of its original investments in an information technology solution which was at risk of becoming outdated. There was general agreement among the group that the company had become dependent on a few clients and serving them with variations on their original solution. To restore their innovative edge, the culture would need to overcome "in-the-box" thinking. They would also need to understand and identify more strongly with the health consumer in contrast to the current weighted focus on partner customers who represented the role of the "middlemen" in the chain of improving health. Building cross-functional collaboration and testing into the development process would be critical, and would require a significant shift to the existing business model and processes. Collaboration would also need to be expanded to executing in new product development to ensure that products brought to market met the requirements of the marketplace and most importantly, the health consumer. In the previous culture, there had been somewhat of a silo mentality, which had caused the roll out of products that were not sufficiently vetted through the organization to optimize marketability. A new cultural norm was established to assure collaborative effort throughout the product development process.

Change enablers to address these cultural challenges and build organizational change capability were defined in terms of the following:

- model the new business direction and culture through empowered leadership
- recognize and reward actions which help advance the new direction
- identify strategic priorities aligned with the longer-term vision and ensure they are completed
- become research-grounded and proficient in the changing healthcare landscape and health consumer needs
- collaboratively identify, test and evaluate Catalina Health™ offering alternatives with key stakeholders, including partners and customers
- measure change progress.

An organizational culture aligned around a new strategic direction

Culture change progress was assessed a year after the strategic visioning workshop. Catalina Health™ changed its name to reflect its new identity. Prior to its strategic business change, Catalina Health™ had been called Catalina Health Resources, which did not adequately communicate the company's essence as a positive "influencer" of healthcare, in contrast with being only a "resource." Catalina Health™ implemented a number of initiatives that began to shape the new cultural paradigm and business strategy. The organization had embarked on a pilot projects with major healthcare organizations outside of its current customer base. Investments were made in research studies to further understand consumer behaviors and need gaps in healthcare. The organization re-launched its fourteen-year-old brand highlighting its understanding of the health consumer and the patient journey®. A brand campaign was launched to create awareness of its new consumer-centric strategic approach.

Given the significant changes occurring as a result of healthcare reform, a second comprehensive healthcare landscape research project was performed which provided the platform for the leadership team to collaboratively identify, evaluate, and propose additional innovative business opportunities for Catalina Health™ to pursue in continuing to realize its new strategic direction. Additionally, performance expectations of the leadership team and other members of the organization included criteria for demonstrating and advancing the new direction and culture.

In preparation for the healthcare landscape research, the consultants interviewed the leadership team over the course of a month to collect their views on healthcare landscape opportunities and to get a sense of the cultural progress. Across the team, there was general agreement that the culture had advanced in significant ways, including considerable increases in:

- openness in exploring new opportunities, markets and customers
- collaboration and input around product development
- health consumer-centric approach.

The evidence demonstrated that the company's culture had significantly coalesced around its new strategic direction.

Conclusion

Business change will always be a challenging endeavor for organizations, but we believe that learning from the collective past of change management will enhance the probability of change success. It is our hope that the concepts, examples, and methodology presented in this book will aid you to more effectively assess the need for change, design the change, implement the change, and make the change stick.

We believe that a key aspect of business change management learning is having a solid grounding in the foundations of change management and its evolution, which have led to Business Change Management (Chapter 1). We also place a great deal of importance on learning the common change risks and best practices to mitigate them (Chapter 2). We have shown the importance of the make-up and role of change leadership, an area vital to successful change efforts (Chapter 3). We have examined change resistance, one of the greatest challenges to organizations, which any serious change effort must address (Chapter 4). And lastly, we looked at culture change, the heart of successful transformative change (Chapter 5). The Appendices which follow provide you with a methodology for Business Change Management and enabling tools, which you can customize in planning and executing your change initiative. Armed with this methodology and a knowledge of Business Change Management we are confident your change initiative is much more likely to be completed on time, on budget, with a greater percentage of the benefits realized.

Notes

1 Lagace, M. (2002) "Gerstner: Changing Culture at IBM—Lou Gerstner Discusses Changing the Culture at IBM." *Harvard Business Review Working Knowledge for Business Leaders.* 12/9/2002. http://hbswk.hbs.edu/archive/3209.html
2 IBM News Room. (News Release, IBM Media Relations). IBM Global Study: Majority of Organizational Change Projects Fail: Changing Mindsets and Culture Continue to Be Major Obstacles. 14 October 2008.

3 Schein, E.H. (1992). *Organizational culture and leadership*. 2nd ed. San Francisco. Jossey-Bass. 12.

4 Schein, E.H. (2009). *The corporate culture survival guide*. San Francisco. John Wiley and Sons, Inc. 44.

5 Schein, E.H. (1992). *Organizational culture and leadership*. 2nd ed. San Francisco. Jossey-Bass. 5

6 Anderson, D. & Anderson, L. (2001). *Beyond change management: Advanced strategies for transformational leaders*. San Francisco. Jossey-Bass/Pfeiffer. 99

7 Levasseur R. "People Skills: Ensuring Project Success—A Change Management Perspective." *Interfaces* [serial online]. March 2010;40(2):159-162. Ipswich. MA. Business Source Premier.

8 Georgescu, P. & Dorsey, D. (2005). *The source of success: Five enduring principles at the heart of real leadership*. San Francisco. Jossey-Bass.

9 Denning, S. (2001). "How Do You Change An Organizational Culture?" *Forbes*, July 23.

10 Schein, E.H. (1992). *Organizational culture and leadership*. 2nd ed. San Francisco. Jossey-Bass. 388.

11 Schein, E.H. (1992). *Organizational culture and leadership*. 2nd ed. San Francisco. Jossey-Bass. 22.

12 Jones, D. & Kirzecky, M. (2009). "Health Care Reform and Comparative Research: The Case for Building Change-Capable Organizations." White paper. http://www.tkghealthcare.com/.

13 Griffin, M. & Bradley, T.D. (2010). "Organizational Culture: An Overlooked Internal Risk." *Bloomberg Businessweek*. October 1, 2010.

14 Schein, E.H. (1992). *Organizational culture and leadership*. 2nd ed. San Francisco. Jossey-Bass. 5

15 Schein, E.H. (1992). *Organizational culture and leadership*. 2nd ed. San Francisco. Jossey-Bass. 375.

16 Urch Druskat, V. & Wolff, S.B. (2001). "Building the Emotional Intelligence of Groups." *Harvard Business Review*. March 2001.

Appendix A

BUSINESS CHANGE MANAGEMENT (BCM) METHODOLOGY DESCRIPTION

BCM methodology description contents

An overview of the methodology

Our fast-cycle Business Change Management methodology (BCM) incorporates best practices and has been used to lead over 100 successful change management projects. The methodology is based on a systems approach and therefore takes into consideration how change will impact the technology, organization, and process architecture. The methodology incorporates concepts embedded in concurrent engineering to dramatically shorten cycle times. The methodology addresses needs in today's environment for change teams to hit the ground running, work on change activities in parallel and interdependently, and apply real-time data and learnings to precisely calibrate change plans.

This overview section provides a summary of each phase of the methodology, including a mapping of the common deliverables and tools that are used in each task. A full description of each of the tasks within each phase follows.

Business Change Management methodology is comprised of four distinct phases of work:

- Phase 1: Create Change Platform
- Phase 2: Design Change
- Phase 3: Implement Change
- Phase 4: Institutionalize Change.

Each *Phase* is broken down into *Tasks* (e.g. P1-1.0) which are further subdivided into *Steps* (e.g. P1-1.1). The framework provides flexibility to address simple projects ranging in scope from a single location or within a function to enterprise-wide across multiple locations. Not every task will need to be followed in rigorous detail depending on the complexity and scale of the change. Also many of the tasks are described in a linear fashion. This is done for simplicity in describing the process. However, change management is a discovery and iterative process. Therefore, some information or decisions that will be made later in the process can and should be used to enrich and/or revise previously made decisions which affect the change plan. Finally, the tasks and supporting tools may be modified and tailored to a unique situation. The user of this methodology should adapt this framework to the needs of his or her business change situation.

Figures A.1 to A.4 depict each phase of the methodology. The shaded boxes represent the critical path of the methodology suitable for simple change projects (i.e. the minimum path or "light version" of the methodology with the required tasks to be performed). Within the task boxes are references for tools and deliverables that can used to perform the tasks. The tools and deliverables are discussed in Appendix B.

Phase 1: Create Change Platform (overview)

Phase 1 of the methodology includes thirteen tasks and focuses on establishing the project governance, creating a sense of urgency, rallying stakeholders around a common threat or opportunity, and completing a stakeholder analysis that provides valuable input into developing a communications plan. See Figure A.1.

Phase 2: Design Change (overview)

Phase 2 is composed of thirteen tasks. During this phase of the methodology the emphasis shifts from rallying the troops to completing a high level design of the change. As data is collected and the design becomes more clear the Project Team will have a much better understanding of how the change initiative will impact the organization. An underlying precept of the framework is to design a balanced solution that addresses the technology, organization, and process architecture. Since so much about change relates to culture one of the key tasks is focused on culture alignment and transition (Task 10). See Figure A.2.

Phase 3: Implement Change (overview)

Phase 3 consists of nine tasks that evolve the design of the change solution for deployment in the implementation stage. Most change initiatives impact the technology, organization, and process architecture creating capability gaps. The design and delivery of knowledge transfer activities, such as training, will enable stakeholders (i.e. executives, members of functions that will implement the change, and the change teams) to be better able to roll out these modifications. See Figure A.3.

Phase 4: Institutionalize Change (overview)

The final phase consists of ten tasks. Institutionalize Change revolves around a series of activities to make the change become the new status quo. During this phase a concerted effort is made to embed and reinforce the desired change in practice. The change impact is periodically reviewed to compare actual vs. planned performance to identify any performance gaps or unintended negative ripple effects from the change. If necessary, additional action might be taken in the form of remedial initiatives to address gaps or negative ripple effects as well to reinforce the change. See Figure A.4.

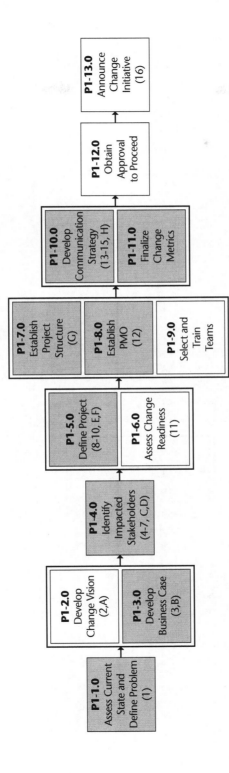

FIGURE A.1 Phase 1: Create Change Platform process flow (simple change initiative shaded)

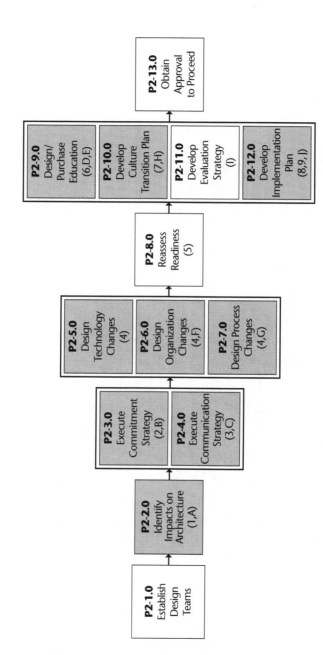

FIGURE A.2 Phase 2: Design Change process flow (simple change initiative shaded)

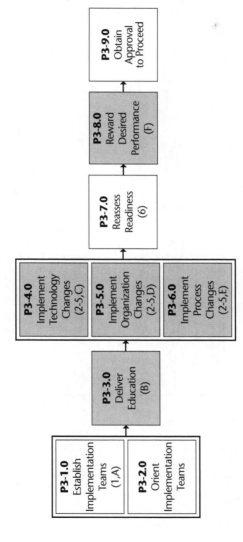

FIGURE A.3 Phase 3: Implement Change process flow (simple change initiative shaded)

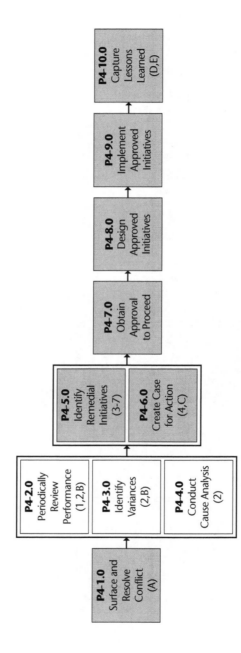

FIGURE A.4 Phase 4: Institutionalize Change process flow (simple change initiative shaded)

Loan Receipt
Liverpool John Moores University
Library Services

Borrower Name: Raza Moula
Borrower ID: ********

Managing successful projects with
PRINCE2.
31111015075631
Due Date: 30/01/2018 23:59:00 GMT

Leading and implementing business
change management : making change
stick in the contemporary organization /
31111015034356
Due Date: 30/01/2018 23:59:00 GMT

Total Items: 2
23/01/2018 12:48

Please keep your receipt in case of
dispute.

BCM methodology tool kit

Thirty three different assessment, design, and implementation tools are included for use with the methodology. They are located in Appendix B. Included are tools, change topic primers, assessment instruments and completed examples. Most tools include a brief description, when the tool is most likely used in the change methodology, the steps for effectively using the tool, and a completed example that can be customized to support the unique needs of your organizational change initiative.

BUSINESS CHANGE MANAGEMENT METHODOLOGY

Phase 1: Create Change Platform

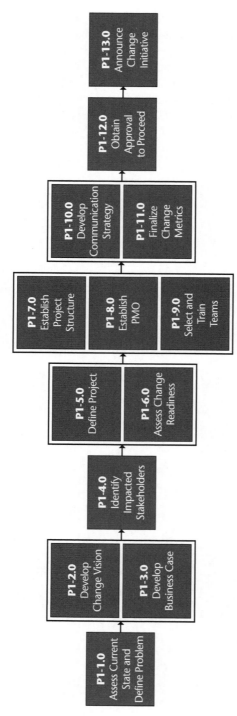

FIGURE A.5 Phase 1: Create Change Platform process flow

Task P1-1.0 Assess Current State and Define Problem

Roles:

Led and performed by senior management, and supported by stakeholders in the organization at different levels and in different functions.

Steps:

1.1   Frame the organization's situation and need for change. The need for change exists in the form of a key problem that the organization needs to fix or a result that needs to be realised. The problem can also be something the organization must obtain or become to realize its aspirations. Obtain from multiple members of senior management:
- organization's desired performance vs. actual levels
- perceived symptoms of the key internal problem(s) which are holding the organization back
- previous change initiatives, their results and what was learned
- the data needed to define the problem, including what data is available and what data needs to be collected
- the stakeholders who need to be involved in the assessment, including front line as well as management.

1.2   Conduct document review and research. Determine organization's status relative to key business drivers:
- organizational performance internally as well as relative to competition and industry
- industry trends and innovation
- comparison of organizational capabilities to best practices
- customer satisfaction levels and specific needs based on recent market research.

1.3   Perform the current state problem assessment with the identified stakeholders. Collect and synthesize input to provide:
- what is working and not working for the organization
- perceived root cause of problem
- what needs to change and why it would effectively address the problem
- solution ideas and how they would address the problem.

Use multiple methods to obtain a well-rounded sample of input:
- interviews
- focus groups
- observation
- pulse survey
- document review.

1.4   Develop and confirm general direction of change strategy:
- synthesize and analyze collected input

- conduct root cause analysis relative to problem that was defined
- define problem complexity
- define high-level change strategy and solution in response to problem and why it would effectively address the problem
- review the findings and change strategy with senior management.

1.5 Establish high-level parameters regarding change strategy:
- degree of alignment with overall business vision and strategy
- timing (historical, current, and projected profitability trends)
- fit with culture
- effect of other planned changes
- level of stakeholder commitment
- sufficiency of budget based on Rough Order of Magnitude (ROM) estimate.

How performed:
- inputs: interviews, focus groups, observation, survey
- off-line work: analysis of data collected.

Tools:
- Impact Analysis Template (P1-T1)

Task P1-2.0 Develop Change Vision

This task may be optional in cases for situations where the problem complexity is low, the scope of change is narrow, and in particular, the requirement for organizational transformation is non-existent or minimal.

Roles:
Led by the designated change initiative Sponsor (from the senior management team), and supported by senior management, and pre-selected members of the change initiative team.

Steps:
2.1 Craft the change vision.
- Align the change vision with the organization's business strategy. The change vision should not be confused with the organization's overall business vision. However, the change vision needs to link tightly to organization's strategic business direction for consistency, substance, and credibility.
- Paint a picture that appeals to both the "head" and "heart".
- Be dynamic and evolving, not static.
- Be both behavioral and motivational.
- Be easy to understand.

- Communicate desired values.
- Include challenging goals (i.e. BHAG: big, hairy, audacious goals).

2.2 Share the change vision with key stakeholders to obtain and incorporate their feedback, including senior management.

2.3 Prepare to use the change vision as an integral part of the communications plan. Even at this early stage of conception, consider how the change vision will be communicated to the change initiative team, stakeholders, and other members throughout the organization who will be affected by the change.

How performed:
- facilitated team exercise

Tools:
- Backwards Imaging (P1-T2)

Deliverables:
- Change Vision Statement (P1-A)

Task P1-3.0 Develop Business Case

Roles

Led and performed by the change initiative Sponsor, and supported by senior management and pre-selected members of the Change Leadership Team.

Steps:

3.1 Understand and articulate drivers behind the change:
- customers/markets
- business imperatives
- benchmarking
- other.

3.2 Identify the one-time and ongoing benefits of realizing the change vision and goals, both qualitative as well as quantitative.

3.3 Identify the one-time and ongoing costs of realizing the change vision and qualitative and quantitative goals.

3.4 Identify the risks of inaction and the specific consequences to the organization's future if the change vision and goals are not achieved, i.e. "the burning platform."

3.5 Understand and articulate the gap between current and desired performance.

3.6 Translate the business case into quantifiable change targets and identify initial change metrics.

How performed:
- off-line work: analysis and documentation development

Tools:
- Business Case Template (P1-T3)

Deliverables:
- Business Case Summary (P1-B)

Task P1-4.0 Identify Impacted Stakeholders

Roles:
Led and performed by the change initiative leadership team, and supported by cross-functional stakeholder representatives (executive level).

Steps

4.1   Identify internal and external stakeholders who will be impacted by the change and consequently need to participate in the change initiative in some way. Determine the most appropriate level of segmentation.

4.2   Identify the impacts the change will have on the identified stakeholders:
- understand their concerns/issues about the change
- assess their current level of commitment to helping achieve the change and supporting the change initiative
- prioritize stakeholder groups by level of importance to the success of the change initiative
- obtain consensus on the "critical few" stakeholder groups (the ones who are most impacted and critical to the overall success of the initiative).

4.3   Categorize stakeholders as winners, those negatively impacted, and those unaffected resulting from the change.

4.4   Identify responses for groups most heavily impacted and try to address their concerns.

4.5   Identify opinion leaders and informal group leaders in the organization who can influence others to move the change forward.

4.6   Select Champions and Missionaries for each level in the organization who will participate in the change initiative.

4.7   Identify specific actions to optimize the commitment of the key stakeholders.

4.8   Perform stakeholder analysis as a way to collect data. Learnings should be integrated into the work plans, communication, and risk management plans.

How performed:
- off-line work: definition, identification and selection

Tools:
- Stakeholder Assessment and Commitment Planning (P1–T4)
- Champion Assessment Instrument (P1–T5)
- Missionary Assessment Instrument (P1–T6).

Deliverables:
- Commitment Plan (P1–C)
- Stakeholder Summary (P1–D).

Task P1-5.0 Define Project (Change Initiative)

Roles:
Led and performed by the change initiative leadership team.

Steps:
5.1   Develop the change initiative charter. This typically addresses:
- scope of the change initiative, what is included and excluded
  - from a value chain perspective
  - locations/geography
  - organizational functions
  - stakeholders
  - SBU's, sectors and brands
- change master project plan (high-level)
  - phases or stages
  - major activities
  - milestones
  - dependencies
  - critical path
- deliverables
- timelines and schedule
- budget.

5.2   Identify initiative constraints and underlying assumptions.

5.3   Develop first draft of metrics for evaluating the success of the initiative.

5.4   Develop or confirm change drivers or critical success factors for the initiative.

5.5   Develop operating principles for the initiative. These could include:
- Communication within and across the initiative (methods, timing, frequency, etc).
  - meeting management
  - decision making

- interfacing and collaborating with groups inside and outside the change initiative
- issue management
- governance.

How performed:
- planning work sessions
- off-line work: plan draft definition and development.

Tools:
- Chartering Template (P1-T8)
- Change Process Primer (P1-T9)
- Change Scorecard Tool (P1-T10).

Deliverables:
- Completed Project Charter (P1-E)
- Change Scorecards (P1-F).

Task P1-6.0 Assess Change Readiness

This task may be scaled back if the change initiative must be implemented (for survival) or if the change initiative has low change complexity or transformational needs.

Roles:
Led and performed by the change team (change management specialists), and supported by various members inside and outside the change initiative, including key stakeholders.

Steps:
6.1   Specify the participants of the initial assessment. Consider the:
- leadership team
- key stakeholders and others who will be participating in the change initiative
- selected members of the organization who will be affected by the change.

6.2   Prepare the assessment process, and readiness questions. Consider using:
- interviews
- surveys
- other online tools.

6.3   Conduct the assessment. Clearly communicate the change vision, business case, and boundaries (scope) of change to ensure that the respondents clearly understand:
- what the target of the assessment is, the desired change

- how the organization could be impacted if the change goals are realized and if they are not
- what the expectations are of key stakeholders surrounding the change.

6.4   Determine the sources of change resistance or other concerns and their root cause(s). Analyze the collected respondent input to determine:
- what are the primary causes of resistance to the change
- where is resistance the strongest
- what level of confidence exists in the change initiative and leadership
- what suggestions and ideas participants have for overcoming resistance in or designing the change initiative.

6.5   Establish a strategy for addressing the resistance, including:
- adjustments or additions to the change initiative
- interventions
- modifications to appropriate HR practices, such as performance management, rewards and recognition.

How performed:
- inputs: interviews, survey
- off-line work: analysis.

Tools:
- Readiness Assessment Instrument (P1-T11)

Task P1-7.0 Establish Project Structure

Roles:
Led and performed by the change initiative leadership team.

Steps:
7.1   Specify levels of management and team structure for the initiative (steering committee, task forces, committees, etc.) and specific people for key management roles.
- program manager (if multiple work streams)
- project manager
- sponsoring executive (if not previously identified during the change visioning).

7.2   Clarify roles and responsibilities, including decision-making authority levels.

7.3   Select influential participants for the change initiative, including Change Champions and Missionaries, as well as:
- corporate representatives
- management

- employee representatives (it is best to get people from each key stakeholder group involved)
- local and national union representatives, if applicable
- suppliers and customers.

7.4   Select team leaders.

7.5   Determine tollgates and reviews for the change initiative life cycle.

How performed:
- planning work sessions

Deliverables:
- Project Structure Chart (P1-G)

Task P1-8.0 Establish PMO (Change Program Management Office)

Roles:

Led and performed by the change initiative leadership, and supported by senior management.

Steps:

8.1   Establish PMO processes, including:
- governance
- risk management
- issue management (including escalation)
- project portfolio management (managing change initiative work streams)
- variance analysis
- performance reporting
- cross-team integration.

8.2   Create PMO tools and templates.

8.3   Provide education/coaching for PMO processes and tools to change leaders and key participants of the change initiative (which can be cascaded to the full team if necessary).

How performed:
- off-line template development and customization
- process design work sessions
- training and orientation work sessions.

Tools:
- PMO Best Practice Assessment (P1-T12)

Task P1-9.0 Select and Train Team

Roles:
Led and performed by change initiative leadership (training specialists) and supported by change team members.

Steps:
9.1 Identify needed competencies for carrying out the change initiative.

9.2 Define a competency profile for change initiative participants relative to experience with change management, as well as business, project and communication skills.

9.3 Identify, orient and select team candidates.

9.4 Assess potential members relative to style and chemistry.

9.5 Confirm team members have appropriate competencies.

9.6 Provide appropriate training relative to change methodology and tools.

How performed:
- off-line: definition, selection.

Interviews:
- training and orientation work sessions.

Task P1-10.0 Develop Communication Strategy

Roles:
Led and performed by the change initiative Sponsor and change management communication specialists, and supported by the change initiative leadership team.

Steps:
10.1 Select communication channels. Examples include:
- task forces
- meetings
- committees
- videotapes
- intranet site
- publications.

10.2 Identify external groups who need to be informed about the change and ongoing progress of the initiative.

10.3 Identify the type of information each channel will convey (e.g. initiative status, financial data, etc).

10.4 Develop a Communication Plan. This should address:
- key messages for each stakeholder group
- specific channels
- timelines
- responsibilities
- feedback mechanisms.

10.5 Identify a strategy to counteract rumors.

10.6 Develop mechanisms to evaluate communications effectiveness.

10.7 Develop mechanisms to incorporate feedback into the change plan, including risk management as well as the change design.

How performed:
- off-line: identification, development

Tools:
- Focus Group Primer (P1-T13)
- Interview Primer (P1-T14)
- Communication Planning Template (P1-T15).

Deliverables:
- Communication Plan (P1-H)

Task P1-11.0 Finalize Change Metrics

Roles:
Led and performed by the Change Leadership Team and supported by Finance business partners.

Steps:
11.1 Develop perspectives or categories of metrics, incorporating the initial metrics defined at a high level early in this phase.

11.2 Finalize financial targets (e.g. ROI, cost savings).

11.3 Finalize operational targets (e.g. cycle times).

11.4 Finalize stakeholder perceptual targets (e.g. of customers, suppliers, employees and project team members).

11.5 Specify how data will be collected.

11.6 Determine process for reviewing metrics.

11.7 Cascade metrics down to each change team member.

11.8 Tightly align change metrics with performance management and compensation decisions (i.e. base, bonus and equity).

How performed:
- off-line development
- communications: group and individual.

Task P1-12.0 Obtain Approval to Proceed (to Design Phase)

Roles:
Led and performed by the Change Leadership Team and supported by senior management.

Steps:
12.1 Confirm that the change initiative, as represented by the plan, program processes, and participants, will address the organization's vision for change and change scorecard.

12.2 Review the change vision.

12.3 Review the change charter, change metrics, and communications plan.

12.4 Obtain approval to proceed.

12.5 Solicit management input on how to support the change initiative, including helping promote the critical success factors and resolving major organizational roadblocks.

How performed:
- meetings review

Task P1-13.0 Announce Change Initiative

Roles:
Led and performed by the change initiative Sponsor and supported by the Change Leadership Team.

Steps:
13.1 Identify and profile audience segments for change initiative communication. The segments will need to hear the common themes and messages (such as change vision, business case, plan of action, etc. described in 12.2, but there will be customized messages (e.g. WIIFM and levels of detail) and styles that differ across the segments, including:
- change team
- stakeholders
- employees

- customers
- suppliers
- partners.

13.2 Develop communication messages, address:
- the change vision and goals
- the business drivers behind the change
- the business necessity, including what's broken
- urgency for doing change now, and the consequences of failure (i.e. the burning platform)
- what will change
- what will not change
- a bottom-line business theme--provide employees with information on the competitive environment (e.g. information on costs, quality, etc., in relation to competitors)
- how management will support effort
- cost/benefit analysis at both the employee (i.e. WIIFM) and organizational level
- timelines and key milestones
- potential impact on individuals (employment, retraining, outplacement, etc.)
- what training is planned
- performance expectations
- how employees will be kept informed throughout the change implementation.

13.2 Deliver communication. Use multiple venues for reinforcement:
- group (e.g. town hall)
- face-to-face
- videoconferencing
- organizational website and newsletter.

How performed:
- off-line development
- communications: group face-to-face, videoconferencing, e-broadcast, organization website.

Tools:
- Elevator Speech (P1-T16)

Phase 2: Design Change

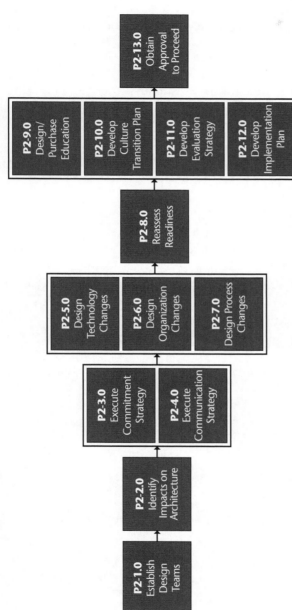

FIGURE A.6 Phase 2: Design Change process flow

Task P2-1.0 Establish Design Teams

Roles:

Led and performed by the Change Leadership Team (Business Architect), and supported by the change team (senior process, organization and technology specialists).

Steps:

1.1 Provide detailed orientation to candidates for the design team, including:
- phase 2 (design) objectives and approach
- change management methodology
- reporting relationships
- data collection, design and analysis tools.

1.2 Identify roles and responsibilities, for example:
- collect and analyze data
- design and implement changes in technology, organization, and process domains
- perform interventions
- assist in communications.

1.3 Select team members (vertical cross section of employees from each impacted area).

1.4 Identify limits of decision-making authority.

1.5 Select leaders for each team.

1.6 Establish interfaces and collaborative protocols with other teams.

How performed:
- orientation session
- off-line work: identification, selection, development.

Task P2-2.0 Identify Impacts on Architecture

Roles:

Led and performed by the Business Architect and process, organization and technology specialists on the change team.

Steps:

2.1 Identify change impacts on technology architecture. This typically includes:
- information and data
- hardware
- information technology applications
- technology used to deliver core products and services.

2.2   Identify impacts on the organization architecture. This typically includes:
- organization design and business model
- culture
- HR practices
- administrative policies.

2.3   Identify impacts on process architecture. This typically includes:
- core and support processes
- physical infrastructure and existing facilities.

2.4   Confirm or update all impacts to stakeholders and organization architecture.

2.5   Incorporate impacts into the change design plan and model (i.e. TOPS architecture).

How performed:
- work sessions for analysis
- off-line work: plan updates.

Tools:
- Impact Analysis Template (P2-T1)

Deliverables:
- Impact Summary (P2-A)

Task P2-3.0 Execute Commitment Strategy

Roles:
Led and performed by the Change Leadership Team and Sponsor, and supported by the Change Champions, Missionaries and change team members.

Steps:
3.1   Identify and implement engagement activities.
- Periodically sense group members' behavior and attitudes and incorporate learnings. This includes collecting data to see how people are embracing the change, what they are feeling, what is working and what is not working, and soliciting input to improve the change initiative's effectiveness. Focus on both:
  - individuals who are negatively impacted and stakeholders who are most critical to the success of the change initiative, and who might pose resistance or lack motivation to move the change forward
  - individuals who have a strong positive organizational impact, influence and passion for the change which can be leveraged to motivate others
  - design feedback and integration procedures
  - develop mechanisms that incorporate stakeholder suggestions and concerns into the plan

- Develop strategies to increase commitment, empower stakeholders, provide adequate resources, increase dissatisfaction with the present state, benchmark, provide education, etc.

3.2 Coach the Change Leaders, Champions, and Missionaries on how to model the desired "engaged" behaviors and attitudes and encourage them in others.

How performed:
- work sessions for design and development
- off-line documentation.

Tools:
- Stakeholder Assessment and Commitment Plan (P2-T2)

Deliverables:
- Updated Commitment Plan (P2-B)

Task P2-4.0 Execute Communication Strategy

Roles:
Led and performed by the Change Leadership Team and Sponsor, and supported by the Change Champions, Missionaries, and team members.

Steps:
4.1 Design communication messages to change initiative team, associated stakeholders, and others affected in the organization by the change.

4.2 Execute each communication event.

4.3 Periodically evaluate the effectiveness of communications. Determine if communications were:
- timely
- believable
- understandable
- useful, e.g. they address issues of concern to targeted audiences.

4.4 Solicit stakeholder input and feedback.

4.5 Integrate feedback into design plan, risk management plan, work plans.

How performed:
- off-line work: design, plan updates
- communication: group face-to-face and electronic
- interviews
- meetings.

Tools:
- Communication Planning Template (P2-T3)

Deliverables:
- Updated Communication Plan (P2-C)

Task P2-5.0 Design Technology Changes (to Technology Architecture)

Note: Activities 5.0, 6.0 and 7.0 are performed in parallel. Technology, organization and process architecture activities are interdependent.

Roles:
Led and performed by change initiative technology design team.

Steps:
5.1 Specify changes to technology architecture. Apply the change design principles and drive out the technology impacts to specific changes. (e.g. requirements, IT capabilities and IT structure).

5.2 Determine if change will create new users and identify new service requirements.

5.3 Identify the effect the change will have on current IT capabilities:
- hardware
- applications
- technology
- data
- communications
- skill sets of IT staff.

5.4 Design changes to technology architecture:
- data base structure
- technology used to deliver core products and services
- applications
- IT hardware.

How performed:
- Work sessions: design and development
- Off-line: documentation

Tools:
- Design-Implementation Challenge Questions (P2-T4)

Task P2-6.0 Design Organization Changes (to Organization Architecture)

Roles:
Led and performed by change initiative organizational design team.

Steps:

6.1 Specify changes to organizational architecture. Apply the change design principles and drive out the organization impacts to specific changes.

6.2 Design changes to appropriate human resources systems:
- reward/incentive programs
- performance management system
- recruiting and selection practices
- talent management
- other.

6.3 Design changes to communication systems.

6.4 Design changes to administrative control policies and informal business rules:
- administrative policies/procedures
- other.

6.5 Design changes to the business model and organization structure, including roles and responsibilities.

How performed:
- work sessions: design and development
- off-line: documentation.

Tools:
- Design-Implementation Challenge Questions (P2-T4)

Deliverables:
- Detailed Modifications to People Practices (P2-F)

Task P2-7.0 Design Process Changes (to Process Architecture)

Roles:
Led and performed by change initiative process design team.

Steps:

7.1 Obtain final consensus on appropriate processes to modify.

7.2 Determine targeted improvements:
- customer satisfaction
- cycle time
- cost
- other.

7.3 Determine type of process change required i.e. whether you need to do Process Improvement (focus is on improving the existing process by analyzing and optimizing the current way activities are completed) or BPR (focus is on redesigning processes for maximum performance (thinking not constrained by current way of doing things).

7.4   Design the process changes and supporting business rules.

How performed:
- work sessions: design and development
- off-line: documentation.

Tools:
- Design-Implementation Challenge Questions (P2-T4)

Deliverables:
- Updated Process Documentation (P2-G)

Task P2-8.0 Reassess Readiness

Note: This task should be based on how task *P1-6.0 Assess Change Readiness* was performed. It is situational and does not need to be performed automatically.

Roles:
Led and performed by change management specialists, and supported by various members inside and outside the change initiative.

Steps:
8.1   Confirm the participants for the readiness assessment and target context. Consider using the same participants from the initial readiness assessment in Phase 1 (P1-6.0) to measure progress, and expand sample if necessary. The assessment should not only be relative to the change vision, but also to the key changes resulting from the design.

8.2   Conduct the assessment. Use the assessment process and tool applied earlier in Phase 1 (P1-6.0).

8.3   Evaluate readiness progress relative to initial assessment benchmark.

8.4   Determine the problems of change resistance/concerns and their root cause(s).

8.5   Identify or augment the change enablers and interventions that will address change resistance root causes.

How performed:
- inputs: interviews, survey
- off-line work: analysis.

Tools:
- Readiness Assessment Instrument (P1-T5)

Task P2-9.0 Design/Purchase Education

Role:
Led and performed by the change team (education specialists) and supported by training vendors.

Steps:

9.1 Identify skill gaps relative to the desired organization, process, technology, and culture changes.

9.2 Determine the skill gaps that can be addressed through formal education.

9.3 Create the curriculum of education needed to address skill gaps.

9.4 Conduct "make/buy" determination for training method and materials.

9.5 `If "buy" decision is reached:
• identify vendors
• review materials
• identify areas for customization.

9.6 If "make" decision is reached:
• develop detailed outlines
• develop participant guides.

9.7 Pilot the training.

9.8 Incorporate learnings into education curriculum and course outlines.

How performed:
• work session for definition, requirements
• research, solicitation, and acquisition with training vendors
• training session.

Tools:
• Competency Gap Tool (P2-T4)

Deliverables:
• Curriculum of Education (P2-D)
• Detailed Course Outlines (P2-E).

Task P2-10.0 Develop Culture Transition Plan

Role:
Led and performed by the change team (organizational development specialists).

Steps:
10.1 Assess fit between change and existing cultural characteristics.

10.2 Translate the change vision and/or business strategy into four to six strategic thrusts needed to transform the culture.

10.3 Identify desired employee values and behaviors needed to successfully implement the change.

10.4 Identify desired cultural characteristics.

10.5 Specify changes to each element of the organizational architecture that will:
- promote desired cultural characteristics
- reduce/eliminate undesired values and behaviors
- enhance the likelihood of realizing desired values/behaviors.

10.6 Incorporate changes into the design and implementation plans.

How performed:
- work session for identification, design
- off-line plan updates.

Tools:
- Culture Mapping Tool (P2-T7).

Deliverables:
- Culture Alignment Plan (P2-H)

Task P2-11.0 Develop Evaluation Strategy

Role:
Led and performed by the Change Leadership Team.

Steps:
11.1 Identify data collection methods for evaluating how the change is succeeding. Look at both qualitative and quantitative results to measure the progress and effectiveness of the initiative, including unintended ripple effects on the organization.

11.2 Develop procedures for updating implementation.

11.3 Clarify roles and responsibilities.

How performed:
- work sessions for identification, development

Deliverables:
- Change Evaluation Plan (P2-I)

Task P2-12.0 Develop Implementation Plan

Role:
Led and performed by the Change Leadership Team, and supported by the change team.

Steps:
12.1 Overall, assess gap between current and desired state for the organization prior to implementing the change
  • identify specific initiative and action items to close gaps

12.2 Determine the scope, speed, and amount of involvement to implement the change model (design), which potentially includes:
  • pilot
  • simulation
  • full implementation.
12.3 Determine whether a power sharing or holding strategy will be used. This will be used to determine which power base is most effective influencing audiences impacted by the change initiative.
12.4 Develop a detailed change implementation plan with milestones.
12.5 Estimate and finalize the budget.
12.6 Develop mechanisms to showcase and communicate the results of the pilot.

How performed:
  • work session for assessments, plan design
  • off-line plan development and estimating.

Tools:
  • Risk Management Tool (P2-T8)
  • Risk Assessment Instrument (P2-T9)

Deliverables:
  • Detailed Plan for Roll-Out (P2-J)

Task P2-13.0 Obtain Approval to Proceed (to Implementation Phase)

Roles:
Led and performed by the Change Leadership Team and supported by senior management.

Steps:
13.1 Review architectural changes (i.e. change model) with management.
13.2 Obtain management approval.

How performed:
  • meeting

Phase 3: Implement Change

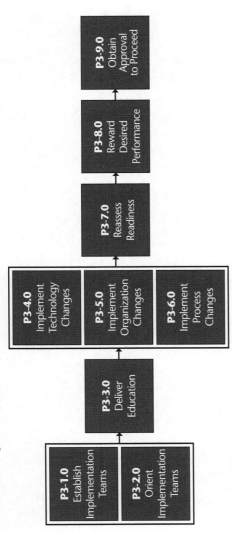

FIGURE A.7 Phase 3: Implement Change process flow

Task P3-1.0 Establish Implementation Teams

Roles:

Led and performed by the Change Leadership Team.

Steps:

1.1   Identify roles and responsibilities for implementing the change.

1.2   Select the implementation team members.

1.3   Identify the limits of decision-making authority that will affect the change in practice.

1.4   Select leaders for each team.

How performed:
- work session for team requirements, selection

Tools:
- Chartering Template (P3-T1)

Deliverables:
- Implementation Team Charter (P3-A)

Task P3-2.0 Orient Implementation Teams

Roles

Led and performed by the Change Leadership Team.

Steps:

2.1   Provide change initiative overview.

2.2   Develop charter and operating principles.

2.3   Develop roles and responsibilities matrix.

How performed
- orientation session
- work session for defining team guidelines.

Task P3-3.0 Deliver Education

Roles:

Led and performed by the change team (education specialists).

Steps:

3.1   Develop training materials from the course outlines, incorporating knowledge needed for designed changes.

3.2   Select trainers.

3.3   Define training program logistics and schedule attendees.

3.4   Conduct training.

3.5   Design/implement other mechanisms for knowledge transfer:
• coaching
• job aids
• on-the-job training (OJT).

3.6   Evaluate sessions and learning.

How performed:
• off-line: design, development, selection
• training session.

Deliverables:
• Job Aids and Formal Training Materials (P3-B)

Task P3-4.0 Implement Technology Changes

Roles:
Led and performed by the change initiative technology team and supported by the Change Leadership Team.

Steps:
4.1   Implement "early wins."

4.2   Implement all other technology changes.

4.3   Recognize and celebrate successes.

How performed:
• communication to group (organization)
• enablement and enforcement of structural systems and policies
• group events for recognizing and rewarding change progress.

Tools:
• Champion Assessment Instrument (P3-T2)
• Stakeholder Assessment and Commitment Plan (P3-T3)
• Communication Planning Template (P3-T4)
• Communication Assessment Pulse Survey (P3-T5).

Deliverables:
• Updated Technology Architecture (P3-C)

Task P3-5.0 Implement Organization Changes

Roles:
Led and performed by the change initiative organizational development team and supported by the Change Leadership Team.

Steps:
5.1   Implement changes to appropriate human resources systems:
- reward and incentive programs
- performance management system
- recruiting and selection practices
- recognition
- outplacement
- other.

5.2   Implement changes to communication systems.

5.3   Implement changes to administrative control policies and informal business rules.

5.4   Recognize and celebrate successes.

How performed:
- communication to group (organization)
- enablement and enforcement of structural systems, policies and business rules
- group events for recognizing and rewarding change progress.

Tools:
- Champion Assessment Instrument (P3-T2)
- Stakeholder Assessment and Commitment Plan (P3-T3)
- Communication Planning Template (P3-T4)
- Communication Assessment Pulse Survey (P3-T5).

Deliverables:
- Updated People Practices (P3-D)

Task P3-6.0 Implement Process Changes

Roles:
Led and performed by the change initiative process team and supported by the Change Leadership Team.

Steps:
6.1   Implement "early wins."

6.2 Implement changes to:
- work processes
- physical layout/infrastructure
- business rules.

6.3 Recognize and celebrate successes.

How performed:
- communication to group (organization)
- enablement and enforcement of structural systems, policies and business rules
- group events for recognizing and rewarding change progress.

Tools:
- Champion Assessment Instrument (P3-T2)
- Stakeholder Assessment and Commitment Plan (P3-T3)
- Communication Planning Template (P3-T4)
- Communication Assessment Pulse Survey (P3-T5).

Deliverables:
- Updated Process Design (P3-E)

Task P3-7.0 Reassess Readiness

This task should be based on how tasks *P1-6.0 Assess Change Readiness* and *P2-8.0 Reaccess Readiness* were performed. This task is situational.

Roles:
Led and performed by the change team (change management specialists), and supported by various members inside and outside the change initiative, including key stakeholders.

Steps:
7.1 Confirm the participants for the readiness assessment and target context. Consider using the same participants from the previous readiness assessments to measure progress, and expand sample if necessary. The assessment should not only be relative to the change vision, but also to progress in realizing key change initiatives.

7.2 Conduct the readiness assessment.

7.3 Evaluate readiness progress relative to previous benchmark (established in P2-8.0).

7.4 Determine the problems associated with change resistance and other concerns, including their root causes.

7.5 Identify or augment the change enablers and interventions that will address resistance root causes.

How performed:
- inputs: interviews, survey
- off-line work: analysis.

Tools:
- Readiness Assessment Instrument (P3–T6)

Task P3-8.0 Reward Desired Performance

Roles:
Led and performed by the change team (organizational development specialists) and supported by the Change Leadership Team.

Steps:
8.1 Reward desired behaviors representative of changed culture.

8.2 Reward desired outputs representative of changes to the organization (e.g. reward early wins, recognize role models).

How performed:
- communications to group and individuals
- organization rewards (tailored to individual aspirations).

Deliverables:
- Modified Compensation and Recognition Systems (P3–F)

Task P3-9.0 Obtain Approval to Proceed (to Institutionalization Phase)

Roles:
Led and performed by the Change Leadership Team and supported by senior management.

Steps:
9.1 Review implementation activities.

9.2 Obtain management approval to proceed with institutionalizing the change.

How performed:
- meeting

Phase 4: Institutionalize Change

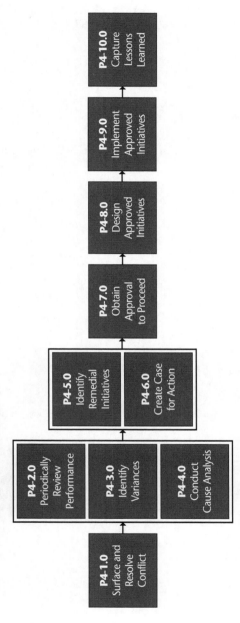

FIGURE A.8 Phase 4: Institutionalize Change process flow

Task P4-1.0 Surface and Resolve Conflict

Roles:
Led and performed by the Change Leadership Team, Change Champions, Missionaries, and organizational development specialists and supported by change team members and stakeholders.

Steps:
1.1 Develop formal conflict escalation procedures:
- identify situations when conflict escalation process should be used
- clarify roles and responsibilities
- specify decision rights
- make sure conflict escalation process is integrated into other appropriate PMO processes.

1.2 Proactively resolve conflict through targeted interventions.

How performed:
- off-line: procedure development
- interviews
- facilitated techniques
- conflict management.

Deliverables:
- Conflict Management Process (P4-A)

Task P4-2.0 Periodically Review Performance

Roles:
Led and performed by the Change Leadership Team and supported by change team.

Steps:
2.1 Identify types of data to collect and data collection methods to assess organizational performance relative to expectations for the changed organization (applying scorecard measures).

2.2 Determine frequency of data collection.

2.3 Identify roles and decision rights.

2.4 Collect performance data using focus groups, interviews, and surveys.

2.5 Compare baseline metrics with actual performance.

How performed:
- inputs: focus groups, interviews, surveys

- off-line: definition, analysis.

Tools:
- Change Scorecard Tool (P4-T1)
- PMO Best Practice Assessment (P4-T2).

Deliverables:
- Variance Analysis Summary (P4-B)

Task P4-3.0 Identify Variances

Roles:
Led and performed by the change leadership.

Steps:
3.1   Identify variances between expected organizational performance and actual results.

3.2   Determine if variance is critical.

3.3   Categorize variances:
- root cause is known – the solution is obvious
- root cause is unknown – additional data needs to be collected.

How performed:
- off-line analysis

Tools:
- PMO Best Practice Assessment (P4-T2)

Deliverables:
- Variance Analysis Summary (P4-B)

Task P4-4.0 Conduct Cause Analysis

Roles:
Led and performed by the Change Leadership Team and supported by the change team and stakeholders.

Steps:
4.1   Apply cause analysis tools to the variance where root causes are unknown.

4.2   Separate symptoms from possible root causes.

4.3   Verify root causes.

4.4   Share findings with key stakeholders to build consensus.

How performed:
- interviews for inputs, probing
- off-line analysis.

Tools:
- PMO Best Practice Assessment (P4-T2)

Task P4-5.0 Identify Remedial Initiatives

Roles:
Led and performed by the Change Leadership Team and supported by stakeholders.

Steps:
5.1   Identify remedial initiatives to address identified root causes and additional change needs, including appropriate elements of architecture.

5.2   Perform risk analysis and update to risk management plan.

5.3   Share findings with key stakeholders to build consensus on initiatives to address change needs and how to most effectively apply them.

How performed:
- work session and off-line analysis, identification
- communication group (stakeholders).

Tools:
- Impact Analysis Template (P4-T3)
- Business Case Template (P4-T4)
- Stakeholder Assessment and Commitment Plan (P4-T5)
- Communication Planning Template (P4-T6)
- Communication Assessment Pulse Survey (P4-T7).

Task P4-6.0 Create Case for Action

Roles:
Led and performed by the Change Leadership Team and supported by the Sponsor.

Steps:
6.1   Identify potential financial justification approaches (net present value, cost benefit analysis, internal rate of return, etc.).

6.2   Select the most appropriate approach (work closely with financial partners or specialists).

6.3   Agree on underlying algorithm for calculating cost of desired initiatives.

6.4   Quantify costs and benefits.

6.5   Prioritize solutions.

How performed:
- work session: identification, approach development
- off-line: financial analysis, documentation.

Tools:
- Business Case Template (P4-T4)

Deliverables:
- Business Case (P4-C)

Task P4-7.0 Obtain Approval to Proceed

Roles:
Led and performed by the Change Leadership Team and supported by senior management.

Steps:
7.1   Review the following with management:
- sources/causes of variation in organizational change outcomes
- prioritized list of modifications
- proposed remedial interventions, including cost/benefits, and required resources.

7.2   Present high-level recommendations.

7.3   Obtain management approval to proceed.

How performed:
- meeting

Task P4-8.0 Design Approved Initiatives

Roles:
Led and performed by the Change Leadership Team (Business Architect) supported by change team.

Steps:
8.1   Design modifications to organization architecture.

8.2   Design modifications to process architecture.

8.3 Design modifications to communications strategy and plan.

8.4 Design modifications to technology architecture.

8.5 Identify/design needed education.

How performed:
- work sessions for design
- off-line: documentation development.

Task P4-9.0 Implement Approved Initiatives

Roles:
Led and performed by the Change Leadership Team and supported by senior management.

Steps:
9.1 Synchronize the timing of initiatives.

9.2 Implement the initiatives using a multi-phased approach.

How performed:
- communication to group (organization) verbally and electronically

Task P4-10.0 Capture Lessons Learned

Roles:
Led and performed by the Change Leadership Team and supported by the change team and stakeholders.

Steps:
10.1 Develop data collection plan for capturing lessons learned from the change initiative, including how the data will be collected and from whom:
- collect data from project manager
- collect data from team members
- collect data from business leaders
- review data from communication pulse survey
- review data from readiness and pulse surveys taken from impacted groups (if performed).

10.2 Evaluate the change initiative:
- strengths – what worked
- weaknesses – what did not work.

10.3 Identify key learnings.

10.4 Update change methodology and tools.

How performed:
- off-line: approach development
- focus groups and interviews: lessons learned collection.

Deliverables:
- Lessons Learned Summary (P4-D)
- Updated Methodology and Tools (P4-E).

Appendix B

BUSINESS CHANGE MANAGEMENT (BCM) METHODOLOGY TOOLS

BCM methodology tools contents

An overview of the tool set

We have developed a set of tools for use with the Business Change Management methodology, which have been successfully used to support many different change initiatives. Tools consist of assessments, templates and guides, which can be used to help complete change tasks.

In the section which follows, each tool is identified by the methodology phase in which it is first used. The tools are referenced within the methodology task boxes as numbers. Below each diagram and within the methodology task descriptions (Appendix A), the tools are identified by the phase in which they appear (e.g. P1 means the first of the four phases), then by "T" for tool, followed by the specific task in the phase (e.g. P1-T1.1).

Also referenced in the methodology task box mappings are the types of deliverables or common outputs of each task. Within task boxes deliverables are referenced as a single letter (e.g. A). Deliverables are outputs of the described tasks and can be constructed by the practitioner to meet needs for acceptance regarding progress based on the change initiative requirements. In some instances tools may be used to help produce the information needed for deliverables. Although they are referenced, unlike tools the deliverables do not appear as practitioner artifacts in the appendix.

Methodology mapping to tools and deliverables

Phase 1: Create Change Platform task mappings

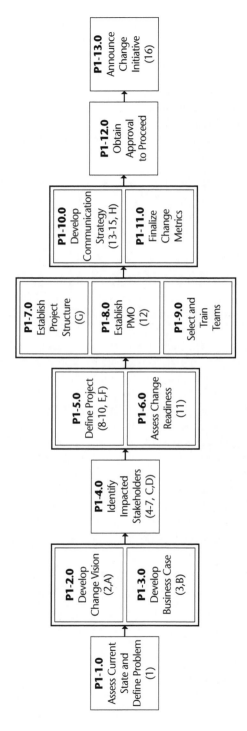

FIGURE B.1 Phase 1 with tools and deliverables mapped to tasks

Figure B.1 shows the tools and deliverables associated with the tasks of Phase 1. The tools and deliverables are listed in Table B.1.

TABLE B.1 BCM tools and deliverables referenced in Phase 1

Tools		Deliverables	
• P1-T[1]	Impact Analysis Template	• P1-[A]	Change Vision Statement
• P1-T[2]	Backwards Imaging	• P1-[B]	Business Case Summary
• P1-T[3]	Business Case Template	• P1-[C]	Commitment Plan
• P1-T[4]	Stakeholder Assessment and Commitment Plan	• P1-[D]	Stakeholder Summary
		• P1-[E]	Completed Project Charter
• P1-T[5]	Champion Assessment Instrument	• P1-[F]	Change Scorecards
		• P1-[G]	Project Structure Chart
• P1-T[6]	Missionary Assessment Instrument	• P1-[H]	Communication Plan
• P1-T[7]	Risk Assessment Instrument		
• P1-T[8]	Chartering Template		
• P1-T[9]	Change Process Primer		
• P1-T[10]	Change Scorecard Tool		
• P1-T[11]	Readiness Assessment Instrument		
• P1-T[12]	PMO Best Practice Assessment		
• P1-T[13]	Focus Group Primer		
• P1-T[14]	Interview Primer		
• P1-T[15]	Communication Planning Template		
• P1-T[16]	Elevator Speech		

Phase 2: Design Change task mappings

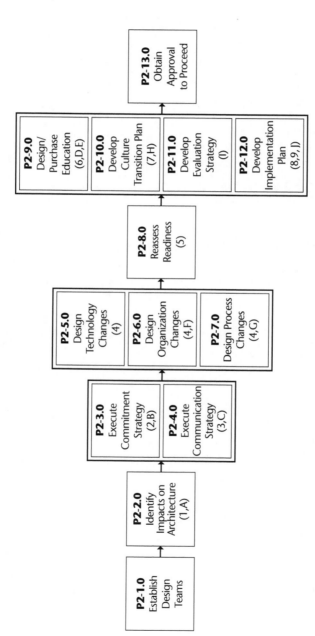

FIGURE B.2 Phase 2 with tools and deliverables mapped to tasks

Figure B.2 shows the tools and deliverables associated with the tasks of Phase 2. The tools and deliverables are listed in Table B.2.

TABLE B.2 BCM tools and deliverables referenced in Phase 2

Tools	Deliverables
• P2-T[1] Impact Analysis Template	• P2-[A] Impact Summary
• P2-T[2] Stakeholder Assessment and Commitment Plan	• P2-[B] Updated Commitment Plan
• P2-T[3] Communication Planning Template	• P2-[C] Updated Communication Plan
• P2-T[4] Design-Implementation Challenge Questions	• P2-[D] Curriculum of Education
	• P2-[E] Detailed Course Outlines
• P2-T[5] Readiness Assessment Instrument	• P2-[F] Detailed Modifications to People Practices
• P2-T[6] Competency Gap Tool	• P2-[G] Updated Process Documentation
• P2-T[7] Culture Mapping Tool	• P2-[H] Culture Alignment Plan
• P2-T[8] Risk Management Tool	• P2-[I] Change Evaluation Plan
• P2-T[9] Risk Assessment Instrument	• P2-[J] Detailed Plan for Roll-out

Phase 3: Implement Change task mappings

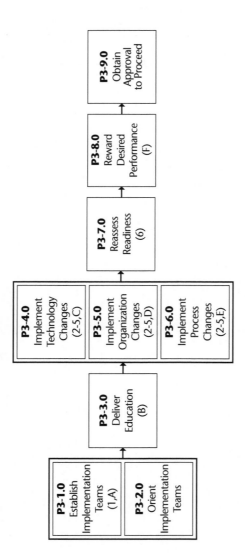

FIGURE B.3 Phase 3 with tools and deliverables mapped to tasks

Figure B.3 shows the tools and deliverables associated with the tasks of Phase 3. The tools and deliverables are listed in Table B.3.

TABLE B.3 BCM tools and deliverables referenced in Phase 3

Tools	Deliverables
• P3-T[1] Chartering Template	• P3-[A] Implementation Team Charter
• P3-T[2] Champion Assessment Instrument	• P3-[B] Job Aids and Formal Training Materials
• P3-T[3] Stakeholder Assessment and Commitment Plan	• P3-[C] Updated Technology Architecture
• P3-T[4] Communication Planning Template	• P3-[D] Updated People Practices
• P3-T[5] Communication Assessment Pulse Survey	• P3-[E] Updated Process Design
• P3-T[6] Readiness Assessment Instrument	• P3-[F] Modified Compensation and Recognition Systems

Phase 4: Institutionalize Change task mappings

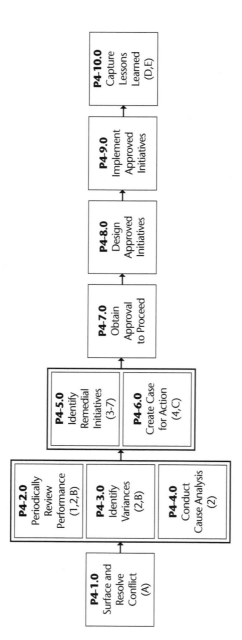

FIGURE B.4 Phase 4 with tools and deliverables mapped to tasks

Figure B.4 shows the tools and deliverables associated with the tasks of Phase 4. The tools and deliverables are listed in Table B.4.

TABLE B.4 BCM tools and deliverables referenced in Phase 4

Tools	Deliverables
• P4–T[**1**] Change Scorecard Tool	• P4–[**A**] Conflict Management Process
• P4–T[**2**] PMO Best Practice Assessment	• P4–[**B**] Variance Analysis Summary
• P4–T[**3**] Impact Analysis Template	• P4–[**C**] Business Case
• P4–T[**4**] Business Case Template	• P4–[**D**] Lessons Learned Summary
• P4–T[**5**] Stakeholder Assessment and Commitment Plan	• P4–[**E**] Updated Methodology and Tools
• P4–T[**6**] Communication Planning Template	
• P4–T[**7**] Communication Assessment Pulse Survey	

Business Change Management tools

1. Backwards Imaging

Description of tool:

For large and complex change efforts it is sometimes necessary to develop a vision that describes what the future state will "look like" for the desired change. This change vision in many instances will be aligned to the overall vision for the organization. This tool guides the team's thinking to focus on what people will be *doing* in the future state, rather than staying with a vision that is so lofty that few truly understand what the future will really be like when the organizational change effort comes to fruition.

Backwards imaging is an excellent way to help teams wrestle with the specifics of what the future state will be like in terms that can uncover both support and resistance. It asks people to describe the future as they expect to see it when the change effort is successful, and to do so in specific, behavioral terms.

When it is most likely to be used:

This tool is most commonly used during **Phase 1: Create Change Platform** when completing the **Develop Change Vision** task. It is updated during the design and roll out phases of change.

Steps:

1. Team members are asked to individually imagine a time in the future when the organizational change is completed. Often this is framed as the end-of-the-year party when the team is celebrating its success. Or, ask individuals to think forward to a front page *Wall Street Journal* article that describes the result of the organizational change initiative. If the business implemented the initiative flawlessly, what would the article say? When people have had the opportunity to create their own article, they can discuss their thoughts as a group and begin to build the future state change initiative vision.
2. With this "picture" of the future in mind, team members then try to describe what they see, hear, or feel as they observe key stakeholders and other constituents behaving in the changed state.
3. Compile the various views of this future state from individual team members and discuss similarities and differences. Use learnings from the stakeholder assessment which was created earlier to "test" this view of the future on key stakeholders, including the organizational change effort sponsor.
4. OPTION: Some teams may wish to actively solicit ideas from key stakeholders as a way of building this picture rather that doing the work themselves and then sending the vision out for comment and critique.

5.   Make sure that the vision meets four key criteria:
   •   the vision is clear
   •   the vision is easy to communicate
   •   the vision is compelling
   •   the vision is measurable.

Figure B.5 provides an example of a vision.

> We are a team-based organization that is organized around core processes that are tightly aligned to our key customer segments. Our employees exhibit initiative and calculated risk taking, have a sense of urgency, and are strongly focused on impacting the bottom-line results of the organization.

FIGURE B.5 Example of a completed vision

2. Business Case Template

Description of tool:
A business case is used to create a justification to undertake a change initiative. When designing the change solution set it can also be used to evaluate different solutions to create a prioritized list of alternatives. A business case is best used in conjunction with other decision variables but should not be used as the primary criteria to select one design alternative over another one.

   The business case should show where the organization is today and compare it to where the organization is expected to go in the future. It is used to gain the support and commitment from key stakeholders.

When it is most likely to be used:
This tool is typically used during **Phase 1: Create Change Platform** during the **Develop Business Case** task. It is also used during Phase 2 when designing technology, organization, and process modifications to architecture.

Steps:
1.   To build the business case, refer to the guidelines listed below and work closely with your Finance partner to build and analyze the business case. After building the business case, hold a management review session to finalize the formula for calculating the business case costs and benefits. Each business case is unique. Using the example of a restructuring project the following steps have been annotated below.

   Guidelines:
   •   What are the major categories of costs and benefits (e.g. infrastructure, outside vendors)?

- For each category of benefits and costs brainstorm potential line items. Potential costs associated with infrastructure can be moving expenses, the purchase of new real estate, site assessment, or rent during the transition.
- Finalize the appropriate cost and benefit categories and line items you will use to create the business case.
- Populate the business case with data. Check for reasonableness. When documenting benefits also take note of non-quantifiable benefits. For all benefits and costs note the timing when they will accrue and whether they are one time or reoccurring. Capture the assumptions underlying each of the key benefits/costs.

2. There are a number of financial formulas that can be used to evaluate each design including; discounted cash flow (DCF), cost benefit analysis (CBA), payback period (PB), internal rate of return (IRR), and net present value (NPV). When the financial analysis is complete, have a management review session to obtain consensus.

3. The final design alternative decision is best made by "blending" a number of decision criteria, including risk assessment, to select the final design.

Table B.5 contains an example of a completed business case.

TABLE B.5 Example of a completed business case

	Years ($ Thousands)						
	2003	2004	2005	2006	2007	2008	Total
Implementation costs	($960.48)	($1,199.52)	—	—	—	—	($2,160.00)
Migration to shared services							
Severance packages	—	($167.86)	—	—	—	—	($167.86)
Retention bonuses	—	($120.00)	—	—	—	—	($120.00)
Training	($34.00)	($119.00)	($17.00)	—	—	—	($170.00)
Initial cash outflows	($994.48)	($1,606.38)	($17.00)	—	—	—	($2,617.86)
Technology HW/SW	($192.00)	($288.00)	—	—	—	—	($480.00)
Ongoing costs (IS outsourcing)	—	—	($1,333.65)	($1,400.34)	($1,470.35)	($1,543.87)	($6,748.45)
Additional cash outflow	($192.00)	($1,288.24)	($1,333.65)	($1,400.34)	($1,470.35)	($1,543.87)	($7,228.45)
TOTAL INVESTMENT	($1,186.48)	($2,894.62)	($1,350.65)	($1,400.34)	($1,470.35)	($1,543.87)	($9,846.31)
Bill-to-Cash - FTE reduction (44-34)	—	$195.05	$780.22	$819.23	$860.19	$903.20	$3,557.89
Bill-to-Cash - Volume growth absorption	—	—	$43.52	$140.08	$193.12	$236.64	$613.36
Bill-to-Cash - Comp adj elim (on eliminated employees)	—	$29.26	$40.96	$43.01	$45.16	$47.42	$205.81
Bill-to-Cash - Subtotal	—	$224.31	$864.70	$1,002.32	$1,098.47	$1,187.26	$4,377.06
Procure-to-pay - FTE reduction (22 to 18)	—	$68.86	$275.45	$289.23	$303.69	$318.87	$1,256.10
Procure-to-pay - Volume growth absorption	—	—	$38.62	$77.25	$130.29	$236.64	$482.80
Procure-to-pay - Comp adj elim (on eliminated employees)	—	$10.33	$14.46	$15.18	$15.94	$16.74	$72.65
Procure-to-pay - Strategic sourcing spend reduction	—	$154.20	$1,156.52	$1,542.03	$1,696.23	$1,865.85	$6,414.83
Procure-to-pay - Subtotal	—	$233.39	$1,485.05	$1,923.69	$2,146.15	$2,438.10	$8,226.38
IS - FTE reduction (103 to 95)	—	$405.73	$540.97	$540.97	$540.97	$540.97	$2,569.61
IS - Comp adj elim (on eliminated employees)	—	$27.05	$28.40	$29.82	$31.31	$32.88	$149.46
IS - Outsourcing (17 FTE's)	—	$1,333.65	$1,778.21	$1,867.12	$1,960.47	$2,058.50	$8,997.95
IS Subtotal	—	$1,766.43	$2,347.58	$2,437.91	$2,532.75	$2,632.35	$11,717.02
Division office lease reduction	—	—	—	$38.34	$76.69	$191.72	$306.75
TOTAL BENEFITS	—	$2,224.13	$4,697.33	$5,402.26	$5,854.06	$6,449.43	$24,627.21
Net cash flow (NCF)	($1,186.48)	($670.49)	$3,346.68	$4,001.92	$4,383.71	$4,905.56	$14,780.90
Cumulative NCF	($1,186.48)	($1,856.97)	$1,489.71	$5,491.63	$9,875.34	$14,780.89	
Discounted cash flow (DCF)	($1,036.23)	($511.42)	$2,229.45	$2,328.34	$2,227.48	$2,176.98	$7,414.60
Cumulative DCF with WACC = 14.50%	($1,036.23)	($1,547.65)	$681.80	$3,010.14	$5,237.62	$7,414.61	
Internal rate of return (IRR)							
Payback period							
Discounted payback period							

3. Business Rules Tool

Description of tool:
A business rule is a written or informal rule that governs employee behavior. Common business rules include:

- formal administrative policies
- informal stories/anecdotal comments that describe what employees can and cannot do
- constraints imposed by funding authorities
- constraints imposed for compliance purposes.

This tool identifies business rules that run counter to the change you are trying to implement. The informal business rules are the hardest to uncover and are often not part of documented processes. These rules "run in the background" and when you ask employees why they do certain things they will often reply "that's the way my predecessor did it." Many of these rules may have been appropriate when they were originally developed but may not be helpful in the future-state environment. See Figure B.6 for an example of business rules that are operating behind the recruiting process.

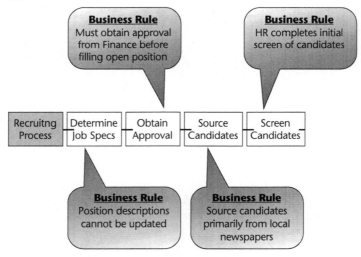

FIGURE B.6 Sample business rules for a recruiting process

When it is most likely to be used:
This tool is used during **Phase 2: Design Change** when completing the **Design Process Changes** task. The data collected in this tool can also be very useful when trying to align the culture to support the business plan or the change initiative.

Steps:

1. **Catalog all of the current business rules.** The first place to start is to look in the book cases of the business managers to become familiar with the formal administrative policies. The identification of informal policies can be collected via focus groups, a pulse survey, or a series of structured workshops. Generally speaking, we have found the latter method to be the most economical while providing the best data capture. The workshops tend to work best when they are organized by process. A strong facilitator can walk participants through each activity in the process, carefully noting the current business rules, who "owns" each rule, how long it has been in place and those that will impede the planned change.

2. **Propose new/modified business rules.** During this step the facilitator identifies how the proposed change initiative will impact each formal and informal business rule. The rules that are most problematic are noted and an initial determination is made as to whether the rule can be amended. If so, alternative business rules are identified.

3. **Create an implementation plan.** Make the final recommendation of business rule changes to management. For those that are approved identify the implementation steps. Remember that significant changes to business rules will cause ripple effects throughout the organization. Depending on the magnitude of these changes training may be required, process documentation may need to be updated, and jobs redesigned. If the business rule changes have significant downstream impacts it may be necessary to either pilot test or simulate the new rules before implementing them. See Table B.6 for a completed example of business rules using the tool.

TABLE B.6 Example of completed business rules tool

Business Rule	Owner	Problem(s)	New Rule	Integration Points
Purchases over $200 require the sign-off of the department Director	VP Purchasing	Creates a bottleneck that results in numerous stock-outs	All staff can order supplies up to $200 without manager approval	
Employees have the freedom to order IT equipment as needed	CIO	Employees order computer peripherals that are not approved by corporate IT and are not fully compatible with existing IT equipment	Can only order equipment from an approved IT vendor that is aligned with Corporate IT policy	On-line catalog

4. Champion Assessment Instrument

Directions:

Utilize this instrument to either identify potential people to act as champions or to assess a champion's strengths and weaknesses.

The champion...

	Not at all				A great extent
1. has a clear vision of the change and why it is important to the business	1	2	3	4	5
2. is highly committed to the change	1	2	3	4	5
3. is able/willing to commit the necessary resources	1	2	3	4	5
4. understands the need for developing financial, operational, and perceptual metrics to guide and evaluate the change	1	2	3	4	5
5. can mediate cross-functional squabbles and ensure cross-functional commitment	1	2	3	4	5
6. will hold stakeholders accountable for achieving the vision and removing roadblocks	1	2	3	4	5
7. understands that change requires an approach that balances process, technology, and people issues	1	2	3	4	5
8. is an active role model who walks the talk	1	2	3	4	5
9. recognizes the need to develop a compelling case for action and believes the existing state needs to change	1	2	3	4	5
10. understands the importance of and is willing to utilize rewards/consequences to ensure the success of the change	1	2	3	4	5
11. is trusted by key internal/external stakeholders	1	2	3	4	5
12. has the formal authority to mobilize action to move the change forward	1	2	3	4	5

5. Change Process Primer

Description of tool:

The Change Process Primer is used to orient change leaders, members of the change initiative team and stakeholders on the process of change from organizational and human dynamics perspectives.

Figures B.7 to B.16 can be incorporated and/or customized for use in a change orientation presentation:

FIGURE B.7 Overview of the change process from an organizational perspective

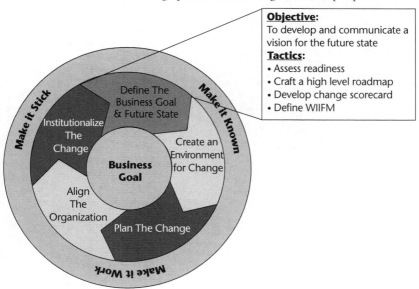

FIGURE B.8 Develop and communicate a vision for future state

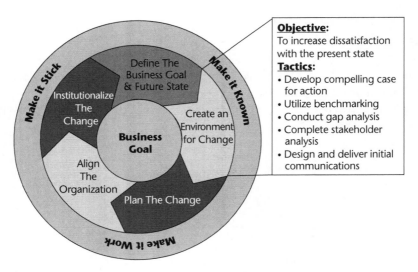

FIGURE B.9 Increase dissatisfaction with the present state

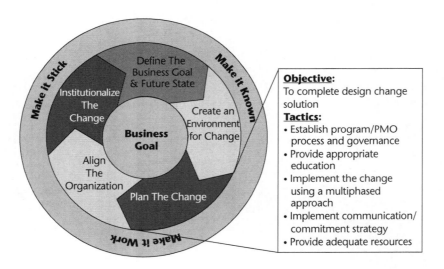

FIGURE B.10 Complete design of change solution

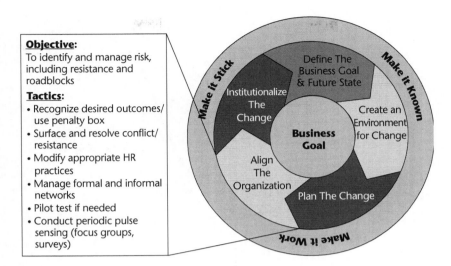

Objective:
To identify and manage risk, including resistance and roadblocks

Tactics:
• Recognize desired outcomes/ use penalty box
• Surface and resolve conflict/ resistance
• Modify appropriate HR practices
• Manage formal and informal networks
• Pilot test if needed
• Conduct periodic pulse sensing (focus groups, surveys)

FIGURE B.11 Identify and manage risk, including resistance and roadblocks

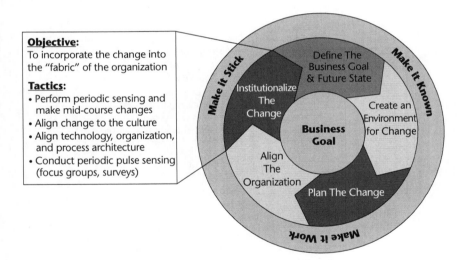

Objective:
To incorporate the change into the "fabric" of the organization

Tactics:
• Perform periodic sensing and make mid-course changes
• Align change to the culture
• Align technology, organization, and process architecture
• Conduct periodic pulse sensing (focus groups, surveys)

FIGURE B.12 Incorporate the change into the "fabric" of the organization

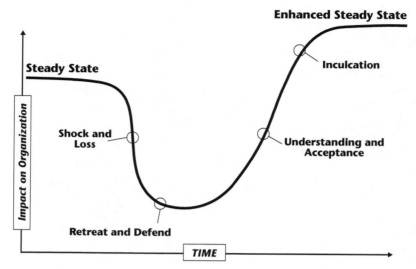

FIGURE B.13 Overview of the human dynamics of change

Phase I: Shock and Loss

<u>Colleague reactions</u>	<u>Management actions</u>
• disbelief • anxiety • apprehension • avoidance.	• acknowledge opportunities and threats • don't overload • provide support networks • utilize 3-way communications • provide conceptual education.

FIGURE B.14 Phase I of the human dynamics of change

Phase II: Retreat and Defend

<u>Colleague reactions</u>	<u>Management actions</u>
• anger and inability to engage issues • frustration and isolation • confusion • activism.	• link new to old • stress opportunities • establish transition structures • be patient • provide a buffer to employees.

FIGURE B.15 Phase II of the human dynamics of change

Phase III: Understanding and Acceptance

Colleague reactions	Management actions
• letting go of the past • disengaging old behaviors • limited risk taking.	• reward desired behaviors • don't penalize honest mistakes • involve employees in planning • provide skill education.

FIGURE B.16 Phase III of the human dynamics of change

Phase IV: Inculcation

Colleague reactions	Management actions
• enthusiasm • consistency of actions • considerable risk taking • change is now the new norm	• provide adequate resources • put "blockers" in the penalty box • utilize informal leaders as role models

FIGURE B.17 Phase IV of the human dynamics of change

6. Change Scorecard Tool

Description of tool:

This tool is to be used to develop a scorecard to guide the efforts and ultimately evaluate the impact of the change initiative. A scorecard can be crafted to measure different aspects of change. Depending on situation, it may be necessary to develop a scorecard to measure the *overall impact of the project* or focus on only the *change management aspects*.

Like an organizational balanced scorecard, a change scorecard should include several categories of measures that are ultimately cascaded down to each change team and team member. Table B.7 provides examples of the different scorecard perspectives for both an overall and change scorecard as follows:

TABLE B.7 Examples of change scorecard perspectives

Types of overall scorecard perspectives	Examples of change process KPI's
Financial	Cash flow
Project	Communications effectiveness
Operational	Operating cost
Market	Customer retention
Process	Cycle time

When it is most likely to be used:

This tool is most commonly used during **Phase 1: Create Change Platform** within the **Define Project** and **Develop Business Case** tasks. The scorecard is commonly updated throughout the life cycle of the project.

Steps:
1. Identify whether you are crafting a scorecard for the overall change project or just the effectiveness of the change process. In many instances it will be at both levels.
2. The key inputs into developing a scorecard are the vision, the change project charter, the business case, and any other pertinent information that details the problem, the gap between where you are and where you aspire to be, and the desired results. Developing a scorecard is an iterative process so build in a healthy amount of "show and tell" and incorporate the learnings.
3. Identify and define each category or perspective of measurement. For each perspective identify three to five specific qualitative and quantitative targets. Examples of perspective definitions for an overall M&A acquisition scorecard are listed below:
   - **Financial:** This perspective is defined as the degree to which the integration creates additional shareholder value. Common targets include revenue growth, headcount reduction, and cost reduction.
   - **Project:** This perspective is defined as the effectiveness of both the PMO and project manager at achieving the other targets. Common targets include retention of key talent, performance to budget, and effectiveness of communications.
   - **Operations:** This perspective is defined as the degree to which the integration rationalizes assets and achieves desired economies of scale. Common targets include reducing the cycle time of a core process, reducing inventory, and improving asset utilization.
   - **Market/Customer:** This perspective is defined as the degree to which the integration enhances market image and increases market share. Common targets include retention of key customers or an increase in market share.
4. Make sure your scorecard is tightly linked to your progress reporting, issue escalation, risk management, and communication activities. Develop a variance analysis process that will identify the source/cause of performance gaps when actual performance does not meet/exceed planned targets.
5. Cascade the overall scorecard down to each change team. Make sure each change team member's performance expectations are tightly aligned with their team's scorecard. See Table B.8 for an example of a completed integrated scorecard.

TABLE B.8 Example of an overall integrated scorecard

Synergy Performance Indicators	100 Day Targets	
	Actual	Plan
Financial Synergies		
Reduce operating costs	$36 MM	$30 MM
Reduce S,G, & A headcount expenses	120K	150K
Operational Synergies		
Decrease inventory	$13.5MM	$15MM
Reduce headcount	167 F.T.E.	130 F.T.E.
	16 Temps	0
	32 part time	32 part time
Market/Customer Synergies		
Retention of key customers	72%	92%
Increase market share	27%	27%
Project Management		
Retain key talent	63%	95 %
Key "critical path" milestones are completed on time	91%	100%
Performance to budget	67%	100%
Communications effectiveness (as measured by pulse survey – an average score of 4/5 on trust, timeliness, believability, and appropriateness of communications)	4/5	4/5
Deliverables quality (accepted by Integration Leader)	97%	100%

7. Chartering Template

Description of tool:
A project charter is a PMO tool that is most commonly used to formalize and clarify a large piece of project-related work. A well-crafted charter will minimally identify the project team members, the objectives or desired outcomes, deliverables, a detailed work plan, and resource requirements or budgeting. When completed, this tool can be combined with a roles and responsibilities chart to specify team member decision rights.

When it is most likely to be used:
The chartering template is most commonly used during the **Phase 1: Create Change Platform** during the **Establish PMO** task.

Steps:

1. Depending on the size/complexity of the change you may need to break the project into a number of different work streams. It is critical to clarify the key roles of the team including the sponsor, project leader, and core and ad hoc team members.

2. Identify the performance objectives or desired impacts. These should be translated into both quantitative and qualitative performance targets.

3. Scope creep is one of the most difficult PMO challenges to address. Clarifying specifically what is and is not in scope can be a valuable use of time to keep the team focused on crafting deliverables that are completed on time, within budget, and of acceptable quality.

4. Deliverables are defined as "concrete" outcomes, *not* activities a project team focuses on that directly impact the desired outcomes or objectives.

5. The next section focuses on developing a detailed work plan. Care should be exercised to appropriately decompose the tasks into activities noting start/end times. For complex projects it might also be advisable to use more sophisticated functionality like critical path management or PERT to understand the relationships between tasks (predecessors) and provide much more clarity around task responsibility.

6. The final template can be used to forecast capacity and resource requirements, which can bubble up to a project budget if desired.

See Table B.9 for a completed example of a Chartering Template.

TABLE B.9 Example of a chartering template

Project/work stream	*Improve Disbursements Payment Process*	
Sponsor	Michael Harris	
Project Leader	Michael Pagani	
Team Members	Ahmad Jones	Faye Ray
Core	Frank Barber	Mario Genovese
Ad Hoc	Joe Thomas	

OBJECTIVES
1. Shorten disbursement payment cycle time by 35 percent.
2. Reduce invoicing errors to 1 percent.
3. Improve internal and external customer satisfaction.
Some of the above numbers to be finalized later in work plan.

SCOPE OF WORK

Included in the Scope	Excluded from the Scope
• Contract processing and payment	• Receiving activities
• Processing Miscellaneous Payments	
• Processing PO payments	
• Document Scanning and Records Management	
• Competency and skill requirements definition	
• Organization and job design for AP	
• Maintenance of vendor records	
• Invoice receipt	
• Handle vendor payment inquiries/problems	
• Activities to ensure contract payment compliance	

DELIVERABLES
• A/P process design documentation.
• Procedure documentation (if different than the above).
• Audit of implementation effectiveness.
• Performance measurement reports.

Item	Period					Project Total
	Q1/07	Q2/07	Q3/07	Q4/07	2007	
Team Members	*Days by Period*					
Michael Pagani	10	30	20	10		70
Ahmad Jones	8	24	16	8		56
Frank Barber	8	24	16	8		56
Mario Genovese	8	24	16	8		56
Contractor(s)						0
Consultant(s)						0
Resources Days Sub-Total	34	102	68	34	0	238
Project Cost Summary	*Dollars by Period*					
Employees	17	51	34	17	0	119
Consultants & Contractors	0	0	0	0	0	0
Travel & Entertainment						0
Capital Item Depreciation	0	0	0	0		0
Training & Education						0
Other						0
Project Cost Sub-total	$17	$51	$34	$17	$0	$119
Capital Expenditures	*Dollars by Period*					
Capital Expenditures Sub-total	$0	$0	$0	$0	$0	$0
Savings/Revenue Increases	*Dollars by Period*					
Not Estimated						0
Saving/Revenue Sub-total	$0	$0	$0	$0	$0	$0
Net Present Value	N/A					

8. Commitment Planning Primer

Description of Tool:

Developing a critical mass of commitment is one of the key success factors for effective change. The initial foray into commitment building begins when a stakeholder assessment has been completed. The output of the stakeholder analysis, a stakeholder summary, becomes the primary input into crafting the communication plan, risk management plan, and commitment strategy.

When it is most likely to be used:

Change management is all about engaging stakeholders around a common solution. These tools can be used at any point in the change methodology.

Steps:

1. Identify the various "chunks of work" and players within your change scope and assess whether the change initiative you are involved in will considerably impact any internal/external stakeholders. Don't overly constrain your thinking by narrowing the commitment planning process to individuals and groups only *within* your organization or the immediate scope of the change initiative. Depending on the scope and complexity of the change initiative it may be necessary to identify stakeholders throughout the entire value chain, which can include individuals from suppliers and channel partners to alliance and joint venture (JV) partners.
2. Obtain the latest version of your organization chart and make sure your commitment plan adequately addresses people at each level in the organization who fall into the following roles:
    *   **Executive Sponsor:** The executive sponsor is the senior-most leader who has the position power to mandate the change. Part of commitment planning is to work with the sponsor to ensure there is a well-thought-out vision for the change initiative and the initiative has been translated into project performance expectations (tangible metrics). The metrics need to be cascaded down to each work stream and project team to ensure "line of sight" so that the sponsor can ultimately hold individuals accountable. The executive sponsor must demonstrate their visible support throughout the project. Lastly, large-scale change is usually very disruptive to an organization. Coach the sponsor, when appropriate, around being decisive to make timely and tough decisions when issues are elevated. Consistency will minimize the rumor mill and demonstrate to stakeholders that the executive's words and actions are tightly aligned.
    *   **Champions:** This key role is defined as individuals who absolutely must support the change initiative for it to be successful. One of the most common oversights is to think that just because a senior executive advocates change all the employees under that person will just "salute and follow orders." Depending on the scope of change and size of

organization this assumption is often a prescription for failure. In large organizations that are involved in an enterprise-wide change initiative it is not uncommon for employees in the lower levels of the organization to never have met, or at times, even heard of the sponsoring executive. Just because he or she provides direction does not mean employees will support the change. It is important to identify champions at *each* level in the organization who are impacted by the change. For example, if the change impacts employees in an offshore customer service group, the person with the most influence over that group is generally *not* the CEO but the direct supervisor of that group. An effective commitment strategy will identify who these individuals are and target specific actions to engage them to ensure their strong commitment.

- **Missionaries:** These are individuals who are "change agents" and are responsible for "rolling up their sleeves" and becoming actively involved in the change efforts. At *each* level of the organization make sure you are sufficiently resourced with enough staff who can actively assist you in the change efforts. This can include people who are core and ad hoc members of the project team, subject matter experts, and internal consultants. Make sure you use the right channels to engage these individuals – you are soliciting their input to understand their concerns/suggestions – and that communications have been specifically targeted to this group.

- **Opinion shapers:** This group of stakeholders is most commonly overlooked. They are the individuals who may or may not possess formal authority but have considerable *informal influence* on a number of other stakeholders. Examples include union leaders and individuals with long tenure whose opinion is sought after. At each level in the organization identify the informal group leaders. Get them involved at the earliest stages of the change starting with the business case. They must understand and buy into the premise that something meaningful is broken. They must also understand and value "what's in it for me" (WIIFM). The more support these individuals provide, the less active the grapevine and resistance you will encounter. The obvious question is "how does one identify who the informal groups are?" Experience suggests observing interactions. After a town hall meeting who do people cluster around? Who is asked "what were the key points of management's presentation in your own words" and "what does it mean?" These folks are the informal group leaders. If you are unfamiliar to a location ask who the informal group leaders are. Another indicator can be that the most vocal folks are often the informal group leaders. Getting the informal group leaders to be active supporters provides a "force multiplier" effect to your commitment plan. For every informal leader that gets on board 20, 50, 100+ others will also become supporters.

- **Impacted:** These individuals or groups are the people who are most heavily impacted by the change. If you are not careful you can easily get overwhelmed with the size of this group. In most instances this large group needs to be subdivided. *The individuals you typically need to focus on the most are the ones who perceive themselves to be the most negatively impacted, the stakeholders who are most important to the success of the change, as they are the ones most likely to resist.* Take the time to clearly understand how the change will affect them. In some instances people resist change because *they incorrectly perceive the change will adversely affect them* in which case you have a communications problem. In other situations they *will* be negatively impacted so it is critical to understand/address their concerns in an equitable manner, and make sure you sense this group periodically via a survey, focus groups, etc. to incorporate their feedback into the change design and roll-out.

3. Take the time to segment stakeholders at the most appropriate level of aggregation. The more you lump large groups of individuals together, the more you dilute your stakeholder assessment and commitment plan. Unfortunately there is no universal algorithm you can use to mathematically identify the optimal size of groupings. It's a judgment call. Experience suggests that the greater the influence and impact a stakeholder group has relative to the change the more you should consider a more focused approach to segmentation. You can segment stakeholders by organizational level, by location, by part of the value chain, by brand, and so on. For example, do you lump all senior managers together or do you target the CHRO and COO individually, if the initiative warrants it? Stakeholder analysis is very similar to developing a work plan. If you do not take the time to decompose tasks into steps, you are likely to underestimate resources, budget, and the timeline. If you are doing an enterprise-wide change initiative and you have your stakeholders segmented at a very high level you will likely have problems with resistance and communications downstream.

4. Collect stakeholder data using multiple channels. Data can be collected via interviews, structured workshops, focus groups, and pulse surveys. The final data collection method will trade off costs, time, and accuracy. Avoid turning the process into a "report card" exercise whereby individuals are labeled as winners, losers, those who support, blockers, etc. The focus needs to stay on what are the issues, who needs to support the change, and how to maximize support at each level in the hierarchy. If you are using project team members in structured workshops it may be useful to have each team member evaluate the stakeholders individually and without discussion, and then compare evaluations and discuss obvious differences. It is not necessary to obtain complete consensus since you are really looking for directionally accurate assessments. It is important to use some technique (e.g. focus groups, pulse surveys) to validate your (the team's) assessment of each stakeholder's level of commitment. Remember for each stakeholder it is important to determine the following:

    *   **The level/type of impact the change will have on them.** Take the time to understand from their perspective how the change will impact

them from a day-to-day operational standpoint, career standpoint, power/political standpoint, etc.

- **Their concerns.** Stakeholder concerns commonly range from issues surrounding project design and roll-out to issues surrounding their personal agendas. When collecting data from individuals pay careful attention to what is said, what is implied, and what is observed from non-verbal behavior.
- **Their current level of commitment**. Develop a continuum of definitions that depict where each stakeholder is in terms of their current level of support. Examples include, are they:
  - enthusiastic or strong supporters?
  - providing verbal support that is not backed up by actions or are mildly supportive?
  - non committal or neutral?
  - uncooperative or moderately against?
  - or hostile/strongly against?

  Identify the drivers of change for each particular stakeholder: what's in it for them? What will make this change worth the energy required to bring it about? Identify those forces which act as restraints to change for this stakeholder. These may be technical, cultural, political or of some other origin. It is useful to understand the nature of the resistance for those key stakeholders who have a medium-to-strong degree of resistance to the change. This information is useful when developing a strategy to influence the stakeholders to support the change. It is important to validate your team's perceptions by seeking input from others.
- **Their ability to influence the ultimate success of the project.** This can be categorized as high, medium and low. Focus more attention on stakeholders who have a high level of influence but low levels of commitment.
- **Actions to optimize their support**. After taking the time to think through the level of commitment required from each stakeholder, as well as the issues and concerns important to them, it is critical to formulate a strategy to influence those whose commitment must be strengthened, or at a minimum, maintained. Think about the stakeholder's style and history as well as those forces that serve as drivers for this individual regarding the change, and those which serve as restraints. It is also important to consider the relationships between the stakeholders you (your team) have identified in terms of who might assist you (your team) in gaining the support of others. For example, a key stakeholder who has a *high* degree of commitment to the change may be able to influence the thinking of another, less committed stakeholder. Your influence strategy should determine *what* the stakeholder's issues might be, *who* can best influence each individual, and *how* to best influence him/her. Your influence strategy should also address *when* the influence process begins.

Remember that stakeholder engagement and commitment planning is *not* static. It is a dynamic process that needs to be continually worked throughout the project life cycle. It is also a discovery process where learnings are treated as outputs that become inputs into downstream change activities. Specifically the learnings from stakeholder engagement must be tightly integrated and used to update the risk management plan, communication plan, overall project road map, and individual work stream work plans.

The commitment plan has to be treated like any other action plan. Attention to detail and execution are critical. Crafting the plan is only half of the equation. The more challenging half is proper execution. There are a myriad of ways to influence a stakeholder. Before executing the plan take your time to ensure you have the right action in place that exerts a force consistent with the behavior change or result you would like to see. It can be conceptualized as understanding "cause and effect."

Make sure you have consensus around the *effect* you want to see with regard to each stakeholder in the plan and then determine what can be done (the cause) to advance the change. For example, you can provide targeted communications, education, use one stakeholder to influence another, provide meaningful rewards (for compliance) or penalties (sanctions which are financial or non-financial for non-compliance). The key is to make sure leaders' actions and words are consistent. If they are not aligned most employees with a long work history will model behaviors that are aligned to leaders' actions much more than words.

As a last resort, the executive sponsor and other leaders *must* demonstrate decisiveness. If key position incumbents are either unwilling or unable to support the change after repeated interventions, these blockers must be removed. If you leave them in their current position they are likely to become pernicious, like a cancer that invades the body, and employees will read management's actions as not really being supportive of the change.

9. Communication Planning Template

Description of tool:

A communication plan is a structured planning tool for communicating top down, across the organization, and bottom up. The latter is very important because it can be used to gauge understanding, communications effectiveness, and message receptivity of each audience. Listed below are the common purposes of communications:

- information dissemination
- data gathering
- evaluating effectiveness of communications
- idea generation
- shaping behaviors

- mobilizing stakeholders
- dispelling rumors or inaccurate information.

There are three types of affected individuals in change initiatives. "Winners" are those groups or individuals who perceive themselves as being better off. Their status, power, impact, etc. have grown as a result of the change or they are the sponsors of the change. Winners generally *support* the change. A second group of individuals are relatively "unaffected." This group is conceptually on the fence. They can *either support or resist* the change. If the communications are sufficiently targeted and a commitment plan is effectively implemented, a large percentage of the individuals on the bubble will become supporters. The last group of individuals are the "negatively impacted." These individuals or groups are most likely to *resist* the change because they perceive it as negatively impacting them. A considerable amount of effort must be allocated to the latter two groups to assess and equitably address their concerns, assess their level of understanding, and continually solicit their thoughts and opinions.

It is critical to tightly link the communication learnings into other related project activities such as stakeholder analysis/engagement, risk management, and overall project management.

When it is most likely to be used:
This tool is typically first used during **Phase 1: Create Change Platform** when completing the **Develop Communication Strategy** task. It is updated during the life cycle of the project.

Steps:
1. The first step in developing a communication plan is to complete a stakeholder assessment. This entails identifying all stakeholders who are either affected by the change and/or whose support is needed to make the change a success. This should include both *internal* (employees) and *external* (unions, suppliers, customers) stakeholders. Once identified it is sometimes beneficial to *prioritize* (high, medium, or low) each stakeholder group relative to how much they are impacted by the change and the degree to which they impact the success of the change. Specific actions for the communication plan which address the key stakeholder concerns and achieving a cascading level of commitment typically occur during the design of a commitment strategy:
    - **Agree on how you will segment stakeholder groups (at an individual or group level).** For example, do you group all of the executive team together or do you segment the CEO and EVP of HR and address them differently? Generally speaking, the finer the segmentation, the better and more actionable the data.
    - **Brainstorm the internal and external stakeholders who will be impacted by the change.** An example of an internal stakeholder is the

shared services function while examples of external stakeholders include external suppliers, owners, and Wall Street.

- **Identify the impacts the change will have on each stakeholder group.** The more specific, the more actionable the communication plan.
- **Complete stakeholder analysis.** This entails assessing each stakeholder's perceived level of commitment, identifying their influence on the success of the initiative, and fully understanding how the change will impact them individually. A rule of thumb for determining influence is that individuals tend to have greater influence when they control key resources that are needed, the stakeholder is perceived to have high levels of formal authority, and the stakeholder is capable of forming broad coalitions across the organization.
- **Identify stakeholders concerns.** Concerns should not be looked upon as a problem or a nuisance. Often stakeholders will identify very valid issues that need to be addressed in order to fully realize the benefits of the change.

2. **Develop actionable messages to optimize commitment levels.** Time and effort should be allocated to executing actions that foster cascading commitment throughout the organization.

3. **Identify the *specific message*(s) that need to be sent to *each* stakeholder group.** Communications should progress from broad to specific. The initial communications should lay a conceptual framework of understanding answering what is being done, why, when, and how.

4. **Identify *which* channels to use when communicating with each stakeholder.** Take the necessary time to fully discuss the best communication vehicle for each key message. Some messages are nothing more than a data download and do not require much interaction. Others necessitate dialogue and interaction. Listed below are common communication channels:

Examples of One-Way Communication Channels
- emails
- voicemails
- homepage/website
- letters/memos
- banners
- town hall meetings
- posters
- videotapes/videoconferencing
- newsletters
- FAQs (frequently asked questions)
- surveys.

Examples of Two-Way Communication Channels
- supervisor/direct report meetings

- one-on-one meetings
- brownbag lunches
- telephone hotlines
- email or chat support
- department meetings
- rumor/communication Czars
- focus groups.

The example in Figure B.18 can be modified to assist you in deciding the most appropriate communication channel. It illustrates channels for sharing and shaping information.

How to Communicate	Purposes of Communication	
Channel	Share Information	Shape Behavior
Face-to-face (one-on-one)		
Symbolic (meeting, rally)		
Interactive media (telephone, voicemail, fax, email)	**Aligned**	
Personal static media (letter, memo, report)		
Impersonal static media (bulletin, flyer, newsletter, video)		

FIGURE B.18 Communication channel identification

5. **Identify who (line executive, direct supervisor, etc.) is the best person to complete each activity in the communication plan.**
6. **Ensure each activity within the communication plan has a specific timeframe by which it is completed.**
7. **Develop feedback mechanisms to solicit input and/or address concerns of key stakeholders.** This information should be tightly integrated with the commitment, risk, and project plans. Feedback mechanisms can also be very helpful in assessing the effectiveness of your communications by collecting data on:
    - **were the key message bytes useful?** Did they answer the questions or address the concerns of the target stakeholder group?
    - **was the communication timely?**
    - **was the communication understandable?** Did the target audience understand the intended message?
    - **did the target audience believe the communications?**

Data concerning communications effectiveness is commonly collected via pulse surveys or focus groups. This quickly identifies themes and next step actions.

Listed below are some general communication guidelines:

- **Employ simplicity**
  - jargon and unnecessary abstract language should be eliminated
- **Target communications to each stakeholder group**
  - focus on areas of concern to each group
  - think carefully about why you are sending the communication and what you hope to achieve
- **Use metaphors, analogies and examples**
  - a picture is worth a thousand words
- **Use multiple channels**
  - select appropriate channels for the objective of the communications (e.g. if you want to foster two-way interactions and dialogue don't select a town hall meeting)
  - make sure relevant external announcements are preceded by internal communications
- **Be repetitive regarding key messages**
  - ideas sink in deeply only after they have been heard many times
- **Lead by example**
  - make sure your leaders' behavior is aligned with the messaging
  - use scripts to ensure message consistency
- **Do not send mixed signals**
  - address concerns/rumors as quickly as possible
  - acknowledge if you don't know the answer to something
- **Encourage give-and-take**
  - two-way communication is always more powerful than one-way communication.

Table B.10 provides an example of a completed Communications Planning Template.

TABLE B.10 Example of completed communications planning template

Stakeholders	Priority (H,M,L)	Concerns	Key Messages	Communication Vehicles (memosw, video, etc)	Resp	Timing
Union reps	H	Reduced job classifications	Will not close plant, expect no more than 3% reduction in union jobs, will try to get new tiger product to this plant which will increase union jobs after first 9 months	1–1 meeting	J King	Feb 28
First line supervisors	H	Position will be eliminated	With SDWT that functionality will be leveraged into the team. Will provide job retraining. Estimate 40% of current supervisors will be able to transition into Process Excellence function	1–1 meeting	J House	Mar 3
Printing, Security, Grounds keeping Depts	H	Functions will be outsourced	Walk them through the manpower redeployment strategy, look for other divisions that can utilize these sets	TEAM meating	DIRECT SUPV	Mar 7

10. Communication Assessment Pulse Survey

Directions:

This survey is used to assess the effectiveness of the communications efforts for the change initiative. The data collected should be used to better target communications and also serve as an input to the risk management, project work plans, and stakeholder engagement plans.

The survey should be administered to impacted stakeholders, members of the change initiative team, senior management, and change leadership. Have participants read each question carefully and select the response that most closely corresponds to his/her perception. At the end of each section there is a place to note any additional comments they feel are pertinent.

Communications effectiveness

	To a very great extent	To a consid- erable extent	To a moderate extent	To a limited extent	Not at all
1. I understand the purpose of Project XXX and how its benefits both the organization and me as an employee	1	2	3	4	5
2. Project XXX communications to-date have been timely	1	2	3	4	5
3. I trust and believe the Project XXX communications	1	2	3	4	5
4. The communications to-date have addressed topics that were of high value to me	1	2	3	4	5
5. Overall, the communications to-date have been easy to understand	1	2	3	4	5
6. Key project milestones have been communicated to me	1	2	3	4	5
7. Overall communications to-date have been consistent (messages don't conflict) across different sources	1	2	3	4	5
8. The communication channels used (e.g. town halls, intranet, small group break-outs) were appropriate for the purpose of the event	1	2	3	4	5
9. The project team provided ample opportunities for me to contribute my ideas and voice my concerns	1	2	3	4	5
10. Performance expectations have been clearly communicated to me	1	2	3	4	5
11 What questions would you like answered relative to Project XXX?					

11. Competency Gap Tool

Description of tool:
Most change projects impact the technology, organization, and process architectures causing considerable modifications to the way work get completed. Examples of the common impacts are listed below:

- business model/structure
- processes
- applications
- roles, responsibilities, decision rights.

These types of changes require new competencies (knowledge, skills, and abilities) to be able to fully realize the targeted synergies of the vision. This tool can be used to identify the gaps between the current and future competencies required and identify actionable methods to facilitate new skill acquisition.

When it is most likely to be used:
This tool should be used during the **Phase 2: Design Change** when completing the **Design/Purchase Education** task. In some instances it will be completed earlier during Phase 1.

Steps:
1. **Determine the appropriate level of segmentation.** Depending on the quality and comprehensiveness of the stakeholder assessment completed earlier, often you can cut and paste the same stakeholder groups into this first column. If the stakeholder groupings are too broad you should segment the stakeholders down to either a job family level (e.g. business analysts, HR generalists) or specific job titles. The more narrow the segmentation the more accurate and useful the analysis.
2. **Determine the importance of each group that has been segmented.** In most environments there are more things broken or opportunities for improvement than there are available resources. Prioritization is critical so you must identify or update the populations of stakeholders that are impacted the most and have the greatest impact on the success of the change. These groups represent the stakeholders with the highest need for knowledge transfer.
3. **Identity change impacts.** A thorough understanding of *how* the change will impact each group is needed before you can determine competency gaps. Collect data to identify how the change will impact the technology (platforms, applications, data requirements) organization (administrative policies, job design, etc.) and process (how work gets done) architectures. Use the impact analysis tool developed earlier as an input. You will likely need to bring that deliverable down to a more finite level of analysis to understand competency gaps.

4. **Identify new competencies.** For each stakeholder group you segmented earlier identify the new competencies required. Take the time to prioritize the gaps so you can strategically allocate your resources to the competency gaps that are most mission critical.

5. **Identify specific methods of new skill acquisition.** There are a myriad of ways to transfer knowledge ranging from self-study and job aids to on-the-job training and computer-based training. Utilize your internal training and development staff to assist you in determining the most appropriate way to advance the skills of the stakeholders. Remember that there are many ways to transfer knowledge and formal classroom training is the most expensive.

6. **Determine resource requirements.** Resource requirements have both hard and soft costs. Don't assume using your internal training and development staff is not a cost. Depending on the scope and complexity of the change you may find that your internal training staff may not have the unused capacity or bandwidth to provide the full range of expertise. Develop realistic budgets that detail resources requirements including the usage of outside consultants and training providers.

See Table B.11 for a completed example.

TABLE B.11 Example of completed competency gap tool

Jon/Job Family	Ability to influence (H,M,L)	Degree of Change Impact (H,M,L)	Change Impacts	New Competencies	Job Aids	Formal Training	Coaching	Other?	Resource Requirements
Production Operators 1 & 2 Maintenance Operators, Industrial Engineer	High	High	Work rules changed; less classifications, elimination of seniority rules. Engineers and Maintenance people now report to Team Leader. All members must be fully cross trained	High performance teams, lean manufacturing principles, process redesign, maintenance package, management, change management, tools	No	Yes	No	NA	Budget $25K for training from application vendor, utilize internal training group for other programs
Team Leaders	High	High	New position. They need to facilitate and NOT supervise	Leading meetings, performance measurement, performance management, project management, leading teams, team dynamics	Yes	Yes	Yes	NA	HRBP will provide day to day coaching, OD team will design and lead team training. Engage outside consulting company to develop remainder of eduction – budget $45K

12. Cross Project Coordination Template

Description of tool:

Large-scale change projects are often a compilation of many different mini-change projects (sometimes referred to as work streams) that are interdependent and need to be coordinated. This tool can be used to proactively identify the project interdependencies and manage these projects effectively.

When it is most likely to be used:

This tool should be used in **Phase 1: Create Change Platform** during the **Establish PMO** task. Once developed the tool should then be used to manage each project until closeout.

Steps:

1. **Confirm the projects are interdependent.** If confirmed then assess whether the interdependency requires special efforts to manage so that all projects are successful.
2. **Identify all of the interdependencies.** Obtain copies of each detailed project work plan. Identify all of the interdependencies. Organize the interdependencies according to theme such as technology-, organization-, or process-related interdependencies.
3. **Develop actions for addressing each interdependency.** Specify who is responsible for completing each action as well as a completion timeframe.

See Table B.12 for a completed example.

TABLE B.12 Example of completed cross-project coordination template

Interdependent Projects: *Human capital planning and talent management*

Project Managers: *Alex Arias & Harry Cano*

Date: 1/10/XX

Description of Interdependence	Actions to Coordinate Each Project	Date	Responsible	Notes
The output of human capital is a talent gap analysis. This is an input into talent management	Develop in parallel and have bi-weekly meetings to ensure the processes are synced chronologically	5/20/XX	Team Leads	Map each process from a data standpoint to make sure all of the inputs and outputs are aligned

13. Culture Mapping Tool

Description of tool:

This tool organizes key cultural dimensions across a continuum and can be used in a variety of ways. It can be used to:

- visually map the current culture
- compare and contrast the "as is" to the "desired future state" culture
- assist in determining the specific type of culture needed to achieve the business plan and desired change benefits
- align the culture to closely support the business plan and change vision. There are many different dimensions and indices of culture. The specific cultural indices should be customized for each specific application and organization.

Give careful consideration to how you will collect data and from whom. For example, in most organizations it does not make much sense to ask the general population of employees what type of future state culture is needed to either implement a change initiative or align to the business plan. The rationale is that most are not close enough to the business strategy to be able to answer that question or lack the skill to be able to articulate a future state culture. A mistake might also be made if you just rely on the senior management team to map the "as is" culture. They may be too isolated to have a clear perception of the culture in a global enterprise.

When it is most likely to be used:

This tool is used during **Phase 2: Design Change** when completing the **Develop Culture Transition Plan** task. Data from this tool should be used through the remaining phases. It should be of particular importance when modifying HR practices and people systems.

Steps:

1. Obtain consensus on the specific use of this tool. Focus the initial discussions around what decisions you want to make or questions you want to answer relative to culture.
2. Customize the cultural dimensions (categories) and indices (specific attributes you are measuring) to your organization. There are a number of off-the-shelf culture surveys, books and articles that you can use to customize the culture tool. If your organization has an Organizational Development or internal consulting group they may provide "boots on the ground" support for this activity.
3. The "as is" culture can best be identified by incorporating the culture mapping tool into an intranet-based survey that is administered to a population of employees. Although less accurate, the current culture can also be mapped via

interviews and focus groups. Remember that there is an overall corporate culture and there may be one or more subculture that vary based on location.

4. Customize the directions according to the specific use of the instrument. For example, if you are trying to compare and contrast the "as is" vs. "the desired" culture you might want to request respondents review each of the indices and place a *C* (Current culture) in the column that most closely represents your organization's current culture.

5. In some instances you may opt to ask survey respondents to place *D* in the column that most closely represents their perception of the desired culture.

6. Calculate the absolute difference between each culture. The larger the difference the bigger the culture gap.

7. Discuss where the cultural dissimilarities are material (they can affect the success of the change project). Obtain consensus from the key decision makers where the cultures should be aligned and how. Refer to the culture alignment primer for additional guidelines.

See Table B.13 for a completed example.

TABLE B.13 Example of completed culture mapping tool

Cultural Characteristics	1	2	3	4	5	Cultural Characteristics	Absolute Difference
1 STRATEGIC ORIENTATION Customer/market driven	C			D		**STRATEGIC ORIENTATION** Technology-driven	3
Long-term profit orientation		C,D				Short-term profit orientation	0
Employees understand & committed to strategy			D	C		Employees don't understand and/or are not committed to vision/strategy	1
2 COMMUNICATION Top Down, or Bottom Up or Horizontal	C				D	**COMMUNICATION** Three-way	4
Infrequent			C,D			Frequent	0
Filtered	C	D				Open/candid	1
3 TRAINING & DEVELOPMENT Considerable opportunity for employee development		D			C	**TRAINING & DEVELOPMENT** Limited opportunity for employee development	3
Managers held accountable for developing employees				C,D		Managers not held accountable for developing employees	0
Development focuses on current job		C			D	Development focuses on current & future job	3

TABLE B.13 *continued*

Cultural Characteristics	1	2	3	4	5	Cultural Characteristics	Absolute Difference
4 REWARDS *Individual*						**REWARDS** *Group*	
Employees have minimum involvement in setting performance expectations						*Employees have significant involvement in setting performance expectations*	
Inequity						*Equity*	
Seniority-based						*Performance-based*	
Performance standards are clear						*Performance standards are ambiguous*	
Compensation at/above market						*Compensation below market*	
Employees receive regular performance appraisals						*Employees don't receive regular performance appraisals*	
5 DECISION MAKING *Slow*						**DECISION MAKING** *Fast*	
Centralized/multiple approval levels						*Few approval levels & broad span of control*	
Analytical/cautious						*Intuitive/daring*	
Authority levels are clearly understood						*Confusion exists regarding authority levels*	

14. Design-Implementation Challenge Questions

Description of tool:

Challenge sessions were originated at General Electric and first used to ensure their strategic plans were going to yield the desired results. Strategic planning, like change management, often has a life of its own and if not periodically checked can morph into areas outside of the scope of the initiative.

The challenge questions can be used to provide an objective "sanity check" regarding the change solution being implemented. This tool can be used to ensure the desired "functionality" has been fully incorporated into the change solution and that the solution has a high probability of achieving the desired results outlined in the change scorecard.

When it is most likely to be used:

This tool should be used during **Phase 2: Design Change** when completing the **Design Technology Changes, Design Organization Changes** and **Design Process Changes** tasks. It can also be used during the **Develop Implementation Plan** task.

Steps:

Listed below are some questions that you may selectively use to complete a challenge session:

1. To what extent does the change solution closely support the business strategy?
2. Does the change solution meet the vision and change scorecard objectives?
   - have the entire range of stakeholders (suppliers, customers, channel partners, etc.) been identified and incorporated into a stakeholder analysis and commitment plan?
   - has the communication plan targeted specific messages to each key stakeholder group? Are you confident you are using the most appropriate communication channels for the objective of each communication event?
   - have you periodically evaluated the effectiveness of communications?
3. Have you sufficiently decomposed the work plan into discrete tasks? Remember each activity takes time to complete, consumes resources, and that outputs for one activity often become inputs for others. The more tasks you forget the greater the chance of not completing the project on time and within budget.
4. Does the proposed organizational structure still incorporate the strengths from the current structure but minimize/eliminate key structural weaknesses?
5. Have you identified the new competencies that are required to successfully execute the change?
6. Have you identified the impacts the change will have on your core/support processes and business rules?
7. Were the short list of alternative change designs subjected to risk and financial analysis?
8. Have you identified the specific technology changes that must be implemented to support the new change?
9. Have you identified the specific organization/people changes that must be implemented to support the new change?
10. Do you fully understand the effect the change will have on your existing facilities asset base?
    - number/location of facilities
    - physical layout.
11. Do you have the right people doing the right work across the organization?
12. Does the new change require cultural alignment? What specific values/behaviors need to be enhanced or reduced?
13. Have the appropriate HR practices been modified to support the change?
    - career ladder
    - talent management/succession planning
    - recruiting
    - performance metrics
    - rewards/recognition

- performance management.

14. Have you developed a risk management plan to address the risks with the greatest probability of occurrence and the highest negative impact?

15. Is the change sponsor willing and able to:
    - remove those who are blocking the change?
    - actively and overtly demonstrate commitment to the change?
    - allocate sufficient resources to the project?
    - provide assistance in navigating organizational politics?

15. Elevator Speech

Description of tool:
This tool is used to very *concisely* and *consistently* communicate the key aspects of any change initiative. This includes:

- what is broken/why are you starting a new initiative?
- what is changing/not changing?
- what are the benefits from an organizational and individual perspective?
- general timelines
- high-level impacts.

When it is most likely to be used:
This tool can be used during **Phase 1: Create Change Platform** in the **Develop Communication Strategy** task. It is likely to be used throughout the project.

Steps:
1. **Identify the 4–5 key message bytes of information that all stakeholders need to understand about the change initiative.** As the name of the tool implies, imagine you are in an elevator and have one minute to not only describe, but to begin to solicit support for, an initiative you are involved in. During this first step identify and "test out" the specific information that is most meaningful to a stakeholder. Remember the focus is not on targeting the messages like you would during a communications strategy but is more about identifying the specific information all stakeholders need to know as you begin to announce the change initiative. If you have an internal communications staff they can be a useful resource during this initial step. Additionally, if you have developed a vision statement for the change this can be a key input when identifying the categories of information.

2. **Develop specific communications for each category of information.** Experience has taught us that this second step is iterative. Develop drafts of the script and begin testing it out on key members of the project team. Modify the content until there is consensus that the messages answer the initial blush of questions stakeholders have, are easy to understand, and most importantly, are consistent (to negate the effects of the rumor mill). The focus is a very

high-level conceptual overview of what you are trying to do, *not* a detailed explanation of any element within the change initiative.

3. **Deliver the Elevator Speech**. As you begin to interact with stakeholders deliver the elevator speech in a conversational tone. (It shouldn't sound rehearsed like you are reciting lines in a play). As the initiative begins to roll out, the elevator speech must evolve to coincide with the progress of the project. Once the project is underway communicate "quick wins," key project milestones, deliverables, etc.

4. **Integrate learnings into the communication and risk plans**. During the course of your elevator speeches it is not uncommon to not only share information but also to pick up valuable information that can be used during the subsequent phases of the project. Make sure you have in place a process for capturing these learnings and updating relevant deliverables during the project including the risk management, communications, and stakeholder engagement plans.

See Table B.14 for a completed example.

TABLE B.14 Example of completed elevator speech (organization restructuring)

Questions	Prepared Response
What is broken/why are you starting a new initiative?	• Our cost structure is 25% higher than the industry average. The largest component of cost is headcount. We have lost $20m last quarter.
What is changing/not changing?	• At a detailed level we are not sure yet, but we will be commencing a study to review the current structure, compare it to best practices, identify alternative structures, and select a high level design. • Process will take two months.
What is or is not in scope?	• The project will include only North American supply chain operations. • The sales and after service organizations are NOT in scope.
What are the benefits from and organizational and individual perspective?	• From an organizational standpoint, estimate operating cost savings of $9MM, cost avoidance $3MM, improved responsiveness to market changes, and enhance customer satisfaction. • From an individual standpoint, processes will be streamlined and much of the administrative content will be centralized so the mundane tasks will be ported over to other groups. Will be using a "caseworker" approach and work will be completed by teams who have responsibility for delivering their service from start to finish.

16. Executive Sponsor Assessment Instrument

Directions:

Utilize this tool to assess the level of executive sponsorship for the change initiative. Areas of weakness are opportunities and should be addressed in the overall change road map.

To what degree is the sponsor:	Not at all				To great extent
1. perceived as competent and trustworthy	1	2	3	4	5
2. highly committed to the change	1	2	3	4	5
3. able to influence stakeholders and has a demonstrated track record in being able to successfully implement change	1	2	3	4	5
4. embracing a clear vision of change that has been translated into metrics to evaluate the change initiative's success	1	2	3	4	5
5. decisive and has a track record of being able to make tough decisions	1	2	3	4	5
6. able to hold stakeholders accountable for achieving the vision	1	2	3	4	5
7. understanding that change requires an approach that balances process, technology, and people's needs	1	2	3	4	5
8. able and interested in actively meeting with key stakeholders to communicate his or her personal support	1	2	3	4	5
9. both a strategic and tactical thinker	1	2	3	4	5
10. able to secure sufficient resources to effectively implement the change	1	2	3	4	5

17. Focus Group Primer

Description of Tool:

A focus group is a facilitated, semi-structured meeting of selected individuals to discuss one or more key issues. A designated facilitator leads the focus group through a series of pre-established questions designed to elicit participants' perceptions about the issue. Participants' responses are captured by either the facilitator or a third party (administrative assistant or support staff). Avoid audio or videotaping the meeting because you are likely to get a filtering of answers.

When it is most likely to be used:

Like interviews, focus groups can be used at almost every task in the methodology. A focus group is commonly first used during **Phase 1: Create Change Platform** when completing the tasks **Develop Change Vision, Identify Impacted Stakeholders**, and **Develop Communication Strategy**. As the project progresses the tool can be used any time input is needed from a diverse population of stakeholders.

See Table B.15 for common focus group categories.

TABLE B.15 Common focus group categories

Common Focus Group Information Categories	
Reactions, perceptions, and experiences	What participants *think* about a specific issue
Concerns, obstacles, and opportunities	
Ideas, possible actions, and recommendations	What they *feel* about the issue
	Why they feel this way

The difference between interviews or surveys and focus groups is that focus groups yield rich qualitative information generated in a group context. Focus groups stimulate participant interactions and can yield insights about what influences their point of view. One of the tradeoffs of a focus group is that attendees' opinions can be influenced by the group they are in. The richness and depth of the information gathered during focus groups clarifies participants' thought patterns in a way that a survey can't. It allows the facilitator to drill down on a topic in contrast to a survey which is much more rigid.

Table B.16 presents an overview of the focus group process.

TABLE B.16 The focus group process

The Focus Group Process	
Step	Outcome
1. Identify/Clarify the Need	The purpose of the focus group, the information being sought, and how the results are specified.
2. Identify the Composition and Number of Groups	Specific participants for each focus group have been identified that reflect the characteristics of the overall group affected by the issue.
3. Understand the Facilitator Role, and Select a Scribe	A facilitator and a recorder have been selected.
4. Create the Focus Group Outline, Protocol, and Data Collection Sheets	The flow of the session is presented in the outline, with the discussion questions and probes listed in the protocol. Data collection sheets should be developed ahead of time and provided to each facilitator and scribe to ensure the data can be mapped across the entire effort.
5. Confirm Approach with Sponsor	The sponsor approves the outcomes from Steps 1–4, confidentiality of sessions, the process of inviting participants, and timing of the sessions.

TABLE B.16 *continued*

The Focus Group Process	
Step	*Outcome*
6. Prepare for the Session(s)	The location and logistics required for the focus groups are arranged.
7. Invite Participants	Invitations are sent to participants and their supervisors.
8. Conduct the Focus Group Session(s)	The focus group session(s) is completed and recorded.
9. Analyze Results	The major themes from the focus group(s) are identified and summarized.
10. Report Findings	Findings are reported to the sponsor and other appropriate individuals.

Steps:

1. **Identify/clarify the need**

   The first step in the process is to clarify the reason for conducting a focus group. This step should probably be conducted in conjunction with the person or people who will be sanctioning the effort and using the information from the focus group (e.g. the sponsor of the effort, a project manager). Some of the more common uses of employee focus groups are to:

   • Collect more in-depth information on a perceived problem or need (e.g. communication breakdowns, collecting data on the current culture, or customer service problems).

   • Assess reactions to a new or revised program, policy, or initiative (e.g., performance management program, mandatory training policy, quality initiative).

   • Generate ideas or recommendations (e.g. collecting data as part of a project).

   Before proceeding to Step 2 it is imperative to obtain consensus around:

   • Why are you conducting the focus group? What specific data do you want to collect?

   • How is this different from what we already know or what we can learn from other methods?

   • Who will we share results with? How will they use the information from the focus groups?

2. **Identify the composition and number of groups**

   The next step in the process is to establish the mix or composition of the focus groups and determine the number of focus groups to be conducted.

   Composition: If you have inexperienced focus group facilitators it is a good idea to restrict the size of the attendees to 20 or less. Some experienced facilitators can handle groups in excess of 50 people. When facilitating a larger group "time box" each question to keep the group task focused. This means assigning a specific time for attendees to answer each question and when that time has elapsed proceed to the next question.

The mix of focus group participants should be representative of the overall group of people that are involved or impacted by the issue. This does not mean that people should be randomly selected from the overall group. Representative simply means that the characteristics of the people who participate in the focus groups are similar to those of the overall employee group affected by the issue.

To develop a representative sample you should first identify any key characteristics of the overall group affected by the issue (e.g. their level in the organization, length of employment, department/division, gender). As much as possible, try to ensure that the distribution of participants across the focus groups reflects the distribution of people in the overall group. Each focus group need not be a microcosm of the larger group. Rather, ensure that you have the right mix of participants across focus groups (e.g. a focus group of leaders, a focus group of employees). *Do not create focus groups with either people who will restrict candid discussions (e.g. union leader, secretary to the President, etc.) or who are from different levels within the organization (especially superior/subordinate relationships) because that is likely to curtail the communications.*

Number of Groups: In general, you should run a greater number of focus groups whenever:

- there is a large group of people being affected by the issue
- the issue is more critical (i.e. the consequences of making the wrong decision are greater)
- you need a higher level of data confidence (directionally correct data vs. statistically reliable data).

3. **Understand facilitator role and identify a scribe**

Facilitator: The facilitator has a significant impact on the quality of information gathered from a focus group. A skilled facilitator is able to:

- lead the discussion
- make participants feel comfortable sharing their thoughts and feelings
- maintain objectivity
- probe to further clarify information
- use silence to draw out additional information
- limit digressions.

Scribe: This individual is responsible for capturing the information during the discussion. In addition to taking notes, it is useful if the scribe can synthesize the comments, identifying how it relates to the information that needs to be gathered. The scribe should understand the issue being considered.

4. **Create the Focus Group Outline, Protocol, and Data Collection Sheets**

Outline: Create an outline of how the focus group session will flow. Identify the sequence of events and the anticipated timing of those events. Focus groups typically run for 1–2 hours. See Step 8 for the typical flow of a focus group session.

Protocol: To make sure that the focus group yields the information that you need, develop a focus group protocol that lists the specific questions that will be asked. The use of a protocol ensures that the same questions are asked during each focus group and responses can be compared across focus groups.

Identify two or three main questions about the focal issue. These will serve as the primary points of discussion. Then identify two to three follow-up probes for each question. These can be used to help clarify the question or to draw out additional discussion if necessary.

If you are going to incorporate a "pulse survey" into the focus group session, do so at outset to ensure you have enough time to complete the survey. Make sure you stress anonymity. Do not ask anyone to sign the completed survey. Consider passing around a box so that attendees can put it in the box themselves.

In general, structure the flow of questions from the broad to the more narrow aspects of the issue. Avoid yes or no questions, since you want to stimulate discussion.

Data Collection Sheets: Ahead of time, think about alternative ways the data can be formatted to facilitate analysis. Any pre-formatted data collection sheets should support the type of questions included in the protocol.

5. **Confirm approach with sponsor**

   You may wish to review your progress to date with your sponsor and seek his or her approval. Review or re-confirm the following:
   - the purpose, outline, and protocol to ensure they will yield the desired information
   - the general characteristics of the intended focus groups to ensure adequate representation
   - the facilitator and the scribe (if necessary)
   - how participants will be notified and whether the sponsor needs to endorse or send the notification (see step 7)
   - any confidentiality agreements
   - the timing of the focus groups
   - reporting requirements and timing.

6. **Prepare for the session(s)**

   Once you've determined how many focus groups you will run, you need to take care of the logistics of the sessions. Determine the:
   - **Location.** The room where the focus group(s) are run should be comfortable and provide an environment conducive to open discussion.
   - **Seating arrangements.** The best seating arrangements use a round, U-shaped, or square room set-up. The objective is to have the focus group members able to see one another during the discussion without anyone appearing at the head of the table.

7. **Invite participants**

   Once you have identified participants for the focus group(s), send them a written communication asking them to attend. It should specify the purpose of the focus group, the date, time, location, whether confidentiality is guaranteed, and how the information gathered from the session will be used.

   You will need to inform the participants' supervisors that they have been asked to attend the focus group. It may be helpful to have the sponsor sign the letter to participants and the letter to supervisors to indicate the importance of the focus group.

8. **Conduct the focus group session**

   Most focus group sessions follow a similar flow. The facilitator should conduct the following activities:

   - **Introduce self and scribe (if used).** Explain the facilitator's and scribe's roles.
   - **Ask participants to introduce themselves** if they do not know each other.
   - **Explain the purpose of the session.** Explain why the participants have been selected and the purpose of the session, confirm confidentiality/anonymity, and provide any relevant background on the issue to make sure everyone understands what is being discussed.
   - **Establish ground rules** for the session. For example:
     - only one person to speak at a time
     - ensure anonymity
     - don't deviate from the focus group protocol
     - clearly communicate that your role is to ask questions *not* provide answers.
   - **Ask the questions and probes** contained in the focus group protocol. Encourage involvement among participants. Here are some ideas when asking the questions.
     - Avoid direct criticism of any participants. Criticism can discourage further participation for the person being criticized and everyone else in the group.
     - Don't be judgmental. Participants will assume that you have formed an opinion or perhaps sided with one group and may become reluctant to voice an opposing view.
     - Make sure the participants are doing most of the talking. Monitor your involvement. If you feel that you are talking too much, ask open-ended questions and then follow the next piece of advice.
     - Use silence or pauses to draw out information. The participants should feel the need to "fill the void" when you've asked a question; don't fill it for them.
     - Use paraphrasing to make sure you understand what someone is saying.
   - **Briefly summarize** the information that has been gathered.

- **Clarify** what information will be shared with the participants at the conclusion of the project (if any) and when that might occur.
- **Thank** participants.

  During the session, the scribe should record comments that are made by participants. The scribe should:
  - – Carefully summarize each respondent's points. Speed and timing may preclude the scribe from recording answers in sentences. Key bullet points are typically acceptable.
  - – At the completion of the focus group "scrub" the data to make sure that responses will *not* give away identities. It is important to understand *what* was said *not who* said it.

9. **Analyze results**

   Most focus groups are fast-paced with multiple people participating during the course of the session. Experience suggests that if you are requested to facilitate more than one focus group session that they are not scheduled back-to-back. This gives you a chance to summarize the notes into a more readable format as soon as the focus group has been completed. The best way to summarize information from several groups is to do a "content analysis." Listed below are some guidelines you might want to consider:

   - First, *review all of the notes* that have been recorded.
   - For each major question that was asked, *identify any general themes* in the responses (e.g. "resource shortages" or "ease of use"). Try to identify all potentially relevant themes, understand how prevalent each theme is, and which stakeholders agreed with this theme (e.g. were people from manufacturing more likely to have the same perception?). You can collapse themes later if necessary.
   - Go back through the recorded information and *identify those responses that are related to each theme*. Be aware that some responses to a subsequent question may relate to an earlier theme.
   - *Cluster the responses* that relate to a specific theme. Revise your clusters as necessary.
   - Try to *summarize the results* to each of the major questions. Review the primary purpose of the focus groups. Try to use the conclusions to address the primary purpose of the focus groups. If necessary, revisit prior steps in the content analysis process until the picture becomes clearer.

10. **Report findings**

    Once you have analyzed your findings from the focus groups, you should present them back to the sponsor and other key stakeholders as agreed in Steps 1 and 5.

18. Impact Analysis Template

Description of tool:

This tool can be used to proactively identify how any proposed change initiative will impact the organization.

All organizations, whether they are Fortune 500 conglomerates or "mom and pop" family companies, have an architecture that is comprised of three distinct elements: technology, organization, and process. Technology is comprised of the data employees need to make decisions, the information systems hardware (networks, servers, PCs, etc.), the production/operations technology that is instrumental in delivering your core product/service, and the software applications that interface with process and hardware. The organization is comprised of the business systems (e.g. planning, budgeting), human resource practices (everything from recruiting and rewards to succession planning), workforce competencies, and the organization structure (job design, reporting relationships, staffing levels). The process element is composed of the administrative policies or business rules that drive behavior, the business processes, physical infrastructure of the business (the site strategy–number and location of work sites), and physical layout of work areas (the arrangement of offices, conference rooms, etc.). The value of this tool is that it will allow you to *proactively* identify the *specific* "ripple effects" of any change initiative to both minimize the time needed for implementation and optimize the potential for success.

When it is most likely to be used:

The impact analysis tool is most commonly used during **Phase 2: Design Change** when completing the **Identify Impacts on Architecture** task. It is updated during **Phase 3: Implement Change**.

Steps:

1. **Complete impact analysis template to understand impact on the business architecture.** This matrix can be used to facilitate discussions around the likely impacts any change initiative will have on each element of architecture. Make sure you spend sufficient time vetting each element of architecture. Pay careful attention to understanding impacts to each function/ department and job/group. This matrix can be used to ensure your future state solution addresses all of the necessary change management elements.

2. **Complete impact analysis template to understand impact on stakeholders.** This matrix can be used in conjunction with the stakeholder assessment completed earlier to ensure all key stakeholders have been identified, the impacts of the design changes are fully understood, and that the solution has effectively addressed all key stakeholder impacts/concerns.

3. **Integrate learnings into the transition plan**. A well-crafted change project utilizes a discovery process. The completion of each tool provides an output that ultimately becomes an input to some other activity (risk management, communications, detailed change work plans, stakeholder engagement) downstream.

See Table B.17 for a completed example.

TABLE B.17 Completed example of impact analysis template

Technology Architecture	Description of Impact	Criticality
• Applications	• Retirement of legacy systems to SAP • Centralization of customer related credit risk	H
• Data	• Need to create relational databases	L
• Hardware	• None	
• Production technology	• None	
Organization Architecture	**Description of Impact**	**Criticality**
• HR practices	• Align rewards and recognition programs to drive desired behaviors • Modify performance management process	H M
• Competencies	• Major job redesign will create major competency gaps relating to the following areas: XYZ	M
• Structure	• Following functions and jobs are heavily impacted as follows • Function X/Job Y (here are the specific impacts)	H
• Business rules/policies	• Need to change the following policies	M
Process architecture	**Description of Impact**	**Criticality**
• Processes	• Streamlined credit, claims, and collections processes across the organization • Added customer self-service capabilities • Increased automation of processes and status/actions tracking • Centralized issuing of adjustment	M
• Facilities	• Need to close office in New York City • Need to close warehouse in Atlanta	H H
• Physical layout	• Redesign layout in corporate headquarters to better utilize team concept	M
Stakeholder group	**Description of Impact**	**Criticality**
• Customers	• Decreased response time to customer inquiries • Increased capability for audit trail	H
• Suppliers/vendors	• Expect 50% reduction in raw material suppliers	H
• Other?		

19. Individual Progress Reporting Template

Description of tool:
This tool is used to report the progress of an individual change initiative. By customizing the tool you can evaluate the progress of the initiative from a deliverable, targeted result, or budgeting standpoint.

When it is most likely to be used:
This tool should be used during the **Phase 1: Create Change Platform** during the **Establish PMO** task. Once developed the tool should then be used to manage each project until close-out.

Steps:
1. **Confirm the specific attributes you want to track.** This can range from projected targets and budget to team and project effectiveness variables.
2. **Agree on frequency of reporting.** Typically the more complex and the longer the project's duration, the more frequent the reporting. Most projects use a bi-weekly or monthly progress reporting frequency.
3. **Develop a process for addressing variances.** A variance occurs any time desired performance does not meet actual performance.

See Tables B.18 and B.19 for a completed example.

TABLE B.18 Example of completed progress reporting template – task/deliverable status

Overall Project Scorecard
Project Name: Acquisition of SYX company
Report Date: 1/1/XX
Project Manager: Johnny Appleseed

Legend/Key (Green: None; Yellow: Minor Impact, threaten schedule; Red: Major Impact, delay schedule)	Planned Comp. Date	Green	Yellow	Red
Overall Project Schedule		●		
Key Tasks/Deliverables				
• Task 1: Completed physical asset analysis		●		
• Task 2: Completed supply chain analysis		●		
• Task 3: Consolidated Akron and Canton offices		●		
• Deliverable 1: Revised org structure for operations		●		
• Deliverable 2: Inventory reduction plan		●		
• Task/Deliverable 7				
• Task/Deliverable 8				

TABLE B.19 Example of completed progress reporting template – synergy status

Legend/Key (Green: on target to achieve; Yellow: Slightly behind schedule; Red: significantly behind schedule/in danger of not meeting)	Planned Comp. Date	Green	Yellow	Red
Synergy Attainment			●	
• Reduce operating costs by $30MM		●		
• Reduce headcount by 40 FTE		●		
• Increase market share by 2%				●
• Consolidate plant operations and save $40MM			●	
• Synergy/Target 5				
• Synergy/Target 6				
• Synergy/Target 7				

20. Interview Primer

Description of tool:
From a time and cost standpoint interviews utilize the most resources but can be extremely useful when trying to collect politically sensitive information or when confidentiality is critical.

When it is most likely to be used:
Interviews can be used at almost every step in the change methodology. Most often interviews are used during **Phase 1: Create Change Platform** during the **Assess Change Readiness** and **Identify Impacted Stakeholders** tasks.

Interviewing is also commonly used during the design and implementation phases whenever it may be necessary to collect additional information to learn more about a change issue.

Table B.20 contains tips for interviewing.

TABLE B.20 Tips for interviewing

Tips for Interviewing

- Finalize logistics. Interviews can be conducted one-on-one, in a group setting, in-person, or via teleconference. Take the time to determine the most appropriate venue based on budget, time, and the type/sensitivity of information you want to collect. When scheduling interviews, be sure to leave 30 minutes in between interviews to allow sufficient time to summarize your notes and allow for meetings that start/end late.
- Always develop a formal protocol of interview questions. Start with the decisions you want to make as a result of the completed interview, then identify the data you will need to collect, and translate that into a series of questions. Avoid yes/no questions.
- Clarify the purpose of the interview at the beginning of each meeting and confirm any of the ground rules (e.g. will maintain anonymity)
- Ask the easy and general questions first and then after you have built up a rapport segue to the questions that are more complex and politically sensitive.
- Be flexible so that you can ask unscripted questions when a respondents answer opens up an unexpected door.

- Maintain time and information control of the discussion. Don't let the discussion go off on a non-productive tangent.
- At the conclusion of the interview, level set expectations. (What will happen next, how will the data be used, project next steps and timelines, etc.)
- Immediately after the interview, review your notes to make sure they are legible. Add any perceptions you have that echo key points in the interview.
- When reviewing the entire data collected across all of the interviewees analyze the data to identify:
  - General themes
  - Key quotes (if you are going to maintain confidentiality make sure you scrub the quotes to ensure they cannot be linked to a particular individual)
  - Look for any specific and unique findings
  - Remember to let the data drive the conclusion and not have preconceived perceptions and cherry pick data to confirm these perceptions.

21. Issue Escalation Template

Description of tool:
During the life cycle of a change project it is common to identify a handful of issues that need to be elevated to a higher level. This is usually the result of differing perspectives relative to an issue that cannot be resolved, so typically an individual with position power makes the decision. It may also be an issue that goes beyond the decision rights that have been delegated to a project management team.

When it is most likely to be used:
This tool should be used during **Phase 1: Create Change Platform** during the **Establish PMO** task. Once developed the tool should then be used to manage each project until close-out.

Steps:
1. Make sure you have defined roles and decision rights for each of the project teams.
2. Develop formal procedures for surfacing and resolving conflict.
3. When issues arise that either cannot be resolved or exceed the decision-making authority of the project team complete the template below and forward it to the decision-making authority.

See Table B.21 for a completed example.

TABLE B.21 Example of completed issue escalation template

Project Name: Organization restructuring
Date Submitted: 1/1/xx
Person Elevating Issue: Walter Mason

Project Problems Needing Help/ Decisions Requested	Recommendations (if any)	Approved By	Date
• Can we outsource non strategic functionality?	• Outsource printing, landscaping, and security		
• Have excess warehouse capacity	• Hartford location is fully owned. Can we sell it and consolidate operations with Stamford		

22. Meeting Management Template

Description of tool:
This tool should be used in any of the following ways:

1. Assist in *planning* any project related meeting
2. *Leading* meetings to ensure they are completed in a timely manner and achieve the desired outcomes
3. *Project coordination* to ensure action items are completed, for cross team coordination, or filed in a central repository (e.g. E-room) so that they are accessible to key stakeholders (other team members, other project teams, management)

When it is most likely to be used:
This tool should be used during the **Phase 1: Create Change Platform** during the **Establish PMO** task. Once developed the tool should then be used to manage each project until close-out.

Steps:
The most critical learning associated with good project management is a well-defined process with supporting governance and the discipline to adhere to the prescribed approach and supporting tools. Listed below are the key components of the template that need some level of clarification.

1. **Define the meeting objective(s).** Think through the purpose, reasons, and/or outcomes of the meeting. Confirm in your mind that a meeting is the most useful mechanism to achieve the outcome.
2. **Decide who should attend the meeting**.
3. **Develop a meeting agenda and any other background or handout materials.** Sequence items and allocate time on the agenda according to the importance of each agenda item in achieving the meeting objectives. Distribute to each attendee *before* the meeting.
4. **Advise participants what *role* they will play** for different items on the agenda.
5. **Identify the facilities (room) and resources needed** (e.g. flip chart, computers, grease board, overhead projector) to achieve the objectives for the meeting. Schedule the meeting room to ensure its availability.

Leading the meeting:
1. Appoint a person to take notes (decisions made, who is responsible, unresolved issues, next steps, etc.) at each meeting.
2. Begin the meeting by restating the objectives, desired outcomes/products, and meeting process procedures.
3. The leader should moderate the meeting (during conflict it is important to maintain an open, non-defensive style), keep discussions focused, encourage participation, assess group process, and obtain group consensus on actions to be taken.
4. Before ending the meeting summarize the main points of discussion, decisions made, responsibilities and timelines agreed upon, and next steps.
5. Periodically debrief participants to assess their satisfaction with the meeting, issues that adversely affected meeting effectiveness, and suggestions to improve group process.
6. As a group, decide on the next meeting's agenda.

Follow-up:
1. Distribute notes to all participants.
2. Ensure action items do not fall through the cracks.
3. Hold participants accountable for tasks they are responsible for.
4. Develop periodic progress reports.

See Table B.22 for a completed example.

TABLE B.22 Completed example of meeting management template

Team Name:	PMO		Project Mgr: P Carson
Date	Nov 23, 2004	*Meeting Objective*	PMO Planning Meeting
Attendees	• P. Carson • J. Taymor • M. Harmon • M. Smith • R. Recardo		
Agenda Item	*Time Allotted*	*Actions/Decisions*	*Person Responsible*
1. Finalize proposed Sub-Team ground rules	5 min	• Develop first draft	• Mark Harrington
2. Obtain consensus on exercises for each Sub-Team during meeting on W Coast.	15 min	• Identify specific changes to each exercise	• Chris Williamson
3. Obtain consensus on overall project roadmap	15 min	• Identify specific changes	• Lou Perrini
4. Agree on detailed in/out of scope descriptions	25 min	• Final draft	• George Billingsley
5. Agree on draft of project governance procedures and tools	20 min	• Final draft	• Mark Harrington
6. Identify the type, frequency, and key message bytes for Change Leadership Team Clinical Council and 4 Sub-Teams.	15 min	• Communication plan	• VP Communications
7. Finalize GCO past, Present, and Future presentation	10 min	• Presentation draft with modifications	• Harry Ratner

23. Missionary Assessment Instrument

Directions:

Utilize this instrument to either identify potential people to act as a missionaries (individuals who will be actively involved in making the change happen) or to assess a missionary's strengths and weaknesses.

The missionary…	Not at all				To great extent
1. has the appropriate competencies and experiences (strategic change management, project management, team building, conflict management, etc.) relative to the change initiative	1	2	3	4	5
2. is highly committed to the change	1	2	3	4	5
3. understands and has a demonstrated track record in being able to influence people	1	2	3	4	5
4. has well developed verbal and written communication skills	1	2	3	4	5
5. is well organized, detail-oriented, and able to work on multiple tasks at once	1	2	3	4	5
6. will hold stakeholders accountable for achieving the vision	1	2	3	4	5
7. understands that change requires an approach that balances process, technology, and people issues	1	2	3	4	5
8. is an active role model	1	2	3	4	5
9. is both a strategic and tactical thinker	1	2	3	4	5
10. understands the importance of and is willing utilize rewards/penalties to ensure success of the change	1	2	3	4	5
11. is trusted by key internal/external stakeholders and viewed as a "person who gets things done"	1	2	3	4	5
12. is able to work with varying levels of ambiguity without becoming frustrated	1	2	3	4	5
13. is results oriented and *not* activity oriented	1	2	3	4	5
14. is creative and able to "think beyond the box"	1	2	3	4	5
15. is analytical and skilled at problem solving	1	2	3	4	5

24. PMO Best Practice Assessment

Description of tool:

This tool is used to assess performance of the change program management organization (PMO) for the change initiative. Assessment is conducted relative to best practice standards for effective and efficient change program management and operation. PMO best practice dimensions include:

- Process
- Organization/people
- Technology.

The results of the assessment can be used to adjust and tune the Change PMO's processes, infrastructure and resources to best meet the needs of the change initiative. The best practices can also be used in setting up the Change PMO.

When it is most likely to be used:
This tool should be used periodically throughout all four phases to determine if the change initiative is getting what it needs from the change program management organization. It should also be deployed if and when serious and consistent problems are occurring in the program management and operation of the change initiative. Additionally, this tool can be used as a checklist for defining the initial infrastructure, process and resource needs the change PMO needs to establish in **Phase 1: Create Change Platform**, during the **Establish PMO** task.

Tables B.23 through B25 depict the best practice assessment template across the three dimensions.

TABLE B.23 PMO Best practice assessment – process

	Applicability		Currently Utilized	
I. PMO/Project Management Process Best Practices	*Yes*	*No*	*Yes*	*No*
1. Produces and routes project progress and status reports that are appropriate for their audience, and for their timing				
2. Performs variance, trend and exception analysis of Time, Cost, Scope, Risk and Quality planned vs. actual status through the project				
3. Escalates issues/key decisions to those who can act on them, and acts quickly on those within his or her control				
4. Prioritizes the portfolio of projects based on each one's business case and linkages to enterprise strategy				
5. Establishes a formal Project Charter that includes project outcomes, deliverables, delineation of what is/not in scope, and a resource/high level plan				
6. Estimates overall project effort and cost using multiple methods, documenting the assumptions, or key factors that affect the estimates				
7. Develops and executes a risk management plan that identifies actions for delaying, minimizing, or eliminating key project risks				

	Applicability		Currently Utilized	
I. PMO/Project Management Process Best Practices	*Yes*	*No*	*Yes*	*No*
8. Structures project phases with a Work Breakdown Structure and Activity Lists at the detail needed for the activity and the staff				
9. Uses Precedence Analysis (map outputs to inputs and critical path) to identify activity relationships				
10. Performs Resource Analysis to reduce over-commitment or underutilization of staff/PMO resources				
11. Use of a standard methodology with a scalable set of supporting tools that are always used				
12. Completes a formal "Lessons Learned" at the end of each project where the methodology and supporting tools are updated				
13. Performs Post-Project Reviews, including evaluation of how well the project met the business need				
14. Data is collected on past projects and is used to estimate cost/time of future projects				
15. Use contingency funds and queuing buffers to ensure schedule and budget achievement				
16. Formal process is used to manage scope change				
17. Formal process for terminating projects				
18. Use of a formal and effective process for coordinating the efforts of interdependent projects				

TABLE B.24 PMO Best practice assessment – organization/people

	Applicability		Currently Utilized	
II. PMO/Project Management Organization/People Best Practices	*Yes*	*No*	*Yes*	*No*
1. Effectively matches the skills of available staff to phase activities and assures understanding of assignments before work begins				
2. Develops and executes a communication plan that includes audiences, responsibilities, media, content, and frequency				
3. Governance (role & decision making clarity) is formalized across the PMO process and the organisation structures (including teams) that interface with it				
4. Usage of project scorecards that include both project process and outcome metrics				

TABLE B.24 *continued*

	Applicability		Currently Utilized	
	Yes	*No*	*Yes*	*No*
II. PMO/*Project Management Organization/People Best Practices*				
5. Project scorecard metrics are cascaded down into the performance appraisals of project team members				
6. Project managers have direct input into the overall performance appraisals of all team members				
7. PMO reports directly to an executive level				
8. PMO periodically performs project performance audits				
9. Use of certifications and formal development pathways to rationalize capabilities across the function				
10. HR tools/process (recruiting, performance management, rewards) are tightly aligned to PMO				

TABLE B.25 PMO Best practice assessment – technology

	Applicability		Currently Utilized	
	Yes	*No*	*Yes*	*No*
III. PMO/*Project Management Technology Best Practices*				
1. Automated systems (e.g. Microsoft Project, Excel) are used throughout the enterprise for planning/managing all projects				
2. Utilization of project management data base that tracks historical time on task, project learnings, etc.				
3. Knowledge library used				
4. Application tools that provide electronic scorecarding at the project, team, and individual levels				
5. Extensive utilization of e-rooms & intranet sites				
6. Effective use of applications (e.g. I Think) to complete "what if" simulations				
7. Methodologies, tools and templates are available to all Project Managers and key stakeholders electronically				
8. Application tools that manage document version control				
9. Effective use of PERT analysis				
10. Use of Monte Carlo analysis for portfolio management				
11. Use enterprise development tools to develop finanical projections and resource management				
12. Portfolio application used for prioritization and resource allocation				

25. Project Close-out and Lessons Learned

Description of tool:
Most Fortune 1000 companies have many different change initiatives being implemented simultaneously. Many organizations do not have the luxury of a large staff that can support these projects so different individuals are staffing each project. The shortcoming of this model is that organizations often "re-learn" the same things over and over. This tool is used to capture learnings from a completed change initiative. It can be used to identify specific opportunities to improve:

- any step/task within the change management process
- supporting tools/templates
- the capabilities/competencies of change team members.

When it is most likely to be used:
This tool should be used to formally mark the completion of a change project. It should be included as the last step in all work plans completed in conjunction with the project sponsor to acknowledge the successful completion of the project.

Steps:
1. **Schedule a meeting with the project sponsor.** Begin the meeting by discussing the change project in terms of planned vs. actual results achieved and then segue to a discussion on the quality and completeness of each deliverable. Ask for specific feedback on the effectiveness of the project manager and feedback on each project team member. Feedback can also be obtained on the key missionaries.
2. **Identify lessons learned.** Jointly identify or propose specific changes to the existing project management process, change management process and supporting tools/templates. Actively solicit the feedback of line leaders who were impacted by the change.
3. **Identify specific next steps.** Identify the timing and responsibility of changes to either the process or supporting tools. Also identify how these changes will be communicated and the learnings are transferred to relevant staff.

See Table B.26 for a completed example.

TABLE B.26 Example of completed project close-out/lessons learned template

Project Name: XYZ new product intro

Section 1: Project Close-out

Sponsor/customer has accepted all project results:

		Yes/No:
1	Completed by 12/12/xx	Yes
2	Zero deviation from budget	Yes
3		

Sponsor/customer has accepted all other deliverables:

		Yes/No:
1	Deliverable 1	Yes
2	Deliverable 2	Yes
3	Deliverable 3	Yes, deliverable was 2 weeks late
4	Deliverable 4	Yes
5	Deliverable 5	Yes, quality was spotty
6		

Sponsor/customer feedback Project Manager and Project Team Members:

- Project Manager was very knowledgeable but tended to be reactive. Did not follow process and did not use risk management tool that adversely impacted deliverables 3 and 5.

Project Name: XYZ new product intro

Section 2: Lessons Learned

Modifications to specific project management process:
- Use CPM
- Develop process for coordinating interdependent project teams

Modifications to specific project management tools/templates:
- Develop project costing/time estimation template

New knowledge/training opportunities:
- Get more people certified in project mgt

Who should be informed about this Lesson Learned? (check one)

	Mgt Board	×	Project Manager(s)	×	Project Team(s)		All Staff
	Other:						

How should this Lesson Learned be disseminated? (check all that apply)

	e-mail		Intranet/Web site		Tip Sheet/FAQ		Library
×	Other:						

Project Manager: Harry Smith	*Signature:* ____ *Date:* ____
Sponsor/customer: Margaret Potter	*Signature:* ____ *Date:* ____

26. Project Management Process Pulse Survey

Directions:

This survey is used to assess the effectiveness of the project management process for the change initiative. The data collected should be used to better target project planning and also serve as an input to the risk management, project work plans, and stakeholder engagement plans. The survey should be administered to members of the change initiative project team. Have participants read each question carefully and select the response that most closely corresponds to his/her perception. At the end of each section there is a place to note any additional comments they feel are pertinent.

Regarding Project XXX:	*To a very great extent*	*To a considerable extent*	*To a moderate extent*	*To a limited extent*	*Not at all*
1. I understand the Project XXX methods, terminology used, tools, and templates	1	2	3	4	5
2. The project-related training has allowed me to effectively complete the work that has been assigned to me	1	2	3	4	5
3. I have the appropriate resources (facilities, right team members, budget, equipment) to be successful in my role within Project XXX	1	2	3	4	5
4. I understand my role and limits of decision-making authority relative to Project XXX	1	2	3	4	5
5. There are formal procedures in place for:					
• Scope change	1	2	3	4	5
• Dependency management	1	2	3	4	5
• Document management	1	2	3	4	5
• Progress monitoring/reporting	1	2	3	4	5
• Risk management	1	2	3	4	5
• Key decisions/issue escalation	1	2	3	4	5
• Knowledge capture	1	2	3	4	5
6. A detailed overall work plan exists, this work plan cascades down to each team, what's in/out of scope, inputs/outputs between each team are known, and the "critical path" across the entire project is well understood.	1	2	3	4	5

Regarding Project XXX:	To a very great extent	To a considerable extent	To a moderate extent	To a limited extent	Not at all
7. Senior Management is highly committed to the success of the project	1	2	3	4	5
8. My direct manager is highly committed to the success of Project XXX	1	2	3	4	5
9. The deliverables of my team have been clearly communicated to me	1	2	3	4	5
10. My direct manager has proportionately reassigned the responsibilities of my day-to-day job so I can be successful with project XXX	1	2	3	4	5
11. I believe that Project XXX is important to our organization's future	1	2	3	4	5
12. I understand how this project is contributing to realizing the change and business benefits	1	2	3	4	5
13. What is working particularly well from a project perspective?					
14. What do you see are the biggest risks to the project? What are your specific suggestions for addressing these key risks?					

27. Project Team Assessment Survey

Directions:

Utilize this instrument to assess the effectiveness of change teams throughout the change initiative cycle as needed.

The Change Team:	Not at all				To a great extent
1. is measured on clear performance metrics.	1	2	3	4	5
2. periodically evaluates its internal team process (how well it is working as a team).	1	2	3	4	5
3. coordinates efforts with others and interdependent teams.	1	2	3	4	5
4. shares information easily among groups or individuals needing it.	1	2	3	4	5
5. listens to each other.	1	2	3	4	5

The Change Team:	Not at all				To a great extent
6. is not afraid to address issues of importance or politically sensitive subjects.	1	2	3	4	5
7. Uses the terms "we" and "us" instead of "I," "me," or "you."	1	2	3	4	5
8. praises or recognizes individuals efforts, contributions, or successes.	1	2	3	4	5
9. have meetings which are focused and have clear agendas, enthusiastic and equal participation, and result in decisions being made or actions taken.	1	2	3	4	5
10. is open to new information, ideas, and more productive approaches for doing things.	1	2	3	4	5
11. seeks clarification frequently and comfortably e.g. "Did you mean...?" "Tell me more about that..."	1	2	3	4	5
12. surfaces and resolves conflict including team issues.	1	2	3	4	5
13. has a formal charter that specifies performance expectations, roles and responsibilities, decision levels, and internal processes.	1	2	3	4	5
14. is very comfortable taking informed risks.	1	2	3	4	5
15. has confidence and trust in each other.	1	2	3	4	5
16. communicates candidly with each other without filtering difficult messages.	1	2	3	4	5
17. has been provided the necessary education for the team to be successful.	1	2	3	4	5
18. accepts and supports decisions made by the team.	1	2	3	4	5
19. periodically reviews how well it is working.	1	2	3	4	5
20. has rebalanced its members' day-to-day job responsibilities with change project responsibilities.	1	2	3	4	5

28. Readiness Assessment Instrument

Directions:

Utilize this instrument to assess whether the organization and its stakeholders are ready to implement any change initiative.

Part I: Organizational readiness

	Not at all				To a great extent
1. The timing of the project will not adversely affect its success (not too many other competing initiatives, fit with business cycle, etc.).	1	2	3	4	5
2. Senior management actively supports the change	1	2	3	4	5
3. The change initiative is fully integrated with other planned/ongoing initiatives.	1	2	3	4	5
4 The organization has a history of failed change initiatives.	1	2	3	4	5
5. The change initiative has not taken into consideration and addressed organizational "politics."	1	2	3	4	5
6. The organization will be able to allocate sufficient resources to successfully implement the change.	1	2	3	4	5
7. The change process is guided by a vision and cascading measures.	1	2	3	4	5
8. Management "walks the talk" regarding the change.	1	2	3	4	5
9. The organization's existing culture is closely aligned with the change initiative.	1	2	3	4	5
10. The change initiative is based on a well thought out and field-tested approach.	1	2	3	4	5

Part II: Stakeholder readiness

	Not at all				To a great extent
11. The change initiative will require considerably different employee behaviors.	1	2	3	4	5
12. There are plans in place to periodically "sense" stakeholders via pulse surveys, focus groups, etc.	1	2	3	4	5
13. Champions and missionaries are trusted by stakeholders.	1	2	3	4	5

Part II: Stakeholder readiness *continued*

	Not at all				To a great extent
14. Stakeholders understand why the change initiative must be implemented and have a sense of urgency to implement it.	1	2	3	4	5
15. Key human resource systems (e.g. selection, performance management, reward, recognition) will be modified to closely support the change.	1	2	3	4	5
16. Stakeholders believe the change can be implemented successfully.	1	2	3	4	5
17. The organization has a plan for carefully communicating to stakeholders.	1	2	3	4	5
18. Programs will be developed to equitably address concerns of stakeholder who are negatively impacted.	1	2	3	4	5
19. Stakeholders have a history of past unresolved issues with the organization.	1	2	3	4	5
20. There is a process in place to solicit stakeholders input and concerns.	1	2	3	4	5

29. Risk Assessment Instrument

Directions:

Utilize this instrument to assess the risk and ultimately the *potential for success* of any change initiative.

The change initiative...	Not at all				To a great extent
1. will require significant modifications to the existing organizational culture.	1	2	3	4	5
2. will solve a problem or threat that is widely known and understood.	1	2	3	4	5
3. is fully integrated with other planned/ongoing initiatives.	1	2	3	4	5
4 will not impact the organization across a number of functions, locations, or business units.	1	2	3	4	5
5. is not competing with other large change initiatives for senior management's attention.	1	2	3	4	5
6. is designed with the input of key stakeholder groups.	1	2	3	4	5

The change initiative...	Not at all				To a great extent
7. has identified all impacts and ripple effects within the organization.	1	2	3	4	5
8. will not require considerable changes to an existing collective bargaining agreement.	1	2	3	4	5
9. utilizes a detailed project plan that identifies all activities, timelines, and resource requirements.	1	2	3	4	5
10. utilizes a commitment and communication plan.	1	2	3	4	5

30. Risk Management Tool

Description of tool:
One of the key success factors in change management is the early identification and prioritization of risks. This tool is used to either *eliminate* the most critical risks or *reduce their negative impact* on the success of the change initiative.

When it is most likely to be used:
This tool should be first used during **Phase 1: Create Change Platform** when completing the **Establish PMO** task. Risk management is best implemented via a "discovery" process where the plan is periodically updated and executed throughout the project's life cycle. Learnings from the risk management plan should be integrated into the overall project, engagement, and communication plans.

Steps:
1. Collect archival data and information from a variety of impacted stakeholders to identify the risks to the project.
2. Organize the risks according to themes (organization risks, technology risks, process risks, leadership, etc.).
3. Obtain consensus on the probability of occurrence of each risk.
4. Understand the consequences or impact the risk will have on both the organization and the project.
5. Generally, it is a good idea to focus on the risks with the greatest probability of occurrence and largest impact on the project. Fully discuss and then agree on some targeted actions that will either eliminate the risk or minimize its negative impact.
6. For each action assign one person (not a team) overall responsibility for its execution.
7. Identify a date to complete the implementation of each action.

See Table B.27 for a completed example.

TABLE B.27 Example of completed risk analysis tool

Key Risks	Probability of Impact (H,M,L)	Severity of Impact (H,M,L)	Consequences	Response	Owner	Comp. Date
Resources not allocated that were planned or requested (e.g. provide communications people, employees from Research & Policy for process documentation)	High	High	Reduced buy-in, considerable confusion, reduced confidence in project team	Review overall work plan and recommend resource reallocations. Review resource requirements for each project team and make recommendations to PMO.	R Richards	24-Mar
Critical Path Management not being used	High	High	Possible delays at go-live, additional resistance	Project plan being updated with more detail. Will focus additional effort managing work interdependencies between work streams and where critical handoffs are occurring. On a weekly basis PMO will enhance reporting capability regarding monitoring project progress and personnel assignments. CPM will be implemented immediately.	N Thanjan	7-Apr

31. Quick Wins Tool

Description of Tool:
A quick wins tool can be used to identify and implement "low hanging fruit," or those components of the overall change initiative that demonstrate considerable progress/impact and:

- require little design effort (e.g. start/stop doing something);
- minimal budget;
- can be implemented typically within 30–60 days.

When it is most likely to be used:
This tool should be used at any task in **Phase 1: Create Change Platform** or **Phase 2: Design Change** when high impact, clearly beneficial opportunities for change, which are relatively quick and easy to execute (i.e. low hanging fruit), have been identified. Many large-scale change projects can be broken down into sub-projects, change solutions, or mini-projects. Some of these are clearly evident opportunities for showcasing early change results that provide quick wins, immediate benefits, and enhance support for the change. These projects or recommendations should go straight to the implementation phase (Phase 3).

Steps:
1. Review the change scorecard and the overall change road map and work stream work plans. Identify potential synergies or benefits that meet quick wins criteria. Key data inputs include:
   - summary of benchmarking data (if used)
   - interview summary of customers, suppliers, or key stakeholders
   - feedback/recommendations from staff
   - summary of a performance gap analysis.
   Remember that a quick win could be as easy as stopping doing an activity which will yield immediate cost avoidance or cost savings.
2. Assign responsibility for capturing quick wins
3. Execute quick wins rapidly
4. Publicize quick wins via the communications strategy to create enthusiasm and momentum around the integration

See Figure B.19 for a completed example.

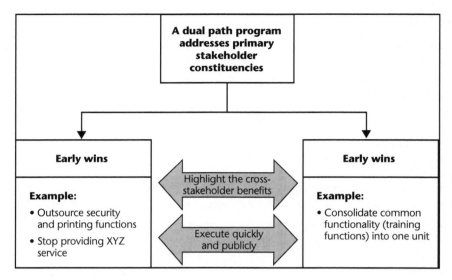

FIGURE B.19 Example of completed quick wins tool

32. Scope Change Request

Description of tool:
Although not recommended, there will be times when it is appropriate to change the scope of a project to be either narrower or broader. This tool is used to ensure that the scope of the project does not mistakenly advance beyond its contracted boundaries. Before the scope can be modified the appropriate individual or team must approve any changes to scope.

Scope changes will impact resource requirements, project timelines, and deliverables. Scope creep is the number one reason why projects are not completed on time and within budget.

When it is most likely to be used:
This tool should be used during **Phase 1: Create Change Platform** during the **Establish PMO** task. Once developed the tool should then be used to manage each project until close-out.

Steps:
1. Make sure you have defined roles and decision rights for each of the project teams.
2. Fully understand the impact and cost of the proposed scope change.
3. Develop formal procedures for surfacing and resolving conflict. When issues arise that either cannot be resolved or exceed the decision-making authority of the project team complete the template below and forward it to the decision-making authority.

See Table B.28 for a completed example.

TABLE B.28 Example of completed scope change request template

Project Name: Project New Look – Redesign of the Talent Management Process		
Date: 2/1/xx	*Project Manager:* Charlie Sutter	*Submitted by:* Otto Karras

Description of Proposed Change:
Upstream activities or inputs that were not part of the original scope are key reasons why our internal talent pools are not sufficient. We need to update the competency model that is comprised of leadership behaviors only. Want/need to create a section for functional competencies. Also need to modify the talent acquisition process, employment value proposition, and the supporting templates.

Reason for Change (Benefits):
After completing the data collection and root cause analysis it was determined that the primary reasons why there are weak internal talent pools is because the competency model is not aligned to the future needs of the business, and the talent acquisition process needs to be redesigned. 70% of external hires at mid-level management and above leave the organization within 16 months.

Implications of Not Making This Change:
Will increase project timelines by two months. Will need to involve HR Business Partners and Corporate Succession Planning group.

Impact Analysis

Manufacturing capacity	X *Project resources*
Cost/budget	*Impact on other projects*
X *Timeline*	X *Project deliverables*
Project outcomes	Other?

Approved:	*Yes:*	*No:*

33. Stakeholder Assessment and Commitment Plan

Description of tool:

A stakeholder is defined as any individual or constituent group within or outside of the organization that can either impact or is impacted by the change initiative. Research studies suggest that stakeholder identification and management is directly linked to completing a change project in a timely manner and to realizing targeted outcomes.

The stakeholder assessment is a key input into the development of several deliverables across a change project including the communication plan, overall change road map and plans for each work stream, the risk management plan, and commitment plans.

When it is most likely to be used:
This tool is first used during **Phase 1: Create Change Platform** when completing the **Identify Impacted Stakeholders** task. It is updated and used throughout the change life cycle.

Steps:
Before using this tool consensus should be arrived at relative to the time/resources available to complete this activity, the scope of analysis and your familiarity with the stakeholders, and the level of accuracy desired (directionally correct information vs. level of validity).

Data is best collected via a "pulse survey" or through focus groups. In cases where you are very familiar with the stakeholders being impacted, the matrix can be completed by assembling a small team of participants. Although the latter method is the most expedient, it also typically provides the least accurate data.

When analyzing the data it is easy to get overwhelmed. For data analysis purposes we suggest you focus on three specific stakeholder roles. "Champions" are individuals or groups of people who absolutely must support the change for it to be successful. "Opinion shapers" are individuals who may/may not possess formal authority but have considerable *informal influence* on a number of other stakeholders. "Impacted" individuals or groups are the people who are most heavily impacted by the integration and who have the greatest impact on the success of the change. This group should be further segmented to identify those with "strong concerns." These individuals represent stakeholders who fundamentally are likely to perceive the change as negatively impacting them. Typically this is the origination point of most resistance and to the extent possible their concerns should be acknowledged, equitable practices should be put in place to treat them fairly, and their concerns should be integrated into the overall implementation and change process.

In order to achieve effective cascading of commitment it is absolutely essential to obtain the latest copy of relevant organization charts. At *each level* within the scope of your analysis make sure you identified people who can act as:

- **Champions:** These are individuals or groups that have the formal authority to make the necessary change solutions "happen" and who absolutely must be strong supporters for the change to be successful.
- **Missionaries:** These are individuals or groups whose are charged with "rolling up their sleeves" and becoming actively involved in the change effort.

Listed below are the steps we recommend for completing a stakeholder analysis:

1. **Agree on how you will segment stakeholder groups (at an individual or group level).** The finer or more specific the segmentation, the better and more actionable the data.
2. **Brainstorm the internal and external stakeholders that will be impacted by the change.** An example of an internal stakeholder would be a shared services function. Examples of external stakeholders include external suppliers, channel partners, and Wall Street.
3. **Identify the impacts the change will have on each stakeholder group.** The more specific, the more actionable the commitment plan.
4. **Complete stakeholder analysis.** This entails assessing each stakeholder's perceived level of commitment, identifying their influence on the success of the change, and fully understanding how it will impact them individually. A rule of thumb for determining influence is that individuals tend to have greater influence when they control key resources that are needed during the change, the stakeholder is perceived to have high levels of formal authority, and the stakeholder is capable of forming broad coalitions across the organization.
5. **Identify stakeholders concerns.** Validate and expand collected stakeholder inputs regarding key concerns. Concerns should not be looked upon as a problem or a nuisance. Often stakeholders will identify valid issues that need to be addressed in order to fully realize the benefits of the change.
6. **Develop actionable responses to optimize commitment levels.** Time and effort should be allocated to executing actions that foster cascading commitment throughout the organization.

See Table B.29 for a completed example.

TABLE B.29 Example of completed stakeholder assessment and commitment plan

Stakeholder	Ability to Influence (H,M,L)	Degree of Change Impact (H,M,L)	Stakeholder Concerns	Change Impacts	Activities	Start Date	Completion Date	Completion Responsibilities	Resource Requirements
Production Operators 1 & 2 Maintenance Operators, Industrial Engineer	High	High	Perception of having to work harder and taking on roles that either mgt or tech support previously did. Changes prior functional to team based on orientation	Work rules changed; less classifications, elimation of seniority rules. Engineers and Maintenance people now report to Team Leader	Provide self directed team training. Get involved in future state design, develop skill based pay reward system that rewards cross functional cooperation	1-Jan	30-Mar	J. Barr	XYZ Consulting Budget $25K
Director of Warehouse Operations	High	High	Job loss, fear of future competence	Job eliminated	Enroll in job bank, offer retraining, offer outplacement	30-Jan	15-Mar	N. Harris	HR will take lead

Appendix C

CHARACTERISTICS OF BUSINESS CHANGE APPROACH EVOLUTIONARY STAGES

Change approach themes	Scientific management & process improvement (origins: early 1900's)	Organizational development (origins: 1960's)	Business process reengineering & structural change (origins: 1980's)	Change as a dynamic system/human transitional needs (origins: 1990's)	Business transformation & change management (origins: 1990's)	Business change management (origins: 2012)
Key theorists, thought leaders	Taylor, Deming	Lewin, Schein, Argyris, Beckhard	Hammer, Champy, Davenport, Rummler, Brache	Senge, Wheatley, Goleman	Anderson, Kotter, Bridges, Conner	Jones, Recardo
Causes/trends that led to	The predominance and expansion of manufacturing; increasing per-worker outputs, productivity goals as means to competitive strength	• Dehumanization resulting from prior scientific, industrial approaches to change • Influence of behavioral science • Emergence of sociology and psychology applied to changing organizational culture	• Frustration with incremental improvement • Rise of IT, office automation • Multinational growth, corporate expansion • Centralization process redundancy from M&A had not been addressed	• Failure of BPR and large scale efforts to lead to true transformation beyond cost savings • Employees disengaged or burned (downsizing effects) • Innovation and differentiation not happening • Counter to over-engineered, top-down change initiatives	• Change efforts lacked strategic focus beyond process or IT change • Need to address change more comprehensively, e.g. overall framework • Remedy for "slash and burn" of structural change that did not fully "transform" the organization • Attempted to address failure causes of BPR - sponsorship commitment, urgency	• Change approaches too conceptual, not easily applied to real world • "Big bang" change as event (one-off), not ongoing process • One size fits all organizations, not scalable and flexible • Too much focus on tactical and "touchy feely" change aspects at expense of business results • It takes an army (FTE's) to make change happen • Change management still needs a seat at the table

FIGURE C.1 The evolution of approaches to business change and the emergence of change management

Change approach themes	Scientific management & process improvement (origins: early 1900's)	Organizational development (origins: 1960's)	Business process reengineering & structural change (origins: 1980's)	Change as a dynamic system/human transitional needs (origins: 1990's)	Business transformation & change management (origins: 1990's)	Business change management (origins: 2012)
Key attributes	• Manufacturing, mechanistic orientation • Increasing productivity through conforming to standards • Process improvement oriented • Quantitative, highly math-based	• Diagnose and address motivation, resistance • Focus on facilitation and engagement of stakeholders • Humanistic "interventions"	• Processes, workflows, redesign to emerging customer needs (blank slate) vs. improving existing • Incorporated some aspects of the OD side – stakeholder management and buy-in (resistance), attention to roles, skills as a means to enable processes • Quantitative measures, metrics	• Organic, bottom-up, productivity and innovation emerge without formal systems but well-seeded environments • High performance teams (human group needs, OD) • Learning organizations • Systems thinking paradigms • Principles, values and conditions • Valued and leveraged human potential as a driver of change	• Frameworks - strategic, comprehensive • Business-oriented rather than reliant on a particular aspect of change, IT • Tools for addressing gaps • Stronger up-front (e.g. burning platform)	• Change cascades from business strategy • Change process is scalable and flexible • Change is viewed holistically in terms of impacts and interventions • Change is not a separate work stream but integrated across the entire solution • Utilizes change lever to focus change efforts to high impact areas

FIGURE C.1 The evolution of approaches to business change and the emergence of change management (continued)

Change approach themes	Scientific management & process improvement (origins: early 1900's)	Organizational development (origins: 1960's)	Business process reengineering & structural change (origins: 1980's)	Change as a dynamic system/ human transitional needs (origins: 1990's)	Business transformation & change management (origins: 1990's)	Business change management (origins: 2012)
Strengths	• Increased productivity/ output through efficiency and consistency	• Elevated the importance of human factors in successful business change (awareness, buy-in, education) • Focused on doing the right thing to treat workers as individuals • Created a discipline "human science" with academic backing (OD) • Emphasized that change was a collective effort vs. a few smart people	• Eliminated or replaced outdated systems and processes that were no longer justified in terms of business value, and a drag on companies' bottom lines • More centralized and standardized global orgs (process perspective) • Cross-functional reengineering lab teams accelerated solution design and development	• Legitimized the importance of creating the conditions/ environment for learning, ideas • Teams used to initiate and drive change – not just carry it out • Probed the human behaviors that were causing resistance or inhibiting people from being empowered participants in the change (ground rules for operating in teams)	• Applied formal lifecycle methodology • Elevated the importance of sponsorship and strategic management • more comprehensive focus on business change	• Change management best practices embedded in the methodology and tools • Methodology and tools evolved and learnings integrated from many large scale change projects • Utilizes strong program and project management governance • Metrics driven • Relies on culture alignment • Manages the white space very effectively • Shorter cycle times, less resistance • Greater realization of targeted results • Less productivity fluctuations during implementation

FIGURE C.1 The evolution of approaches to business change and the emergence of change management (continued)

Change approach themes	Scientific management & process improvement (origins: early 1900's)	Organizational development (origins: 1960's)	Business process reengineering & structural change (origins: 1980's)	Change as a dynamic system/ human transitional needs (origins: 1990's)	Business transformation & change management (origins: 1990's)	Business change management (origins: 2012)
Issues/ weaknesses	• Tactical in focus. Did not question the business direction or assumptions underlying processes • Minimal human factor, treated individual workers as commodities or as common parts of a machine • Tools became religion e.g. Six Sigma, they were misapplied, brought more disruption to processes that needed simpler, less mechanistic solutions • More applicable for operations shop floor than knowledge worker environment	• Became separated from the "hard" aspects of business change, an island unto itself • Treated as the "soft science"	• Human factors relegated to a supporting role in change • Large scale efforts were over-staffed and expensive • Destroyed trust, Too often disguised cost-cutting • Change often became technology-driven (i.e. the cart pulled ahead of the horse problem) • Drifted into tactical change, process improvements that changed roles and headcount efficiently – but not strategically	• Lacked structure, • Preachy tone, even if it appealed to the better side of human nature in unlocking potential • Seen as "soft" • Did not integrate easily with other approaches – became seen more as tools and interventions	• Too formulaic and overly prescriptive • Used an atom bomb to kill an ant • Very top-down; cascade-effect can make employees feel like they are along for the ride • Framework-oriented rather than concrete, tools and activities of change efforts not integrated	• Many of the tools assume a moderate level of business knowledge and consulting skills acumen

FIGURE C.1 The evolution of approaches to business change and the emergence of change management (continued)

BIBLIOGRAPHY

Anderson, D. & Anderson, L. (2001). *Beyond change management: Advanced strategies for transformational leaders*. San Francisco. Jossey-Bass/Pfeiffer.

Argyris, C. (1985). *Strategy, change, and defensive routines*. Marshfield, MA. Pitman.

Beckhard, R. & Harris, R. (1987). *Organizational transitions*. Reading, MA. Addison-Wesley.

Bennis, W. (1995). *On becoming a leader*. New York. Simon & Schuster.

Blanchard, K. & Hersey, P. (1982). *Management of organizational behavior: Utilizing human resources*. Upper Saddle River, NJ. Prentice Hall.

Bohm, D. (1980). *Wholeness and the implicate order*. New York. Routledge.

Bridges, W. (2003). *Managing transitions: Making the most of change*. 2nd ed. Reading, MA. Addison-Wesley.

Connor, D. (1998). *Leading at the edge of chaos: How to create the nimble organization*. New York. John Wiley & Sons.

Csikszentmihalyi, M. (2003). *Good Business: Leadership, flow, and the making of meaning*. New York. Penguin Books.

de Bono, E. (1985). *The Six Thinking Hats*. US. MICA Management Resources.

Drucker, P. (1999). *Management challenges for the 21st century*. New York. HarperCollins.

Gardner, H. (2006). *Changing minds: The art and science of changing our own and other people's minds*. Boston, MA. Harvard Business School Press.

Georgescu, P. & Dorsey, D. (2005). *The source of success: Five enduring principles at the heart of real leadership*. San Francisco. Jossey-Bass.

Goleman, D. (1995). *Emotional intelligence: Why it can matter more than IQ*. New York. Bantam.

Greenleaf, R. (1977). *Servant leadership: A journey into the nature of legitimate power and greatness*. Mahwah, NJ. Paulist Press.

Hamel, G. (2007). *The future of management*. Boston, MA. Harvard Business School Publishing.

"Harvard Business Review on Leading Through Change." (2006). Boston, MA. Harvard Business School Press.

Hammer, M. & Champy, J. (1993). *Reengineering the corporation: A manifesto for business revolution*. New York. HarperCollins.

Kaplan, R. & Norton, D. (2001). *The strategy-focused organization: How balanced scorecard companies thrive in the new business environment*. Boston, MA. Harvard Business School Publishing.

Kegan, R. & Lahey L. (2009). *Immunity to change: How to overcome it and unlock the potential in yourself and your organization*. Boston, MA. Harvard Business School Publishing Corporation.

Kotter, J. (1996). *Leading change*. Boston, MA. Harvard Business School Press.

Kuhn, T. (1962). *The structure of scientific revolutions*. 1st ed. Chicago, IL. The University of Chicago Press.

Rummler, G. & Brache, A. (1990). *Improving performance: How to manage the white space on the organization chart*. San Francisco. Jossey-Bass.

Schein, E. (1992). *Organizational culture and leadership*. 2nd ed. San Francisco. Jossey-Bass.

Senge, P. (1990). *The fifth discipline: The art and practice of the learning organization*. New York. Doubleday.

Wheatley, M. (1994). *Leadership and the new science: Learning about organization from an orderly universe*. San Francisco. Berrett-Koehler.

INDEX

A page number in italics indicates a figure and a table is shown in bold.

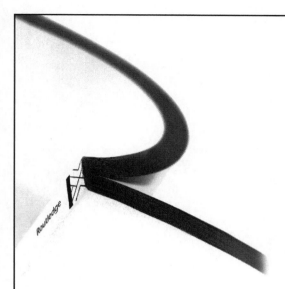